THE
EVERYTHING®
SMALL-SPACE
GARDENING BOOK

Dear Reader,

I am passionate about teaching and inspiring others to experience the joy and benefits of growing a food-producing garden. It was perfect timing when I was asked to write this book. I had just recently downsized, from growing veggies commercially on two acres to living in a condo with a front balcony for my only outdoor space. When I moved I immediately started growing some veggies and herbs in containers and found a new love of growing in my very small space. I was still craving a little bit more garden space and missed chatting with other gardeners, so I signed up for a 4-foot by 12-foot community garden plot. Now I have the best of both worlds: I can run out my front door to pick a handful of salad stuff for dinner, or run down the alley (yes, I created a community garden just a block away) to drop off my compost, pick some carrots or a head of broccoli, and chat with fellow gardeners. An hour or so of "fun" work each week is all my garden takes.

Happy creating and growing in your own small-space garden!

Catherine Abbott

Welcome to the EVERYTHING. Series!

These handy, accessible books give you all you need to tackle a difficult project, gain a new hobby, comprehend a fascinating topic, prepare for an exam, or even brush up on something you learned back in school but have since forgotten.

You can choose to read an Everything® book from cover to cover or just pick out the information you want from our four useful boxes: e-questions, e-facts, e-alerts, and e-ssentials.

We give you everything you need to know on the subject, but throw in a lot of fun stuff along the way, too.

We now have more than 400 Everything® books in print, spanning such wide-ranging categories as weddings, pregnancy, cooking, music instruction, foreign language, crafts, pets, New Age, and so much more. When you're done reading them all, you can finally say you know Everything®!

QUESTION

Answers to
common questions

FACT

Important snippets
of information

ALERT

Urgent
warnings

ESSENTIAL

Quick
handy tips

PUBLISHER Karen Cooper

DIRECTOR OF ACQUISITIONS AND INNOVATION Paula Munier

MANAGING EDITOR, EVERYTHING® SERIES Lisa Laing

COPY CHIEF Casey Ebert

ASSISTANT PRODUCTION EDITOR Melanie Cordova

ACQUISITIONS EDITOR Ross Weisman

ASSOCIATE DEVELOPMENT EDITOR Hillary Thompson

EDITORIAL ASSISTANT Matthew Kane

EVERYTHING® SERIES COVER DESIGNER Erin Alexander

LAYOUT DESIGNERS Erin Dawson, Michelle Roy Kelly, Elisabeth Lariviere, Denise Wallace

Visit the entire Everything® series at www.everything.com

THE
EVERYTHING®
SMALL-SPACE GARDENING BOOK

All you need to plant, grow,
and enjoy a small-space garden

Catherine Abbott

Adamsmedia
Avon, Massachusetts

This book is dedicated to every reader who
wants to grow some of their own veggies, no
matter how small of a space they may have.

An Everything® Series Book.
Everything® and everything.com® are registered trademarks of F+W Media, Inc.

Published by Adams Media, a division of F+W Media, Inc.
57 Littlefield Street, Avon, MA 02322 U.S.A.
www.adamsmedia.com

ISBN 10: 1-4405-3060-2
ISBN 13: 978-1-4405-3060-9
eISBN 10: 1-4405-3128-5
eISBN 13: 978-1-4405-3128-6

Printed in the United States of America.

10 9 8 7 6 5 4 3 2 1

Library of Congress Cataloging-in-Publication Data
is available from the publisher.

This publication is designed to provide accurate and authoritative information with regard to the subject matter covered. It is sold with the understanding that the publisher is not engaged in rendering legal, accounting, or other professional advice. If legal advice or other expert assistance is required, the services of a competent professional person should be sought.
—From a *Declaration of Principles* jointly adopted by a Committee of the American Bar Association and a Committee of Publishers and Associations

Many of the designations used by manufacturers and sellers to distinguish their products are claimed as trademarks. Where those designations appear in this book and Adams Media was aware of a trademark claim, the designations have been printed with initial capital letters.

Illustrations by Eric Andrews

This book is available at quantity discounts for bulk purchases.
For information, please call 1-800-289-0963.

Contents

The Top 10 Tips
for Small-Space Gardening

1. Use containers for growing veggies, herbs, and small fruit trees. Containers do not require a lot of space and can be placed on balconies, patios, or hung in front porches.

2. Grow vertical crops to maximize your space. Some veggies grow better if they are allowed to climb up a trellis or if they are staked. Also, vertical crops allow more space for other plants to be grown around the base of the upright plant.

3. Grow plants that produce a large crop for the amount of space they take. You can get a large harvest of tomatoes or cucumbers from one plant, whereas planting a potato in the same area will not yield as much of a harvest.

4. Grow plants that you can eat more than one part of. For example, with beets you can enjoy the tops as baby greens, and once the plant matures, you can enjoy the root.

5. Grow intensively. Utilize the square-foot growing method to maximize the number of plants you can grow in your small-space or container garden. Just make sure you keep your soil rich and fertile to allow enough nutrients for all the plants to grow well.

6. Interplant fast- and slow-growing plants. Vegetable plants mature at different times and take up different amounts of space. Intermix a variety of plants in the same space—you'll harvest one plant while the slower growing one matures.

7. Plant several different crops throughout the season. Plant an early spring crop, and once it has been harvested, remove the used plant. Replant with a summer crop, and use the area again with a veggie you can harvest in the fall or winter.

8. Avoid planting too many large plants. Some plants, such as potatoes and squash, can take up a lot of garden space. Limit the number of large plants, making more room for a larger amount of smaller ones to increase your harvest.

9. Choose dwarf or small-size vegetable varieties. There are several varieties of smaller vegetable plants and fruit trees being developed as more gardeners are growing in small spaces.

10. Grow perpetual or perennial vegetables. Choose varieties of vegetables that can be harvested over several seasons, such as Swiss chard or kale. Grow asparagus or perennial herbs so you will be able to harvest from the plants for several years with only a little maintenance.

Introduction

VINE-RIPENED TOMATOES. SUCCULENT SQUASH. Plump cucumbers. Growing vegetables is a rewarding and cost-effective way to eat better for less, but you might think you lack the space necessary to grow a food-producing garden. With this guide, however, you will learn how to maximize your space and grow delicious vegetables, herbs, and fruits cheaply and efficiently—whether you have a small backyard or just a window sill.

You're most likely used to seeing your backyard, front yard, or existing flower beds in a certain way and might not even realize that there may be different options for utilizing those spaces. This book will help you take a look around your property, see it with fresh eyes, and find those hidden spots that may have potential for starting a food garden. A green patch as small as a square foot can nourish and grow some lettuce plants or even a tomato plant, so long as the area gets enough sun. Once you see the potential in one area, you will be surprised how every little nook and cranny in your small space could be the next perfect spot for growing some veggies or herbs.

Even a concrete jungle with no green in sight (other than an occasional green storefront canopy) can have great possibilities for supporting food-producing areas. Both your high-rise balcony or the rooftop of your apartment or office building can sustain growing vegetables in containers or hanging baskets. Another great option for the urban dweller is to check out community gardens in your neighborhood, and if there aren't any, perhaps there is a park or empty lot that would be the perfect place to start. There is so much potential for growing food no matter where you live. You just have to know where to look—and this book can help.

Perhaps you are already growing in your small space or on your balcony or patio and are looking for new ideas to improve what you are already doing. Have you thought of growing upward? In this book you will find information on what plants are best grown vertically using trellises or stakes, while maximizing your lower space for growing even more veggies and herbs.

Are you totally new to gardening and not sure where to begin? Or are you on a very tight budget and do not want to waste any money or time on something that may not work for you? In the following chapters you will find several garden designs in a range of price points that will work in a variety of small spaces. You can follow these designs as they are given, or use them as inspiration for making your own garden plan.

This book is divided into chapters focusing on specific topics relating to small spaces, making it easier for you to find what you need to get started. Feel free to jump from chapter to chapter as you have questions about how best to utilize your own small space. You will find specific information on how to plant, care for, and harvest many common vegetables, herbs, and fruits.

Growing in a small space can have its challenges, but the successes will definitely outweigh any concerns you may have. A productive garden can and should be a reality for everyone, regardless of the amount of land you live on. This guide has everything you need to grow fresh produce in any size space, at any time of the year!

CHAPTER 1

Designing a Small-Space Garden

Small-space gardening can be done anywhere you have access to soil, water, and light; it can be in a few pots on your balcony, in your front or backyard, in a community garden, or any kind of space available if used creatively. If you are new to vegetable gardening or just want to reinvent your existing space, this chapter will offer the information you need to make the best choices when getting started.

Why Do You Want to Grow Vegetables?

The first thing to consider when deciding to grow vegetables is *why* you want to start. What you want the vegetable garden to do for you will determine what size you may need and what you may want to grow.

Here are some questions to get started on your plan:

- Do you want to save money on your grocery bill?
- Do you want to feed your family healthy organic vegetables?
- Is gardening a hobby, and you just love to grow things?
- Do you want to spend time connecting with your family?
- Do you want to garden for fun, relaxation, and exercise?
- Do you just want to have pretty plants to look at on your patio?

You can definitely save money on your grocery bill as well as feed your family healthy organic produce by growing your own vegetables. As a hobby, gardening is a wonderful way to connect with other gardeners, neighbors, nature, and most of all, your family. Children love to get into the garden planting; they love watching things grow and then eating the fresh picked vegetables and fruits. You may have many other reasons for wanting a vegetable garden. But for whatever reason you choose to garden, it can be fun and a great way to stay active and enjoy the outdoors.

FACT

Soil contains bacteria, which boost serotonin levels. Serotonin is the neurotransmitter responsible for mood elevation and for staying awake. So to lighten your mood, go play in the dirt.

Planting a vegetable garden can be very rewarding. It is miraculous how a tiny little seed can produce enough vegetables to feed your family for several meals. Your health and the health of your environment are important. Growing some of your own vegetables is a great place to start to get healthier. By growing one or two types of vegetables for yourself, you will save on trips to the supermarket, you will know exactly where your food came from, and you'll know how it was grown. These are all important steps for building a healthier body and environment.

How Much Time and Space Do You Have?

Whatever the reason you want to grow your own vegetables, it is important to consider that gardening does take time, money, and energy. Now that you know why you want to grow, it is important to be realistic with how much time you have to devote to your garden. Do you have a tiny little plot or balcony, or a front or backyard you want to turn into a garden? The size of your space will determine the amount of time it will take. A small-space garden can have its own challenges; for example, many veggies often grown in containers need more watering.

If all you have is a few minutes a day to spend on your vegetable garden, perhaps a few pots are what you want to start with. If you have a few hours a week, you could manage a small garden spot, or perhaps a 4-foot by 8-foot raised bed in your front or backyard is the better choice. If you want to grow enough food to feed your family all year round, you may need to set aside at least one day a week to tend to a much larger garden. No matter where you live, you can find a spot to grow some of your own vegetables.

What Do You Want to Grow?

When choosing to grow in a small space, it is important to know what you would like to grow as well as what will grow best in that space. Certain vegetables need specific requirements to grow well. Some need warmth and lots of sunlight, whereas others can be grown in a shadier spot. Deciding what you want to grow is your second step in choosing the best course of action for your garden.

Planning what you want to grow will save you time, money, and energy in the long run. It is important to grow what your family will eat. Does your family eat a lot of salads, or do they love tomatoes or cucumbers? Write down a list of vegetables that you love to eat and get your family involved so they are part of the decision making. That way they will be willing to help plant and take care of the garden.

Some vegetables take much more effort than others to grow well, so when choosing what you want to grow, consider how you will be growing it. Swiss chard or salad greens are easy to grow and can be harvested several times from just a few plants. A 10-foot row of asparagus will initially take some time to plant, and you will not get a harvest for a couple of years; however once the bed is established you will be harvesting asparagus in the spring for years to come. Some root crops such as carrots, beets, or radishes need to be thinned as they grow and that can be time-consuming, especially if you have large rows of these vegetables. It is important to check to see what kind of time you want to put into gardening before choosing what you want to grow.

ALERT

Children love to garden. Choose quick-growing veggies like radishes or lettuce so the children can watch them grow, or fun-eating veggies like peas or corn. Find a spot where your children can easily be involved in making their own little garden or pot. Teaching them how to plant, weed, water, and take care of that area is an invaluable tool in getting them in touch with where their food comes from.

Picking and eating fresh vegetables from your garden can be a joy. You can experience this with only a few vegetable plants grown in pots; however, if your goal is to preserve food for eating during the winter, it is important to plant more than you would need for fresh eating alone. So here again, planning ahead and deciding what you want to do with your harvest is also important.

Since space is a consideration for you, there are plants that give bigger yields than others in the space they take up. The only root crop that takes up a lot of room is the potato, but read on to find creative ways to plant yours. You can train tomatoes, cucumbers, and beans to grow vertically, giving you more of a harvest for the space used. Consider growing vegetables that have more than one edible part, such as beets; you can eat the root or enjoy the leaves in a salad. Another example is onions: You can eat the greens in your salad and then wait until the bulbs are large enough to harvest to save on space as well.

Here is a list of ten common vegetables you can grow in a small space:

1. Beans
2. Beets
3. Carrots
4. Cucumbers
5. Garlic
6. Lettuce/Spinach
7. Onions
8. Peas
9. Peppers
10. Tomatoes

Growing vegetables (even in a small space) takes effort and your time, so it is important to grow what you or your family will eat. However, do not be afraid to try something new. A vegetable fresh from the garden has much more flavor than most veggies bought at the local grocery store. You could be surprised by what you or your family may eat! If you find you do not like something or have an overabundance of certain veggies, give some away to friends, neighbors, or your community food bank.

Consider Your Climate

When deciding to grow your own vegetables, you need to consider your climate. The United States and Canada are divided into plant hardiness zones ranging from one (the coldest areas, such as Alaska) and up to eleven, which are the warmest areas (like southern California, southern Florida, and Hawaii). These zones are based on temperature variations and first and last frost dates, and give the gardener an idea what plants will grow best in each zone.

These zones can be important when choosing perennial plants. However, with vegetable gardening, most people grow annuals within the growing seasons of the area in which they live. Most areas in the United States and Canada also have four seasons—spring, summer, fall, and winter. The majority of gardeners grow vegetables in the spring and summer. Some gardeners in the South can grow during the fall and winter months as well, but usually only in the southernmost parts of the United States. Growing seasons can be extended by using greenhouses or other structures to give vegetable plants protection from inclement and unpredictable weather.

ALERT

Vegetables have the same basic needs as humans: they need light, food, water, and warmth. The amount of these basic needs given to a vegetable plant will determine how it will grow, mature, and produce healthy food. These four essentials always need to be considered when choosing your garden site.

During the year temperatures go up and down. The length of your growing season will be pretty standard but can vary depending on the weather and the amounts of rainfall you get. You need to be aware of these things when choosing your site. The general climate of your area is important too; however, each garden site will have specific issues to consider:

- Does your small garden site have good soil
- Does it retain water or is it well drained?
- Is the pot large enough for what you are growing?
- Is the area protected from the wind?
- Does the site have many mature trees or a large fence that will block out the sun, or does it get full sun?

Often, all of these factors can be controlled by choosing different ways to grow on your site. For example, growing in raised beds, in a pot on a balcony, or in a greenhouse can solve a multitude of site problems.

Your Light Conditions

Sunlight plays a big part in growing a successful vegetable garden, whether in a pot or in your backyard. One of the most important aspects to growing your own vegetables is sunlight, and often this is the area over which you have the least control. When choosing your garden site, you will need to consider the amount of sunlight the area gets throughout the day. Most vegetables need an average of six hours of sunlight in order to grow. If you only have a shady spot, do not fret too much as there are a few plants that do okay in a bit of shade; perhaps you can grow other vegetables in containers that can be moved around to follow the sun's path. Choose the sunniest spot in your space for your veggie patch. It can often be your front lawn.

The sun alters its path throughout the seasons, so take the time to jot down when the sun hits your area during the different seasons and how long it stays there. The area may not get any sun during the winter months. But likely you will not be growing anything at that time, so it does not matter. However, if you get no sun during the spring and summer, you will need to choose another site. When you first start a garden, these are all things you can learn as you go. If things are not working out exactly as you planned, make a note so you can improve on things in your next growing season.

QUESTION

How do I keep pests away from my plants?
When planning your vegetable garden, include aspects that will attract healthy insects and animals to your space such at butterflies, ladybugs, and some birds. Drawing these creatures in can be done by planting certain veggie plants and shrubs, or including a small water feature. Attracting these insects and animals will help to keep at by any harmful pests that may be attracted to your garden.

You also want to consider how the trees or fences in the area affect the amount of sun your site will get. In the winter months, when the leaves are off the trees, you may get full sun; however, the site will become shadier as the leaves come out. Again, find a sunnier spot if you will be growing your veggies during the spring and summer. Large trees and shrubs will compete for soil nutrients as well, so planning your site near trees will affect how many nutrients your vegetables will get. You always want great soil and it will need to be even more fertile if your garden site is near large trees. Perennial shrubs are not usually that much of a problem as they do not need as many nutrients and as much water as larger trees. Many attractive vegetable gardens use these shrubs as borders to attract beneficial insects to the vegetable patch.

Most gardeners do not have the ideal garden site; however, you can still grow a great vegetable garden with a little knowledge and desire. With the amount of sunlight plants need being such a big consideration, here is some more information on how much certain veggies need.

Here is a list of vegetables that do well with four to six hours of sunlight:

- Carrots
- Lettuce
- Kale
- Peas
- Swiss chard

Vegetables that traditionally need more sunlight and warmth are the ones that produce fruit. These need as least eight hours of full sun to grow best:

- Cucumbers
- Eggplant
- Peppers
- Squash
- Tomatoes

No matter how large or small your garden site is, choosing an area that will get the most possible sunlight, has good drainage, and reasonably good soil will ensure you will have veggies to harvest.

Your Water Source

Water is another very important aspect to having a healthy vegetable garden. You cannot depend on rainfall alone as it can be variable in most areas. A good water source near your garden site is essential. Most people will be less inclined to water if they have to pack it from a long distance. Make sure your garden hose is attached to the water source so it can easily reach across the full length of your garden site, or that you have a large enough watering can to do all your pots at one time. This will make watering easier.

Most vegetable plants need 1 to 2 inches of water each week; some will need more if you live in an extremely hot climate. Containers and raised beds may also need more water, depending again on the temperature in your area, if the plants are under cover, and how much rainfall you get. There are several different ways of watering your vegetable garden—sprinklers, soaker hoses, drip irrigators, or hand-watering containers are some of the most common.

ALERT

A water measuring tip: place small empty cans (tuna or salmon can work well) in four different areas of your vegetable garden. Turn on the overhead sprinkler and leave it on for one hour; then measure the amount of water in each can. This will give you an indication of how much water your garden is getting in that hour.

If you live in an area that gets plenty of rainfall, a rain gauge is a useful tool. This will help you keep track of the amount of water your vegetable garden is getting. Too little water will not allow the vegetable plant roots to grow deep enough to reach the reserves of water and nutrients in the soil. Too much water will saturate the soil, reducing the amount of air space needed for the vegetable roots to grow strong, deep, and healthy. Either way is harmful to your vegetable plants. Stressed plants will not produce as much as they could if they were healthy, so make sure you keep track of the amount of water your vegetables are getting.

Designing Your Site

It is now time to decide on how you want to grow your vegetables. The kind of space you have, the terrain, the soil, and the amount of sunlight your garden site will get can help with your design decisions. Do you have a tiny balcony, porch, patio, or alley way and the only space available will hold just a few pots? Or is the space a large patio that will enable you to have some larger planter boxes, perhaps to grow a dwarf fruit tree? Is the space fairly flat and rows will work best for you? Do you have poor soil and a raised bed would be the best option? These are all great ways to grow a fabulous vegetable garden. Consider the following design options to see what's best for you.

Container Gardening

If you live in the middle of a city and the only sunny area you have available is on a balcony, porch, or in some other small space, growing in containers is the perfect option to make a lovely vegetable garden. Containers come in various sizes and can sit or hang in your space. Some vegetables grow better in containers than others, so to get the best results possible, you want to be informed when choosing your vegetable plants.

In some urban homes or offices all the access you may have to the outdoors is a concrete patio. These are often areas that get a lot of sun. Sometimes these spots are a little too hot, but they might offer ideal conditions for growing your food using containers. Patios are usually big enough to accommodate larger planters, enabling you to easily grow larger vegetables and even some fruit trees and berry bushes.

Row Method

Row gardening is best used if you have a flat area. Even though row gardening is usually used on larger plots, this method of growing can be easily utilized in small spaces, such as in a flat sunny front or backyard. When planning a row garden, it is important to make sure you allow space for pathways between and at the end of each row to accommodate a place for you to walk and use any larger tools, like a rototiller or wheelbarrow. Walking on the soil where you will be planting your veggies can compact it and harm the soil structure. When designing this style of garden, make designated pathways.

Rows can be as long or as wide as you want or need them to be. Often the width is dependent on the type of equipment you will be using to till the beds. If you are going to be using a rototiller, measure the width of the tines. This will give you an idea of how wide you want your bed to be. When choosing the width of your garden bed, consider how long your reach is; if you are weeding on one side, can you easily reach across the bed without straining your back?

Growing in Raised Beds

Raised beds are structures that have four sides and hold soil. They are a great option for a small space, for areas with poor soil, for a hillside garden, or if you want structures in your garden. If you want to grow in a moist area that has poor drainage, the raised bed will allow for better drainage. If you have a sloped or terraced garden site, raised beds will help define these areas and make it easier to grow plants in the more difficult to reach areas. If the garden is replacing your front lawn and you want it to look attractive to your neighbors, using raised beds is a great way to add structure, definition, and tidiness to your vegetable garden. Raised beds are often used in community gardens as they can be easily designated to individual growers.

Even in the smallest garden, make room for a place for at least one person to sit. This adds purpose to the space and will be a lovely place to enjoy your garden. You can place your seating in a shady spot so you can relax after a hot day of working.

Another great reason for using raised beds is that the bed can be made to any height. If you have physical disabilities, have limited mobility, or cannot bend easily, the raised bed can work very well for you. Make sure it is built to the height that works best for you. If it is a low bed, adding a ledge on the top will allow you to sit while gardening. And the ledge is great for older gardeners or those that cannot easily get down on hands and knees to plant or weed.

CHAPTER 2

Prepping Your Small Space

When planning for a successful small-space garden, an important first step is getting to know your garden space. Whether you're growing in front of your home or in your backyard, you'll need to know the nature of your area before you plant the first seed. Read on to learn about different soil types, how to amend garden soil, the proper way to fertilize, easy composting, and the importance of good drainage. Following these crucial steps while prepping your small space will ensure healthy plants and the abundant crop you desire.

Your Soil

Fertile soil is a necessary element to a successful garden in the ground or in containers. Soil supports the vegetable plants by providing them with nutrients, warmth, air circulation, and the moisture they need to grow to maturity. Most gardens do not have ideal soil; however, with a little work and attention, you can develop healthy, fertile soil that your plants will love.

Soil is made up of soil particles, organic matter, humus, water, and air. Soil particles are mineral materials that have been broken down into pieces smaller than pebbles. The organic matter and humus are made from decaying organisms, mainly plants that are at various stages of decomposition. About half of soil is actually solid; the rest is filled with air and water.

Air space is needed so that oxygen and carbon dioxide can move freely in and out of the soil; both are needed for vegetable plant roots to grow. Clay soil can impede airflow, as it is heavy and soil can get compacted by machinery or by being walked on. Either practice can inhibit good air circulation in the soil—another reason to have designated pathways to prevent your garden beds from becoming compacted.

ALERT

When planting containers it is important to use a light soil mix or good compost. If you use soil from your garden, it is often too heavy and will not allow air to circulate in the container. Garden soil will impede the growth of your plants rather than support it.

Proper moisture is another very important ingredient needed in soil to support healthy plants. The water in the soil encases the soil particles and dissolves them; this enables the vegetable plant to absorb the nutrients through the water. If the soil gets too wet, it becomes saturated and does not leave any room for the oxygen and carbon dioxide to reach the plant roots or for the water to dissolve the soil particles. The plants are left nutrient deficient. Your soil needs a healthy balance of soil particles, organic material, water, and air circulation so plants can get the oxygen, moisture, and nutrients needed to grow to maturity.

When used in containers, the soil has more restrictions. So a lightweight soil mix is important to allow proper movement of the water and air. This will ensure the plants get what they need.

Consider What Your Plants Need

Now that you know more about what soil is and what your plants need to grow well, it is time to take a look at your own garden soil. Does it look healthy? Is it dark in color, rich smelling and crumbly, or is it hard, grayish in color, and dry? Are there earthworms when you dig around in it, or is it rocky with some straggly weeds? No matter what you are starting with there are always ways to improve it; soil is a living thing and will need amending and fertilizing along the way.

So what kind of soil do you have? There are four basic types: sand, silt, clay, and loam (sometimes called humus).

Sandy Soil

Sandy soil is mostly made up of sand and is the opposite of clay soil. Sandy soil is made up large particles that do not hold together well. As a positive, sandy soil is often the warmest soil, which can benefit heat-loving vegetables. The main drawback to this type of soil is that it does not hold the water that is needed to move the nutrients from the soil to your plants. To tell if you have sandy soil or not, pick up a small handful, rub your fingers through it, and if it falls apart and feels gritty, your soil is made mostly of sand.

To improve sandy soil you will need to add organic matter such as compost, rotted manures, and shredded leaves. Doing this every year, or even twice a year if you have enough material, is ideal. Organic matter adds nutrients to the soil and helps it to retain moisture. Both nutrients and moisture, which may be lacking in a sandy soil, are needed to grow healthy vegetable plants.

Clay Soil

In clay soil the particles are very tiny and bind together to make the soil heavy and difficult to work with. Another disadvantage is clay soil stays colder than other soils, so plants often have a tendency to grow slower. It also can get waterlogged, and prevent oxygen from reaching the roots of your vegetable plants. On the positive, clay soil is richer in nutrients and retains more moisture than sandy soil, which means it needs less water in the hot summer months. To check if you have clay soil, take a small handful of soil, add a little water, and roll it between your hands. If it forms an elongated shape and does not easily fall apart, you have mostly clay in your soil.

ALERT

Raised beds or containers are always great options if you have poor soil or live in an urban area where there is no open ground available. There are good packaged soil mixtures sold at garden nurseries. Be sure to consider the initial cost; however, raised beds or containers are great ways to grow some of your own veggies.

To improve clay soil, you want to add as much organic matter as you can. By adding in compost, shredded leaves, and rotted manures (such as horse, cow, or chicken manure), you will help to enlarge the amount of space between the soil particles and make the soil lighter. This will increase air circulation, allowing the oxygen and nutrients to be absorbed by the plants.

Silt Soil

Silt soil has medium-sized particles, larger than clay and smaller than sandy soils. Silt drains better than clay soil and holds nutrients better than sandy soils. This type of soil is very rare and is really only found near rivers or in areas that were once under water. The main disadvantage to silt soil is that it lacks organic matter, but that can be easily remedied by adding it in. To test if you have silty soil, put a small amount of soil in your palm, add a bit of water, and rub it between your fingers. Silty soil will have a soapy feel to it.

Loamy Soil

Loamy soil has the ideal soil structure, which is a mixture of sand, clay, and silt. It holds nutrients, retains moisture but does not get soggy, and it is easy to work with. Gardeners who have been gardening for years usually have made what soil they started with into a loamy, rich soil. A rich, loam soil is slightly moist and crumbles easily by just poking your fingers into it. It is very similar to rich well-rotted compost.

Most soils are a combination just with a bit more sand or clay in them. But no matter what your soil type, it will need to be replenished with healthy amendments (organic materials) and organic fertilizers on a regular basis. Your vegetable plants are drawing nutrients continuously while they are growing. Rain and wind can wash or blow away nutrients as well, so it is important to know your soil and to take care of it in order to have healthy vegetable plants.

Drainage Concerns

The amount of moisture present in the soil plays a huge part in allowing nutrients to be used by the plants. Too much or too little water is a concern when trying to grow healthy veggie, fruit, and herb plants. If you have water sitting in your garden after a rain or if your water seems to drain away too quickly, you probably have a drainage problem. In containers, if the plants become waterlogged or dry out, their growth can be affected. So drainage holes in containers are extremely important for keeping your plants healthy.

ALERT

Nature's plants rely on fallen limbs, leaves, seeds, and eventually huge trees that decompose over time, making a forest a blanket of rich humus. High-fiber woody materials are exactly what some soils need. Sawdust and wood chip mulch will conserve water, control weeds, and build long-term soil fertility.

Organic matter in soil helps to lighten it, offering better drainage and the ability to hold the correct amount of water for your plants. Add in as much organic materials as possible such as compost or aged animal manure (several inches if you have that much), and till or dig it under. Mulching with straw or leaves can protect the soil from erosion and leaching of nutrients; the mulch will decompose over time, adding organic matter to the soil. With container gardens, it is important to renew your soil every year before planting a new crop, as well as regularly fertilizing every few weeks.

If your garden area has a drainage problem and you are not sure how to go about fixing it, call a landscaper to assess the situation for you. Drainage pipes, which can help remove any excess water you may have in your garden site, can be placed underground. Well-drained soil helps to keep plant roots from becoming waterlogged, allowing the plants to absorb the nutrients and oxygen needed to grow and mature. Poorly drained soil leaves your vegetable plants more susceptible to root rot and disease.

Backyard Composting

Making compost can be a huge benefit for your vegetable garden. It does take some work but for a little time and effort, the rewards are great! A compost pile makes use of your kitchen waste that otherwise would go into the garbage, and is an excellent spot to recycle your weeds (just make sure they have not gone to seed). You can allow other garden debris to decompose in the pile rather than having it go to the landfill. Having a compost pile is also a great way to keep your garden clean. The resulting compost is perfect for using in your garden beds or containers.

ESSENTIAL

Shredded leaves will decompose much faster than whole ones (any tree leaves will work for mulch). Rake fallen leaves into a pile and then run your lawn mower over them. If you have a bag on your mower, that's even better because you can then just empty it into your compost pile or place the shredded leaves directly onto your garden bed as mulch.

Making a Compost Pile

The best times to make a new compost pile is in the spring or in the fall, as the heat of the summer or the cold in winter will not slow down the decomposition process. A good-sized pile will most likely take from three to six months to decompose into good compost. The final result should be a rich, dark-colored material that smells earthy and easily crumbles in your hands.

To make your compost pile:

1. Lay down 4 to 6 inches of carbon material—for example, straw, shredded or dried leaves, small sticks, corn or broccoli stalks (chopped into smaller pieces or put through a chipping machine, if possible).
2. Cover that with 4 to 6 inches of green material—for example, leaves, grass, and kitchen waste.
3. Add in a handful of organic fertilizer lime if you want.
4. Then cover with a thin layer of soil or animal manure to keep the flies and odor down.
5. Repeat the above steps.

For best results, make the pile at least 3 feet high by 3 feet wide before leaving it to sit. Temperature is an important factor in making compost; the larger the pile, the easier it is for the material in it to get to the high temperatures needed to kill any weed seeds or diseased plant material. A temperature that is either too low or too high can slow down the decomposition process, while warm weather has a tendency to speed it up a bit. The pile usually starts out cool, and then as the materials start to decompose, the temperature inside the pile increases. Once your compost pile has reached approximately 3 feet by 3 feet, let that one sit and start a new pile. Most plastic compost bins will be approximately this size when they are full so you can move the bin, leaving the pile to work, or have two bins if you have a large amount of debris.

ALERT

When making compost, you want to have a balance of green and brown material. Too much green material will attract flies and give your compost a strong odor; too much brown material will slow down the decomposition of the pile.

Moisture is another important aspect to consider when making compost. The amount of moisture needs to be high, so make sure you add water to your compost regularly. Never let your compost pile dry out, especially in the summer months. Keeping the pile covered will keep the sun from drying it out as well as preventing the rain from making it too wet. Here's a way to check to see if your pile has the proper amount of moisture. Take a handful of compost from the middle of the pile, and if it is crumbling and slightly moist to the touch, there is enough moisture. If it forms a hard ball, the pile is too wet.

The moisture in the pile will allow air, which is also needed in the decomposing process, to filter in. Turning your pile will also allow more air circulation, and is especially important if your pile is too wet. A lot of gardeners never turn their compost and that method does work; however, taking the time to turn your pile over regularly will hasten the decomposition process.

Choosing a Compost Bin

Constructing your own bin rather than purchasing one can save you money, as you can use recycled materials. Another benefit is that you can make it any size to fit your needs. A simple compost structure is a three-sided bin made by stacking concrete blocks, railroad ties, wooden boards, bales of straw, or pallets. Wire fencing or wire mesh can also be used to make a less solid bin so long as the holes are small enough to hold the materials you have. Bending the wire into a circular shape is often the easiest and the sturdiest shape to set up. Often, you can get these materials for free; they are also fairly inexpensive to purchase. Make sure the walls are about 4 feet high and the area inside is a minimum of 3 feet by 3 feet.

QUESTION

What, exactly, is topdressing?
Top dressing is a nutritious application of organic materials such as leaf mold, well-rotted manures, and compost that is spread on the surface of the soil or around the base of a plant. You can do this either in the ground or in a container.

There are many different types of plastic compost bins on the market; they are compact, and great for a tiny space. Plastic bins are lighter to move around, can last longer than wooden bins, and are enclosed so they can protect your compost from the rain and sun. They come in round shapes, square shapes, solid-sided containers, tumblers, and ones with removable and stackable sides. Most have a capacity of 12 cubic feet, which is the size needed for your compost to heat up. They are a great addition to any small-space garden!

Apartment Worm Composting

If you live in an apartment or a condominium and do not have access to a backyard, composting with earthworms can be an easy way to turn your kitchen waste into nutritious compost that is great to add to your vegetable containers. An earthworm has the ability to consume its own weight in soil and organic matter each day. It leaves behind castings that are rich compost. Generally, a pound of earthworms will compost 1 pound of kitchen waste, making 1 pound of compost each day. Check with your local nursery or search the Internet to purchase worms.

There are many different worm-composting kits you can purchase online or at local garden centers. However, to save some money you can make an easy and inexpensive worm-compost container using inexpensive plastic bins. To make this worm bin you need the following items:

❑ Two (56-liter) plastic bins
❑ Bucket
❑ Burlap sack or newspaper
❑ Small pail of pebbles
❑ Peat moss
❑ Potting soil (or a mixture of organic materials such as straw, soil, and aged manure, if you have it)
❑ Worms
❑ Water

Here are the steps to making your earthworm compost:

1. Drill at least six holes in the bottom of one of the containers, and then place it into the second container. The second container will hold any liquid that will drain from the first bin. Lift out the top bin every few weeks and use the liquid from the second one as a tea for your garden plants.

2. Prepare the bedding by filling a bucket one-third full of peat moss, one-third full of a combination of good garden soil, dried straw or leaves, and manure (if you have some available): finally, fill the last third of the bucket with water.
3. Soak this mixture overnight, and the next day squeeze out any excess water.
4. Cover the bottom of the plastic bin that has holes with a layer of small pebbles.
5. Lay 4 inches of the bedding mixture over the pebbles. Leave the bin to stand one day, as the mixture may heat up too much and kill the earthworms if they are put in right away.
6. Move some of the bedding to the side of the bin and place the earthworms from their shipping container into the center of the bin. Lightly cover the earthworms with the bedding you pulled aside.
7. Place a burlap sack or some newspapers on top of the bedding and moisten with a watering can. Keep the bedding material moist but not soggy.
8. The bin will begin to drip from the holes in the bottom, so make sure the first bin is inserted into the second one so the second can catch the drippings.
9. Start feeding the worms slowly. If you give them more than they can eat in a twenty-four hour period, the extra vegetable waste will attract flies and heat up the bedding, which can kill the earthworms. Start feeding them soft foods like cooked veggies, bread scraps, and soups, leftover cereal with the milk, cornmeal, or coffee grounds. After a few weeks your earthworms will be ready to handle raw vegetables. Do not give the earthworms strong foods like onions or garlic.
10. Every few weeks add a thin layer of soil on top of the decomposing pile.
11. Every two weeks turn the compost with your hands (wear gloves) to aerate it. Reduce the amount of food you give the earthworms for a few days as the earthworms will not come to the surface for a few days after you turn the compost.
12. After one month, add another 2 inches of bedding to accommodate the increased worm population (they will have increased over the month).
13. After three months the compost will be ready to use; however, you will need to start a new bin in which to move the earthworms. When you are

ready to divide the existing box, use a large table covered with a plastic sheet and dump the bedding and worms onto the table. Heap the compost into a pile in the center of the table. Pick out the rocks and put them back into the bin. Any worms exposed to the light will burrow into the center of the pile. Scrape the top of the pile of bedding into a bucket and wait ten minutes while any exposed worms burrow deeper. After several scrapings your worms will be at the bottom of the pile, making it easy to put them back into the bin you are using. If there are a lot of worms, start a second bin.

14. To make a new bin, go back to steps one through four.

CHAPTER 3

Layered Gardens

If your soil is not the greatest, if you do not have a lot of time to maintain your garden, or if you have physical difficulties in doing the heavier work of maintaining a full-sized garden, the layered or lasagna methods will work well for you to create a new garden bed. This chapter describes what layered gardening is, what kind of materials you will need to get started, and gives step-by-step instructions to get your bed established quickly and easily.

What Is Lasagna Gardening?

Lasagna gardening (also known as no-dig gardening, no-till gardening, and sheet mulching) is a method utilizing layers of organic matter to build up existing or create new soil. In this method there usually is no digging or tilling of the soil; layers of organic matter are continually added on top of the existing bed each season and left to decompose over time. The mulch or organic matter is used to build up the soil fertility, to smother weeds, and to retain water. Less maintenance is needed for this type of garden.

When starting a new plot, the layers of organic matter are placed directly on top of the earth, whether it is sod, rocky or poor soil, or weeds. The layers are then left to decompose over time. The quantity and heaviness of the organic matter (also called mulch) blocks out any light so the sod or weeds will naturally die back. You will want to keep the mulch moist. Moist mulch will hasten the decomposition, adding nutrients to the existing soil, as well as attract earthworms, which will also help in making rich, fertile garden soil.

One of the main benefits to this method of gardening is that it is easy to do. You do not have to remove sod, weeds, or any other debris that may be in the area you want to use to start a new bed. There is no tilling or double-digging involved, so there is less work if you have less time to spend in the garden, or if you have a bad back, knees, or are disabled in any way. If you have a small area, this is an ideal way to make a veggie garden very quickly and with very little effort.

FACT

If you want your materials to decompose faster, you can add some earthworms along with the layers of organic matter. Composting worms can be purchased from most garden centers or through the Internet. This way you do not need to wait for the earthworms to find you; they are immediately working to make the soil better.

To plant seeds, just move some of the mulch aside and set them in. If the seed is large, lightly cover it with some mulch. Seeds do not need light to germinate; however, once they do sprout, they will need it, so make sure the mulch is not too heavy. If you are putting in transplants, just move the mulch aside, set the plant in, and then move the mulch back around the plant. This way light will not be able to reach the soil so weeds will not grow.

One word of caution: with this method of gardening, you can attract slugs. If you live in a rainy climate, layered or lasagna gardening may not be the best choice for you. Moist mulch is the perfect environment for harboring slugs, especially over the winter when they lay eggs.

The term "no-dig gardening" was first demonstrated by a gardener named Ruth Stout in the early 1900s. She wrote the books *How to Have a Green Thumb Without an Aching Back: A New Method of Mulch Gardening* and *Gardening Without Work*. She also made videos demonstrating how to create and maintain a no-dig garden. Patricia Lanza coined "lasagna gardening," which is similar to the no-dig method. She accidentally came up with the idea of layer mulch when she had to work and had less time to spend in her garden. The weeds started taking over, so she would lay cardboard in the pathways; then she would just step on the weeds in her garden beds to trample them down. She found her veggies flourished in this environment, so she kept adding more mulch—hence the term "lasagna gardening." She wrote a book on her method, titled *Lasagna Gardening*.

Planning Your Site

Before you start laying down any organic matter, take the time to look at your garden area and do some planning. Planning is very important. Once you starting layering the organic matter, it can be hard to move it to another spot. Vegetables need a minimum of six hours of direct sunlight to grow well, so make sure the area you choose has at least this much sun. Choose a spot where you have easy access to water, making it easier to keep the mulch moist.

Mark out the area you want to transform into a garden by using a garden hose, string, or lime. Having a visual of what the completed garden bed will look like makes it easier to decide if it is placed in the right spot and what size will work best. A garden hose can be easily moved around so you can experiment with different shapes to make it more accessible or attractive without having to do any of the work. If you are a first-time gardener choosing to use this method, start out small; the amount of organic matter you will need can be overwhelming to start.

A layered garden can be started at any time; however, fall is probably the best time to start, as this is the time of year when more organic matter like leaves and other garden debris is readily available. Starting a new bed in the fall gives the organic matter time to settle and decompose over the winter months; the fall rains and winter snow will help to keep the area moist without any effort on your part. You need to keep the mulch moist like a sponge, but not overly wet, so proper drainage is something else to consider when deciding on a spot for a new bed.

ALERT

The layered gardening method can be used in containers as well. Containers require a lighter soil, so the mixture of organic matter layered in a container is different from the soil of a regular garden bed. Use four times as much brown matter as green matter in a container. The ratio in a regular garden bed is usually one to two.

What Materials Do I Need?

To make a layered or lasagna garden, you can use anything that you would normally put into a compost pile. You want to use organic materials that will easily break down, and then quickly provide the nutrients the plants need to grow. Organic matter or material is defined as matter that has come from a once-living organism and is capable of decay, or is the product of decay.

When using organic materials in your layered garden, you will want to use the same method as you would when making a compost pile. Alternate the green and brown materials in a one-to-two ratio, using twice as much brown material. This way the materials will decompose more quickly than they would if a large amount of only one type of material was placed on the beds.

Here is a list of some common materials separated into green and brown materials that would be great for making and maintaining a layered garden:

GREEN ORGANIC MATERIALS

- Grass clippings
- Kitchen scraps (no meat or bones)

- Animal manures
- Compost
- Coffee grounds
- Weeds (make sure they have not gone to seed)
- Seaweed
- Trimmings from your flower and vegetable plants

These items add nitrogen to the soil and usually break down quickly; if there is too much of this green material, the garden can become smelly and attract flies. The best way is to lay down green materials and then cover them with a brown material, compost, or soil.

BROWN ORGANIC MATERIALS

- Cardboard (nonwaxed)
- Newspaper
- Straw
- Leaves
- Pine needles
- Wood chips
- Sawdust
- Peat moss
- Vegetable stocks, such as corn or brassica stems
- Shredded paper

The lists have the most common and readily available organic materials; however, these are not the only materials that can be used. Whatever you have access to can be used, just make sure it is organic so it will break down over time.

FACT

The smaller the size of kitchen waste material, the more quickly it will break down. One way of doing this is to purchase a used blender from a thrift store or garage sale. Run your kitchen waste through the blender with a little water; then pour the mixture onto your garden bed. The earthworms love the addition, and mixing makes it easier to keep away any unwanted smells.

Continue layering the organic materials while alternating the green and brown materials, until they reach a height of about 2 feet. This pile will shrink to half its height in a matter of days, so when starting a new garden, you may have to add more material every few weeks. That way, no light can reach whatever you are covering up, and the soil will decompose more quickly as well. Gradually you will only need to add materials once or twice a year to maintain your healthy new garden bed.

Gathering Materials

You will need a large amount of organic material, especially when starting a new layered garden plot, so planning and stockpiling is necessary. Set up an area where you can easily put materials into piles, or use a system similar to a compost bin. You can also stockpile using garbage cans, or smaller, plastic bins for smaller items. It is easier to divide the materials into the green and brown piles when you first get them, saving time in having to divide things up later. To maintain a healthy layered bed, it is a good idea to use a variety of materials that can go directly onto the beds as mulch. Once the initial base of the new garden is established and your plants are growing, you can layer the organic materials around the plants as you get them.

ESSENTIAL

Cardboard is one of the best materials to use as a first layer when starting a layered garden as it will block out any light, and it takes about two years to decompose totally. Newspaper will decompose in one season, so it is best used on a regular basis as mulch to keep the annual weeds from growing.

So, where do you get all these materials? Once you start looking around there is usually plenty of debris you can collect from your existing yard, flower beds, or veggie gardens that can be used in your layered garden bed. Let your neighbors and friends know what you are doing so they can collect their garden waste or grass clippings for you. If you are growing your vegetables organically, make sure you ask whether or not the neighbors spray with any pesticides. If they do, stay away from those materials. The pesticides will leach into the soil and into your veggies.

If you live in a rural area, animal manures, straw, and hay can usually be collected from local farms. If, however, you live in an urban area, these are less readily available. Garden centers or animal feed lots will sell bagged manure, and some will sell bales of hay or straw, but if you have a large space, it can get expensive to purchase these materials on a regular basis. A less expensive option for collecting green materials is to talk with your local landscape company to see if you can use their debris (grass clippings, small branches, and shrubs). Often these items are already chipped and very easy to use. For less expensive brown materials, go to local building supply stores, local building contractors, or tree trimmers and ask them to put aside sawdust or wood chips for you.

For cardboard, check your local liquor store; they often give empty boxes away for free. Try collecting from any warehouse or appliance store where you may get some larger pieces of cardboard. Collect your own newspapers or check with your local recycles depot for cardboard and newspapers. Keep all mail and computer paper at home or collect it from the office; invest in a shredder and shred all this paper. Store the shredded paper in a garbage can and spread the material over your garden bed when it is needed. Shredded paper will decompose more quickly than sheets of paper or newsprint.

ALERT

Seaweed is another great addition to your layered garden. If you are lucky enough to live near the ocean, avoid taking any seaweed in February on the western coast of Canada, because during that time the seaweed is needed for spawning salmon.

Most coffee shops are willing to put aside their coffee grounds for you if you ask and make arrangements to pick them up regularly. Even some grocery stores will give away compostable produce instead of putting it in the garbage. These items make great green materials for a layered garden.

Depending on where you live and the size of your layered garden, you may have to get inventive in finding a readily available supply of good-quality organic matter. Take stock of what you can produce in your own yard, see what your friends and neighbors can give you, and then go to your local businesses. There are a lot of items going to landfills that could be used to make a very productive, layered vegetable garden.

Building a Layered Garden Bed

As previously mentioned, fall is one of the best times to start a layered garden bed. However there is no perfect time, and this method can be used at any time of the year. If you choose to make a new bed in the spring or summer and want to plant your veggies immediately, you may want to add more "soil-like" materials like compost, aged animal manures, peat moss, or top soil than you would in the fall, as the materials will not have the time they would in the fall to decompose. You will want at least 3 to 4 inches of usable soil to plant your seeds or transplants so they will have access to nutrients, especially if the area you are using has poor soil.

Here are steps to creating a layered or lasagna vegetable garden:

1. Mow your lawn or a weedy area and keep the clippings for spreading later.
2. Mark out the area you want to make into your garden bed. This can be done using stakes or by edging the area by digging a trench around it. This gives the area a raised bed appearance, and the edges of your garden will be well defined.
3. Cover the area with cardboard, making sure no area is left uncovered; overlapping the cardboard will help. If you do not have cardboard, newspaper can be used—just make sure you put on a thick layer—as newspaper will decompose more quickly than cardboard.
4. Moisten the cardboard or newspaper using your garden hose to wet the area thoroughly.
5. If you have any shredded leaves or grass clippings, put a thin layer over the cardboard, 1 to 3 inches if you have that much.
6. You can then add compost, kitchen scraps, peat moss, or any combination of these.
7. Add another layer of shredded leaves, straw, sawdust, shredded newspaper, or any combination of these. Give the bed another good spray of water; you want it to feel like a moist sponge.

8. Repeat steps five, six, and seven until your layered bed is about 2 feet in height. Each layer should be 3 to 4 inches.
9. If you are starting this bed in the spring or summer you will want to add more compost or garden soil on top of the whole area; 3 to 12 inches is best. If all you can put on is a couple of inches, leave the site for a few weeks so the cardboard can decompose a bit. If you can put on at least 3 or 4 inches of soil-like material, you can start planting your seeds and transplants.

FACT

Black plastic can be used to cover your layered garden. It is usually used for three reasons: first, to warm up the soil so it will decompose more quickly and plants can be put out earlier in the season; second, to keep the soil from getting too wet, and third, to block sunlight so weeds do not grow. Just cut a little hole in the plastic to plant your seed or transplant.

Some people do not like a messy, layered garden, so they compost all their kitchen scraps and then cover their beds with the compost. Layering works either way, but it is definitely easier just to spread the kitchen waste and cover it with some straw, peat moss, or topsoil. A cautionary note is to try not to place weedy organic materials such as hay or animal manures as your top layer. It is better to place these materials on the bottom under other organic materials that will help to prevent any weed seeds from germinating.

The Best Plants to Use

Any common vegetable plant will grow in a layered garden; however, some do better than others. Here are a few that are recommended to grow using this method of gardening.

Asparagus

This vegetable plant loves to be mulched, so it's a perfect match for a layered or lasagna garden. If starting with a new garden, first lay down newspaper and then top with 18 to 24 inches of organic matter such as manure and peat moss. When planting the asparagus roots, add more manure and peat moss around the roots. When the roots start to sprout, add a layer of compost and grass clippings. It takes about three years after planting before you get a good harvest of asparagus, but if well-cared for, the plants will produce for as many as fifteen years. Keep adding layers of these organic materials each spring, and you will have a healthy harvest of asparagus for many years to come.

Cucumber

Before planting your cucumber seeds or setting your transplants out, make sure the soil is warm enough; night temperatures should be at least 10°C or 50°F before planting. Cucumbers like at least 6 inches of mulch such as straw, which will keep their roots moist and cool. Keep adding layers of manure or compost to the cucumber bed as the plant grows, giving it a shot of nutrients to produce fruit.

Garlic

Garlic is another plant that grows best when well mulched. Garlic is usually planted in the fall, so plan on making your new bed in later summer. You can utilize black plastic to decompose your organic matter more quickly. In October or November, set the garlic cloves into the mulch so they are covered. The green tops will start coming through the mulch in January; in the spring the seed heads will start to form—these are called garlic scapes. Cut the scapes off so all the plant's energy can go to forming the cloves rather than the flower. Once the green tops start to die back, the cloves are ready to be pulled. After they are pulled, place another layer of organic matter onto the bed, and it will be ready to plant a summer crop.

ESSENTIAL

The flowering stem of the garlic plant is called a scape and is delicious to eat. The stem grows quite tall once the flower starts to form. Before it opens, cut the scape off the plant. It has a similar taste to a garlic clove, can be chopped, and is great to use in soups, stews, and stir-frys.

Potatoes

Use the layered or lasagna garden method to save time digging trenches or hilling your potato beds. Potatoes do not want a nitrogen-rich bed, so avoid using grass clippings or other nitrogen-rich materials when adding organic material to your potato bed. Never lime the potato bed, but adding bone meal in between the layers of mulch will give you a great potato harvest.

When starting a new bed for potatoes, lay down a thick layer of newspaper, wet it, sprinkle on some bone meal, and then place your seed potato on top. Next, cover the seed potatoes with thick mulch (at least 12 to 18 inches) made of straw, spoiled hay (may contain weed seeds), or leaves; anything dry will work. The potatoes' tops will easily grow through the mulch. To harvest, just push it aside and pick up the potatoes, no digging needed.

Tomatoes

Tomato roots can reach as far down as 6 feet, and they like to stay cool and moist. A regular deep watering, rather than frequent shallow watering, is needed to grow tomatoes well. The layered garden method utilizing mulch will help to retain the moisture in the soil. Once the tomato plant is transplanted and staked, add a layer of damp newspapers around the base, then cover the paper with a few inches of straw or shredded leaves. Give the plants a deep watering around the base of the plant, and then water regularly once a week.

Maintaining Your New Garden

Growing healthy, abundant vegetables takes some time, energy, and usually a little money. The layered or lasagna garden is by far one of the easier methods for saving money and for creating a low-maintenance garden. All you really need to do is keep adding organic matter to your bed on a regular basis. As with any garden, you will need to pay attention to your plants, fertilize on a regular basis, give the plants at least 1 inch of water each week, and weed when necessary (this method helps to keep the weeds in control, however your bed will not always be totally weed-free).

ESSENTIAL

Another easy way to make a garden bed is to place 1 foot of hard-wood chips over the area, plant fava beans in the chips, and then enjoy the harvest throughout the summer. At the end of the season you can till the area under to make a regular garden bed or continue to mulch with more organic material to continue with the layered-garden method.

There are several benefits to using the layered or lasagna gardening method. It is a way to keep your garden fairly weed-free. The mulch helps to retain water, so less time is spent on watering. There is less need to fertilize as the decomposing organic matter feeds your plants and the soil you create is easy to work. This is a great gardening method to use if you cannot make a compost pile—due to animals or neighbors—or do not want to make one. Your kitchen scraps can be put directly on the garden bed and then covered up (so as not to attract animals and to reduce any smell as they decompose). This gardening method is great for those tiny garden spaces, especially ones with poor or very little soil.

CHAPTER 4

Square-Foot Gardens

Using the square-foot gardening method is an excellent way to grow intensively in a small-space garden. In this method, vegetables and herbs are grown in square-foot sections, thereby maximizing how many of each you can grow in that space. In this chapter you will learn the basics of using the square-foot method and gain tips on how to get your site ready, how to decide plant placement, and how to use a step-by-step plan to get you started.

What You Need to Know

If you have a small space or limited time to garden, using the square-foot method can work well to grow an abundance of vegetables. The basics of square-foot gardening are:

- You can grow more food in less ground space.
- Less time is needed to maintain your garden.
- You are growing in 1-foot squares.
- Each square contains one, four, nine or sixteen plants.
- The 1-foot squares can be grouped together into raised beds measuring 4 feet by 4 feet.
- One 4-foot by 4-foot block can potentially feed one person for a season.

A certain number of vegetables, herbs, and fruits are planted into each square foot. For example, one tomato is planted in one square, whereas four spinach or lettuce can be planted in that same space allotment. The size of the plant at maturity determines how many plants are placed into each square. Certain plants have a tendency to sprawl, so they are grown vertically using stakes and netting to maximize space.

The square-foot gardening method is usually done in open-bottomed raised beds with the area is divided into one-foot square sections. These sections are marked off with sticks, string, or some kind of marking to clearly define the square-foot grid. Each section is used to plant a different vegetable; this helps to encourage plant rotation, as each variety of vegetable is moved to another section the following season.

FACT

Square-foot gardening uses the practice of planning small but intensively planted gardens. The phrase "square-foot gardening" was popularized by Mel Bartholomew in his 1981 Rodale Press book and subsequent PBS television series.

If you choose to plant in this way and are starting a new garden from scratch, it is suggested to build 4-foot by 4-foot beds. This makes is easy to divide the area into square-foot sections. Ideally you will want to be able to access your garden box from all sides to make it easy to care for the plants and maintain good soil fertility. If this size or shape is not suitable for your garden area you can make the bed narrower. A box of any length, either 2- or 3-feet wide, will work just as well. Just keep the bed in even-foot lengths to make it easier to make the square-foot grid. If you can only access your bed from one side, two or three feet is the maximum distance that most people can reach without straining, so make the bed no wider.

If you already have an existing garden space and want to start growing using the square-foot method, it can be developed almost anywhere. Look at your existing space and modify it if you need to. Just remember to mark off the area into square-foot sections, so you can plant appropriately. Remember, to manage the bed easily, it is important to be able to reach all the squares comfortably. If your small space does not include any soil area you can still use the square-foot method on a balcony or patio to grow vegetables, fruits, and herbs in containers. Get a pot that is a foot across and start planting.

▼ Square-foot garden grids

Benefits

Gardeners have been using the square-foot method successfully for several decades and there are numerous benefits, including saving time, energy, water, and money.

Less Work

Vegetable gardening can take a lot of time. It can take backbreaking work to turn the soil, and consistent weeding is needed to keep the plants healthy and happy. Using the square-foot gardening method can make vegetable gardening a much easier and enjoyable task. Because it is usually done in a small area, the soil is never walked on or compacted, and the soil remains loose and easy to till or dig. Weeding takes less time than growing in a conventional bed. The plants are grown closely together and block any light from reaching the bare soil so weeds cannot germinate or grow. You can get a large amount of vegetables from a small space because the method promotes intensive planting.

ALERT

If you are going to install a brick or stone patio or pathway, make sure you lay down a heavyweight landscape fabric designed especially for this purpose before installing the materials. This will keep weeds from growing through the cracks and make the area easier to maintain.

Using the square-foot method makes it easy to keep the garden soil more fertile. The area is traditionally smaller than conventional gardens, so less digging, tilling, and amending is needed. At the end of each season and the beginning of the next, just mix in a few handfuls of compost and some organic fertilizer to each square foot and you are good to go.

Less Water

You are growing in a smaller area so less water is required to grow a large amount of food. Hand watering is probably the easiest method for this type of garden. Just remember to water at the base of the plants so the water reaches the plant roots. All vegetables and fruits require regular watering (approximately 1 inch of water per week) and some fertilizing to grow well.

Pesticide- and Herbicide-Free

This type of gardening promotes organic methods for growing vegetables, herbs, and fruits. Marigolds are regularly used as a natural insect repellant in this garden plan; the smell of marigolds has been proven to keep a variety of pests away from your vegetable plants. Growing a few of these colorful flowers in one of the foot squares is all that is needed to help keep your garden free of unwanted insects and pests.

Plant rotation, another principle in organic gardening, is utilized in square-foot gardening. Plant rotation is a process where plants within the same family of vegetables are planted in a different area each year, usually using a three- or four-year rotation. By moving your vegetables to a new spot each year, you will be able to keep the soil more fertile, reduce the amount of pests and diseases in your garden, and ultimately grow more productive and healthier plants.

QUESTION

What is organic gardening?
Gardening without using synthetic fertilizers and pesticides is considered organic gardening. The basis of organic gardening, by adding organic matter, fertilizers, and amendments, is to feed the soil rather than just the plant.

Plant rotation can seem very confusing when you first start learning about it; however, once you learn the basics it is easy to do. Different vegetable plants use varying amounts of nutrients from the soil to grow well. One year you may grow a vegetable that uses a lot of nitrogen in one area. When you rotate your crop the following year, you may plant a crop that uses more phosphorus. The rotation gives the soil time to increase its nitrogen level again. By planning your vegetable layout this way the soil stays healthy because it has time to rebuild.

ALERT

Tomatoes, peppers, eggplants, potatoes, and okra are all in the nightshade family; broccoli, cauliflower, cabbage, brussels sprouts, collards, and kale are from the Brassica family; cucumbers and squash are cucurbits; and beans and peas are legumes. Veggies from the same family should not be planted in the same spot the following year.

Another benefit to moving your vegetables to different areas of your garden each year is to cut down on the pests and diseases in your garden. A few of these little guys can wreak havoc on your vegetable patch so try to keep them out. Some vegetable plants will attract certain pests and diseases, ones that often live in the soil where the plant is growing. By moving this vegetable plant to another area of the garden, the pests or diseases have nothing to feed on and usually will not survive. Other plants will repel certain pests and diseases and these plants, too, will help to keep your garden free of unwanted pests.

Companion planting is another gardening method used to keep plants disease and pest free. This method uses a diverse planting of vegetables, herbs, and flowers to make a more natural growing environment.

Easy Access

The smaller area generally used in the square-foot method makes the beds more accessible from all sides and makes maintenance of the garden easier. If you have limited mobility, an aging back, arthritis, or use a wheelchair, the square-foot gardening method is a great option for you since a raised bed can be built to a height most comfortable for you. You can create a raised bed with a bottom—basically a large container—and place it on top of a table or make it with legs to the height you want.

A garden bed designed at a convenient height will eliminate any unnecessary bending if that is a concern. Using a lightweight soil mix will make digging and planting easier as well and using smaller and lighter tools (children's tools perhaps) can make gardening tasks easier for everyone. Gardening should be fun and easy, so find what works best for you.

Plant Protection

Square-foot gardens are usually grown in small, raised beds, giving the plants extra protection. Staking can be easy to do as well. Stakes for vertical growing, row covers, or plastic for making a mini-greenhouse can easily be constructed utilizing the four sides of the raised bed.

ESSENTIAL

Encourage ladybugs and butterflies to your garden. They eat unwanted pests like aphids, mealy bugs, and whiteflies. To attract the ladybugs, plant marigolds, goldenrod, or butterfly weed around your garden.

Plants may need protection from the cold, especially when they are young transplants or the seeds are just starting to germinate. Likewise, they may need some shade from the hot summer sun, or protection from pests.

Attach a trellis structure of wire or plastic pipe to the side of the bed; then cover it with plastic or a row cover to protect the plants. Place chicken wire around the area to make a quick and easy fence to keep out unwanted pests.

Disadvantages

Even though this method is highly recommended for small-space gardening, there are a few other things to consider before jumping in completely. Square-foot gardening can take a lot more planning and record keeping than some gardeners may want to do. Recording where each vegetable is planted from year to year is necessary to rotate your veggies properly and keep the soil fertile. The record can be a simple drawing of your garden that marks where each plant is grown. However, it takes time and forethought to do even this.

Because you are growing intensely, it is necessary to have the soil as fertile as possible so the plants will have access to the nutrients they need to grow well. This means having a good source of organic matter such as compost, animal manures, and organic fertilizers to add to the garden soil.

Accessible Compost

Compost is extremely useful for any garden; however, it is a necessity when using the square-foot garden method. It is important to add compost to the garden bed twice every season: once before you plant your seeds or transplants, and again after you have pulled any plants that are at the end of their cycle.

Compost can be fairly easy to make, but it is another job that needs to be done when growing a square-foot garden. Before committing to a square-foot garden, decide whether you want to take the time to manage a compost pile or find out if you have access to this material from somewhere else.

Getting Your Site Ready

If you have decided to go with the square-foot gardening method to grow your veggies, you will need to prep your space. As discussed earlier, the traditional square-foot garden bed is a 4-foot by 4-foot square with a pathway around it so it is accessible from all sides. The raised bed is also traditionally made from wood with a height of at least 12 inches.

If wood is not an option for you, you can make your beds out of a variety of materials such as rocks, recycled railway ties (just watch that they are not treated with creosote, which is not recommended in growing food organically), adobe blocks, or bricks.

If you are starting a new garden bed you will most likely be bringing in soil. If you have done your legwork and have healthy, fertile soil, you will not need to be adding any compost or fertilizers the first year. If, however, your soil is not ideal, take the time to add amendments such as animal manures, organic fertilizers, and compost, if you have it.

ESSENTIAL

Garden catalogs often use the terms "full sun" and "partial shade" when describing the amount of sunlight a plant needs. Here are some common terms. Full sun means eight or more hours of direct sunlight; partial shade means fewer than eight hours of sun, or a full day of sunlight coming through leaves from a tree; full shade means no direct sun.

If you have an existing garden bed you want to transition into a square foot garden, mark out the square-foot grid. If the soil has not been amended or fertilized in the past year, make sure you take the time to turn over the soil, adding as much organic matter from compost or animal manures as possible. It is also important to add in organic fertilizers for nitrogen, phosphorus, and potassium.

Plant Placement

In square-foot gardening, every square-foot space contains either one, four, nine, or sixteen plants. The size of the plant when mature will define how many plants can be grown within the 1-foot square. Tall or climbing plants are trellised or staked and supported with netting or lattice to minimize the amount of ground space they need to use. Depending on your garden site, use the vertical plants to give either some shade to the rest of the squares or some protection from cool winds.

Here is a list of some common vegetables and berries, indicating the number of plants that can be grown in each square-foot section, and which plants can be staked vertically to maximize the ground space.

▼ **TABLE 4-1: COMMON VEGETABLES AND BERRIES FOR SQUARE-FOOT GARDENING**

Vegetable	Number of Plants per Square Foot	Grown Vertical
Bean, pole	8	Yes
Beet	9	
Brassica	1	
Carrot	16	
Corn (maize)	1	
Cucumber	2	Yes
Eggplant	1	
Lettuce	9	
Marigold flowers	4	
Parsley	4	
Pepper	1	
Radish	16	
Raspberry	4	
Spinach	9	
Strawberry	4	
Swiss chard	9	
Tomato	1	Yes

Plants that grow underground such a potatoes, beets, or carrots need to be grown in a bed that is at least 1 foot deep to allow enough room for the root to grow strong and healthy. If you are planning to grow these vegetables in a container, make sure the container is deep enough.

A Step-by-Step Garden Plan

The design is based on one or two 4-foot by 4-foot squares. One bed is used to grow small plants, the other for growing larger plants. This design can provide veggies for two people for a season. You can double or triple the area if you have a larger family to feed.

Exchange List

Vegetables and fruits need a certain amount of space to grow their best. If you would prefer to grow something other than what is in the previous table, use the following exchange list to find the most appropriate replacement. Remember to try to keep families of vegetables together so you can properly rotate the vegetables each year.

▼ TABLE 4-2: HEAT-LOVING VEGETABLES

Vegetable	Number of Plants per Square Foot
Tomato	1
Pepper	1
Eggplant	1
Basil	4

▼ TABLE 4-3: BRASSICAS

Vegetable	Number of Plants per Square Foot
Broccoli	1
Cabbage	1
Cauliflower	1
Brussel sprouts	1
Kale	1
Collard	4

▼ TABLE 4-4: ROOT VEGETABLES

Vegetable	Number of Plants per Square Foot
Carrot	16
Beet	9
Turnip	9
Radish	16
Onion	16
Leek	16
Garlic	16

▼ TABLE 4-5: SALAD GREENS

Vegetable	Number of Plants per Square Foot
Lettuce	4
Oriental greens	4
Mizuna	4
Arugula	4
Spinach	4
Swiss chard	4
Celery	1
Salad greens	broadcast

QUESTION

What does broadcast mean?
To broadcast means to scatter seeds—you can lightly throw the seeds onto the top of the soil in the area you want them to grow. This works best when planting small seeds like salad greens or lettuce.

▼ TABLE 4-6: POTATOES, CORN, AND SQUASH

Vegetable	Number of Plants per Square Foot
Potato	1
Corn	1
Asparagus	1
Artichoke	1
Squash	1 plant takes 4 square feet

Planting Instructions

The dates are only guidelines. It is important to consider your climate and garden site so you are planting when your garden area is ready. Whether you are starting seedlings or direct seeding, always plant a few extra as not every seed will germinate.

Early March

Start seedlings in seedling trays indoors.

▼ TABLE 4-7: PLANTING IN EARLY MARCH

Vegetable	Number of Seeds to Plant
Tomato	6
Basil	6
Pepper	3
Cabbage	2
Broccoli	2
Spinach	3
Oriental greens	3
Leek	4

Late March

Plant seeds directly into the garden bed.

▼ TABLE 4-8: PLANTING IN LATE MARCH

Vegetable	Number of Seeds to Plant	Number of Inches Between Seeds
Peas, shelling	8	3
Peas, snow	8	3
Potato	1	12
Marigold	4	2

Make sure your soil is not too wet or cold; if it is not ready, plant in early April.

Early April

Start seedlings in flats indoors.

▼ **TABLE 4-9: PLANTING IN EARLY APRIL**

Vegetable	Number of Seeds to Plant
Cabbage	2
Broccoli	2
Lettuce	3
Spinach	3
Oriental greens	3

Early April

Plant seeds directly in your garden bed.

▼ **TABLE 4-10: PLANTING IN EARLY APRIL**

Vegetable	Number of Seeds to Plant	Number of Inches Between Seeds
Carrot	16	2
Beet	9	3
Radish	16	2

Make sure your soil is not too wet or cold; if it is not ready, plant in late April.

Late April

Set out seedlings to your garden.

▼ **TABLE 4-11: PLANTING IN LATE APRIL**

Vegetable	Number of Plants to Set Out
Cabbage	1
Broccoli	1
Lettuce	2
Spinach	2
Oriental green	2

Choose your healthiest transplants from early March seeding and give the other ones away.

Early May

Plant seeds directly in your garden bed.

▼ **TABLE 4-12: PLANTING IN EARLY MAY**

Vegetable	Number of Seeds to Plant	Number of Inches Between Seeds
Carrot	16	2
Radish	16	2
Potato	2	12

Late May

Set out seedlings to your garden.

▼ **TABLE 4-13: PLANTING IN LATE MAY**

Vegetable	Number of Plants to Set Out
Tomato	4
Basil	4
Pepper	2
Broccoli	1
Cauliflower	1
Lettuce	2
Spinach	2
Oriental greens	2
Leek	4

Choose your healthiest transplants from early March seeding and give the other ones away.

Late May

Plant seeds directly in your garden bed.

▼ **TABLE 4-14: PLANTING IN LATE MAY**

Vegetable	Number of Seeds to Plant	Number of Inches Between Seeds
Bean, green	9	3
Corn	2	12

Early June

Plant seeds directly in your garden bed.

▼ **TABLE 4-15: PLANTING IN EARLY JUNE**

Vegetable	Number of Seeds to Plant	Number of Inches Between Seeds
Bean, yellow	9	3
Corn	2	12

The square-foot gardening method has been used successfully in regions with desert conditions, mountains, high pollution, and even in cramped urban areas. You can use the square-foot method in its exact form, or utilize some of the principles in your existing garden, perhaps with containers. A few seeds planted in a square-foot area, some hand watering, your own compost, and a reasonably sunny spot (back *or* front yard) can produce a lot of veggies in a small space.

CHAPTER 5

Vertical Gardens

Vertical gardening offers easy solutions for growing some of your own vegetables and fruits in a small space. In this chapter you'll learn how to maximize your space by growing upward. You will find information on making and using a variety of trellises, structures, and living walls. You will also find inventive ways of staking your veggies for creating a healthy and successful food garden, and tips and suggestions on what vegetables grow best using these supports.

Things to Consider

Any kind of garden, whether it is small or large, can take advantage of vertical growing to maximize the space. Let your vertical garden do double duty. When planning a vertical garden, look around your house. Are there features that you want to enhance such as a beautiful view, or do you have something to hide like a busy road or an ugly air conditioner? Just remember most veggie plants grown upright like lots of light and heat. Make sure you have an area that gets at least eight hours of direct sun, and wherever you are starting, include a properly built structure to support the plants.

You can utilize existing walls, fences, or structures such as the side of a shed or garage to place a trellis or screen. Or you can make a self-standing structure to support the plants. Constructing a simple screen or trellis is the easiest way to start growing a vertical garden. Use the screen or trellis to divide your garden to make it look bigger, give the garden some depth, or hide some unwanted sight. Placing a mirror on a fence or trellis can give the illusion of a much larger space. Hanging a few baskets or using window boxes for your veggies will also maximize your space.

FACT

Incorporating perennials such as clematis or honeysuckle into your vertical garden will not only add color and fragrance to your garden but these flowering shrubs will also attract bees, hummingbirds, and beneficial insects to help keep your vegetable plants pest- and disease-free.

Certain veggies such as cucumbers, squash, beans, and tomatoes produce best when trained to grow upright. The kind of trellis, stake, or structure you will need depends on which plants you wish to grow; their size and weight at maturity will determine what kind of support they will need. If all you are planning to grow are beans and peas, there are inexpensive options to consider. If you want to trellis heavier vegetables and fruits like cucumbers, squash, or grapes, for example, a stronger structure will be needed. The last thing you want is to put up a flimsy trellis that will fall once the vegetable starts to produce.

Putting up a well-built structure such as a pergola for growing grapes, for example, can take time and some cash. If you are on a budget, there are a variety of materials such as tree branches, recycled wood, wire, iron, and pipe that can be used to train and support your vegetables and fruits. Growing vertically will keep your plants happy, use your small space more effectively, and create beauty and variety in the landscape.

A Trellis

It is possible to double your growing space by simply using a basic trellis to grow climbing veggies and fruits. A trellis can be a simple fence-like structure or an elaborate architectural structure. It depends on what you want to grow and how much you want spend. Your structure can be freestanding, fixed to posts that are secured into the ground, or secured to an existing wall or fence. Again, it depends on what is already existing in your garden that you may want to use and where you want to place the structure. If it is going to be attached to a wall, the trellis needs to be held away from the structure by a few inches; this will allow ventilation for the plant, prevent the trellis from rotting, and give the gardener easier access to harvest and maintain the plant. The spacing can be done by placing bricks on the ground or using a piece of wood that is attached to the existing structure to position the trellis a few inches away from the wall or fence.

FACT

Recycle old pantyhose, twist ties, string, ribbon, or strips of cloth to tie your plants to a trellis or stake. Ties will need to be checked occasionally so they do not get too tight and strangle the plant.

A trellis placed against the wall of a building or fence could also be attached using hinges. This method would allow the trellis to be either raised or lowered allowing easier access to clean and paint the wall or fence, as well making it easier to reach the fruits to harvest and maintain the plant.

Building a Simple Wooden Trellis

A common trellis is an open latticework usually made of wood or iron. Most building supply centers sell various lengths of lattice; however you can easily make a simple trellis out of wood, small trees, or bamboo.

To make this simple 6-foot-high by 36-inch-wide trellis it is recommended to use cedar or redwood for a longer-lasting support; however less expensive fir or pine can also be used and will usually last at least five years.

Supply list: (Note: 1-inch by 2-inch measurements are usually only ¾ by 1¾ inches.)

❑ Four (1-inch by 2-inch) wood strips cut to 6-foot lengths
❑ Eight (1-inch by 2-inch) wood strips cut to 36-inch lengths
❑ Two (2-inch by 4-inch) wooden boards cut to 32½ inch lengths (3½ inches less than the width of the trellis)
❑ Forty (6d) galvanized nails (Extra are always needed just in case you lose or bend some.)
❑ Hammer
❑ Drill (It is recommended to drill as small hole in the wood strips before pounding in the nail so as not to split the wood.)

Follow these steps to make the trellis:

- **Step 1:** Nail one of the 6-foot length wood strips from the top edge of the wood strip to the edge of the 4-inch side of the 2-inch by 4-inch wooden board. Repeat on the other end with a second strip.
- **Step 2:** Nail the other 2-inch by 4-inch wooden board to the bottom back of the strips from step 1.
- **Step 3:** Nail the next 2-inch by 4-inch wooden board 2-inches from the first 2-inch by 4-inch wooden board. Repeat on the other end.
- **Step 4:** Nail one of the shorter wood strips perpendicular to the long strips 2 inches below the top of the longer strip.
- **Step 5:** Nail the next wood strip 4-inches below the first one.
- **Step 6:** Nail the next wood strip 12-inches below the second one.
- **Step 7:** Repeat steps 5 and 6 until all the shorter wood strips are nailed to the frame.

You can now attach the 2-inch by 4-inch wood board directly to an existing wall or fence. Another option is to attach a second set of 2-inch by 4-inch wood boards to the existing structure and attach your trellis to it using eye hooks or hinges; this will make it easier to remove or raise the trellis.

ESSENTIAL

Make a creative garden fence using 18-inch diameter steel stakes, found in the masonry section of any local hardware store, as your fence posts. Attach branches, dowels, copper pipe, or lath horizontally with wire to create a garden barrier. This structure can be easily moved around your garden.

This trellis will work well for beans, peas, and cucumbers. A stronger trellis is needed to support large, heavy vegetable plants such as winter squash, or fruits such as grapes or kiwi. So check out other options. Either way, make sure the trellis is firmly secured either into the ground or to an existing structure.

Other Trellis Ideas

▲ DIY-style vertical planter

There are various materials you can use to create a trellis on an existing wall, fence, or between two sturdy posts secured into the ground.

- Strong twine. This is mainly used if you will be growing peas, beans, or flowers like sweet peas.
- Galvanized wire. This is used for larger, heavier plants such as squash, cucumbers, or some espaliered fruits.
- Green or white plastic-coated netting, which can be purchased in most garden centers and comes with different-sized holes. Choose the 4- or 6-inch holes for growing larger vegetables such as cucumbers for ease of accessing the fruit, or the 1-inch squares for trellising peas or beans.

- Nylon cord strung across between two eyehooks or sturdy nails secured to an existing fence or structure.

Trellises can be used to enhance a garden in addition to growing food. Have fun creating your own personal hideaway in your tiny space by adding a chair in the shade of a trellis, or use a trellis to divide your garden into garden rooms. The rooms will make a small area more intriguing and attractive. Another great idea is to attach a large mirror to a fence or trellis, giving the illusion of a much larger space than what really exists.

Building Structures

You may have a shed, a garage, or the side of your house that you can use to grow some of your food upward; however, if none of these are available or you need other options, constructing a pergola or a terraced garden (especially if you have a hilly space) is another way to maximize space. These structures will be permanent so some planning is important. What do you want to use them for? Where will they be best located in your space? What size do you want or need? What kind of materials do you want to use? How much will they cost to construct? What is your budget? Getting advice from professionals when building permanent support structures can be helpful—they can be very costly to construct and should be built properly to last for many years.

Pergola

Pergolas were originally designed in warm climates to provide shade for a place to walk or sit. A variety of fruits, flowers, and vegetables were grown on the structure to help shade the area below it. The most common materials used for building a pergola are wood or iron. When building a pergola, you can go big and expensive if it is going to be used as a garden room, or you can build more simply if the main use will be to support a few grapes or bean plants.

If you want to make your own pergola to support heavier items such a fruits or squash plants, make it at least 6 feet wide and whatever length will fit into your garden space. The upright posts should be at least 3 inches by

4 inches in diameter at whatever length you want the pergola height to be (usually a minimum of 6 feet high so a person can easily walk under it). The upright posts are held up with sturdy cement or concrete stands that are 12 inches square (commonly used when building a fence). For the material used across the top use wood or sturdy iron that is 2 inches by 4 inches. All these materials can easily be purchased at your local building supply store. Treated wood will last longer; however, make sure a nontoxic preservative is used if you want to grow your food organically.

FACT

Plastic and wire half baskets are easy to hook on to a trellis to make a beautiful living wall. There are plenty of different supports that hang single pots or baskets; check them out at your local garden store.

A smaller pergola structure can be built out of poles, bamboo, or small trees nailed together if you are just wanting to grow lighter plants like beans or peas. Even with this small structure you will still want to make sure the upright posts are sturdy and supported by either being buried in the ground or being connected to stakes that are buried in the ground. The benefit of a smaller structure is it can be moved around your garden, making it easier to rotate your crops.

Terraced Garden

Anyone who has seen the extensive use of terraced gardens in Asia can see the benefit of building, even a very small version of one, in a small space. If you have a hillside that is unsightly, difficult to get to, or hard to keep from a weed nightmare, making a terraced garden can easily turn it into a productive space. Even if you live in a concrete jungle, a terraced garden can be built out of cement blocks or wood to maximize your space.

There are many benefits to a terraced garden:

- It can increase your growing area, especially on a hillside.
- The garden beds are easy to reach, relieving stress to your back or knees and making gardening more accessible if you have a disability.

- Terracing a hillside helps to slow down soil erosion and better retain water.

Growing on a steep bank can be difficult, as the ground is hard to get to and awkward to plant and maintain. Depending on the size of the area you want to develop, the terrace can either be built quickly by hand or, while the project may be more costly, you can hire someone with a machine to do the terracing for you. Either way terracing can make a huge difference in how much you can grow in the space and how easy your garden is to maintain.

ALERT

Raised beds around a patio do not dry out as quickly as containers because they hold more soil. For a more labor-saving garden, grow perennial plants such as asparagus or herbs like rosemary, thyme, and sage instead of annual vegetables.

When building a terraced garden, scope out the area to see how many levels could be built, the depth of each level, and the length you want each to be. Marking out the levels using stakes and string will help you to visualize what the arrangement will look like, and you can use the markers when the digging starts.

- **Step 1.** Dig holes into the ground where posts can be placed and hammered in. You will want a post every 4 to 6 feet. The height of the post will depend on the steepness of the slope. Make sure the post is securely hammered into earth.
- **Step 2.** On the downhill side, nail boards (2 inches by 6 inches) to the posts; this will help to contain the soil.
- **Step 3.** Excavate the soil, making a straight edge below the board, while throwing the soil upward behind the board. Dig down to the height you want your first terrace to be, making a flat area along the bottom where your pathway will be.
- **Step 4.** As you excavate the soil, nail more boards to the now-exposed post to contain the soil (you are basically building a fence against the exposed soil).

- **Step 5.** Continue with steps 3 and 4 until the length of the first terrace is complete.
- **Step 6.** If another level is needed, start at step 1 again.

Note: It is best to used nontoxic, pressure-treated wood or cedar, if available, so the wood will not rot. If wood is not readily available, or too costly, cement blocks or rocks could be used as well.

If you live in an urban area where there is no soil, let alone a hillside to terrace, you can build a structure similar to a stairway using wood or cement blocks. Build each step to a depth of 12 to 16 inches—to whatever length and height you want. Make as many steps as you want, just make sure you can easily reach the beds without straining.

Living Walls

Walls, fences, and the sides of buildings can provide much-needed privacy, especially in busy urban areas, but sometimes they can be very unsightly. Growing a living wall of vegetables can provide a much-needed space for growing food as well as make the area look more appealing.

If the wall is located in a sunny location, the wall can act as a solar store by trapping in heat and offering a warm microclimate for your plants. Heat-loving plants such as tomatoes, peppers, eggplants, cucumber, and basil are some common examples that will benefit with this extra heat.

ESSENTIAL

Colorful, free-blooming flowers offer nectar to bees and seeds to hungry birds. Some common flowers that will attract the birds and the bees to your garden are bee balm, columbine, coreopsis, honeysuckle, impatiens, petunia, sunflower, and morning glory.

If your wall or fence is in a less sunny spot, you can still grow veggies or flowers that will take a bit of shade such as lettuce, spinach, and cabbage family crops. Some shade-loving flowers such as hydrangea and jasmine will attract beneficial insects and butterflies to your garden. Cherry trees can take a little shade as well, so espalier a cherry tree against the side of a wall that gets only four to six hours of sunlight. If the area gets little or no sun use, it will attract insects and other animals to rest and drink by hanging containers of water. Or create a wall with baskets or containers for storing your mulch or recycling materials. When you have a small space, being creative is sometimes necessary.

Staking

Staking is used to support a plant growing upright by attaching the plant to some kind of material, usually a piece of wood, metal, or bamboo with one end driven into the ground. The plant is secured or fastened to the stake at various intervals to hold it upright as it grows.

There are several other benefits to staking your vegetables and fruits:

1. You can potentially grow twice as much food in the same area.
2. It is easier to see the fruits and veggies to harvest them.
3. Having to bend less when harvesting makes vertical gardening easier on your back and legs.
4. Fruits and pods do not touch the ground, which helps keep them from getting moldy or discolored.
5. Better airflow around the plants keeps them healthier.
6. More light and heat can reach the fruits to help them ripen.

FACT

Use a stack of four plastic-seaside buckets (graduated in size) to make a strawberry tower. Make sure each bucket has a drainage hole at the bottom, then fill each bucket with some multipurpose potting soil and stack them with the biggest bucket on the bottom. Fill the spaces between the buckets and plant strawberries (two per bucket).

Vegetable-gardening stakes can be used to support climbing vegetables such as pole beans or peas, and sprawling vegetables such as tomatoes, cucumbers, and squash. The best time to put up stakes or other supports is at planting time, so you do not have to disturb the plant roots once they are developing. You can then train and tie the plant to the stake as it grows.

▲ Wooden garden bed with homemade vertical trellis

Here are some easy-to-make stakes:

❏ Teepee made from wooden poles, small trees, or bamboo. Place three to eight poles in a teepee shape and tie them together at the top. Spread them outward and secure each piece into the ground.
❏ Galvanized fence wire can be easily purchased at a building-supply store. It can be shaped into a circle and placed into your garden or cut to any length you need and secured between two posts.
❏ Wire cages can be purchased at any hardware or garden store and are commonly used for staking tomatoes.
❏ Garden string or twine tied between two posts works well for lighter veggies such as beans or peas. Stretch the string between two pieces of wood that are secured into the ground.

- Wooden frames can be built to whatever sizes you want or need. An old window frame can be leaned against a wall or fence to make an easy structure for cucumbers to climb.
- Nylon trellis made of soft white plastic can be purchased at your local garden center. It is easy to work with, clean, and store, and is strong enough to hold up larger plants like squash and cucumbers when hung between two sturdy, secure posts. The netting usually comes in 6- or 8-foot lengths with 4- or 6-inch squares and can be easily cut to whatever length you need. Once it is up, just train your plants to wind around and through the holes.
- Green garden netting is a plastic mesh with ⅝- by 1¼-inch squares that can be found at most garden centers or hardware stores. This netting works well for peas as their tendrils can easily grasp the material. This type of netting is also placed over cherry trees to protect the fruit from birds.
- Eyehooks drilled into a cement or wooden wall work well for tomatoes or cucumbers. Space the eyehooks every few feet depending on the plants you want to grow. Stretch a piece of wire or string through the hooks and then hang more wire or string downward toward the ground securing each line into the ground.
- X-shaped stakes use two pieces of bamboo or wood connected into an X and tied together with twine. Secure a set into the ground at either end of your bed (no wider than 6 feet for sturdiness) then place another piece of bamboo or wood across the top of the two ends. Run string or wire down from the cross piece to allow the plants to climb up it.
- Concrete grid is the material laid in concrete before it is poured. You can find it at building supply stores. Attach the grid to strong posts or a wall to make a very sturdy trellis. It may rust, however, so if you do not like the rusty look, choose one of the other suggestions.

ESSENTIAL

Climbing annual flowers can be added to your vertical garden for their color, fragrance, and their ability to attract beneficial insects. Some common annual flowers are black-eyed Susan vine, cardinal climber, cathedral bells, hyacinth bean, and moonflower.

The Best Plants for Your Vertical Garden

If you have limited space for growing some of your own food, using vertical space is a great way to increase your overall harvest. Here are some common vegetables best grown vertically.

Beans

There are several varieties of beans. Some, like bush beans, grow to be only 12 to 16 inches high and so do not require any trellising. However, climbing and runner varieties need upright support in order to grow well. Beans are quite a lightweight plant so a simply constructed trellis made out of bamboo or wood poles will work well. A teepee is a great option: set up eight stakes and plant two to four seeds at the base of each stake and let them climb. If you want to grow beans against a fence or wall, string hanging from eyehooks or nails on a piece of wood will work well. Beans like warmth to grow, so make sure you plant where they will get full sun.

ALERT

If the soil is cold, beans seeds will not sprout. To give your bean crop a quick start, presprout the seeds indoors. To do this, spread the seeds on a piece of damp paper towel. Seal the towel in a jar or plastic bag and keep it damp until the seeds start to sprout (usually a few days). Carefully remove the seeds from the towel and plant them into the soil.

Cucumber

There are several varieties of cucumber: slicing, pickling, and the long English are the most common ones. They all do best if grown upright. This way the fruit does not lie on the ground (it can become moldy if it comes into contact with the soil), you can easily water at the base of the plant, and it is easier to see the cucumbers, making harvesting more fun. Cucumbers need a strong trellis system as they get heavy once they start to grow. The white plastic netting or fencing material is probably the best to use, whether the plants are grown in a garden bed, up against a wall, or on the side of a building. Cucumbers like warmth to grow well, so choose a sunny spot.

Peas

Garden netting is one of the best trellis materials for peas, as the plant tendrils are small and they need to attach to something easy and small. Peas are more of a cool, moisture-loving crop, so get them started early in the spring. Like beans, they are a lightweight plant, so they do not need a big, strong structure to grow upright. There are several varieties: shelling, snap, and snow peas. The snap and snow peas can grow up to 6 feet, so make sure you have a trellis that is high enough for them.

Squash

Squash is often grown sprawling along the ground, which can take up a lot of garden space. They are large and heavy when mature, so growing them vertically requires a strong trellis or structure. Fencing wire can be placed in a circular shape in your garden bed, and then the plant can be trained to grow through and around the holes. Growing squash upright will save space and allow lots of light to reach the fruit. This method will also allow for good airflow, which will help to keep the plant free of mildew and keep the fruit from touching the ground and rotting.

ESSENTIAL

You can grow lettuce under the shade of cucumbers by training your cucumber plants to vine over a low arch made of chicken wire. Use 5-foot lengths of 3-foot–wide wire and set it up as a low bridge in your garden bed.

Tomato

The tomato is one of the most popular veggies grown and eaten in North America. They are much tastier when freshly picked, rather than picked up at the grocery store. Some gardeners find them difficult to grow, as they need a lot of heat and regular deep watering. But tomatoes may not grow well if they are overwatered; a once-weekly, deep watering is usually all they need. Tomatoes can become diseased if their leaves get wet or if the fruit touches the earth, so it is best to trellis them in some way.

For staking tomatoes, the most commonly used material is the wire cage that all gardening stores sell. This works well for some smaller varieties of tomato; however, the X-shaped stake is a great way to support the taller tomatoes.

As well as increasing your garden space, vertical growing can add interest to a garden space. Even if all you have are a few containers on a balcony, you can utilize the vertical space by putting stakes into your pots or attaching a trellis to the side of your balcony or an eaves trough. You can be as creative as you want when it comes to vertical gardening. Have fun.

CHAPTER 6

Container Gardens

Do you want to grow some veggies but live in a concrete jungle where the only outdoor space you have is a balcony or porch? Do you have a tiny garden space but the soil is rocky and hard? Growing your vegetables in containers is a great solution to these problems. In this chapter you will find great advice and information on everything you need to know about growing your vegetables in containers.

The Containers

If you do not have any soil available that can be easily moved, you can mix your own, or it can be purchased in bags of scientifically formulated potting mixes. This convenience means you do not need a lot of space to grow some of your own veggies. Tomatoes will thrive in a hanging basket, potatoes can be grown in a large bushel-sized container, and lettuce will grow great in a window box. Containers take up very little space and can be placed on a balcony, porch, or patio; they can sit on a windowsill, be attached to balcony railings, or hung in baskets from the rafters. They can also be positioned in a backyard among traditional garden beds to add structure and attractiveness to your overall garden.

When choosing a container for your vegetables, there are three important rules to remember. First, the container must be able to hold soil; second, it must be large enough for the plant to grow to maturity (some vegetables have shallow root systems whereas others have much deeper roots and need more space to grow); and third, water must be able to drain easily from the bottom of the container so the soil does not get waterlogged. The container can be any shape so long as it can fulfill these three essentials.

ESSENTIAL

Practical and attractive hanging planters can be made from using two recycled-plastic containers, one inside the other (leave at least 1 inch space around between them). Cut drain holes in the bottom of the smaller one; then fill it with potting soil. In the bottom of the larger container, lay some gravel or Styrofoam. The smaller pot sits inside the larger one. Trim the top edges if necessary.

Containers can be purchased at your local nursery or hardware store. The most common kinds available are traditional oak barrels, pots made from reconstituted paper, terra-cotta, ceramic, wood, plastic, and resin. If you are planning to grow your vegetables in a container for several years choose a good quality one that will last. Containers need to be cleaned on a regular basis to keep them looking good, as well as pest- and disease-free, so choose a container that you can take care of easily.

To save money, you can recycle items that are no longer fulfilling their original purpose. Some ideas for small containers for growing lettuces, for example, are tin cans, bricks with a center opening, milk cartons, a bucket, or an old cooking pot (a great place to use that kitchen pot that got burnt and will never come clean again!). When you purchase garden pots, there usually are holes in the bottom of them already; however, if you are recycling a container, make sure you make at least one good drainage hole so excess water can easily drain.

If you want to grow root crops or beans and peas, you need a little larger container. Some suggestions that might work are Styrofoam coolers, wooden crates, plastic crates (which may need a liner such as landscape fabric in order to hold the soil), and plastic ice cream buckets (ask at your local ice cream parlor for their empties). Garbage cans, wooden barrels, metal washbasins, old wheelbarrows that have become rusty and full of holes, or plastic clothes hampers are great options for planting larger crops such as tomatoes, potatoes, and squash. Or try your hand at woodworking. Cedar, redwood, or teak are your best choices for wood if you choose to build your own box, and building your own is a great way to get the size you want for that special spot. When it comes to funky containers, be creative and save money!

Container Soil

In a garden bed you use the soil that exists; however, with a container you usually need to purchase the soil. The amount and cost will depend on how many containers you need and the sizes and types of containers you choose to use. Some or all of the soil in your containers needs to be replenished every year, since the vegetable plants will draw all the nutrients that are in it. Some new soil every year is necessary unless you make your own compost, which works well in containers, and plants love it.

ALERT

Tomatoes, peppers, and cucumbers need a minimum depth of 18 inches of soil to support their roots. Use 18-inch pots or a 5-gallon bucket at a minimum. Lettuce roots require only a few inches of soil, so they can be grown in a window box or even a little red wagon.

There are many different products to choose from when buying potting soil. All potting soil consists of composted bark, compost, humus, sphagnum or peat moss, and either perlite or vermiculite (the white particles), which is used to lighten the soil mix. The proportion of each of these materials is different with each brand and varies the quality and price of the soil mixture you are purchasing. Here is some information on your options.

All-Purpose Potting Mix

Pricewise, this is your cheapest option. This type of mix usually has less perlite or vermiculite, which means your pots may not drain as well and will require more watering and fertilizing. This is a good option if you have compost or other soil amendments to add to the mix and you remember to fertilize your plants on a regular basis.

Premium Potting Mix

This mix has a higher content of perlite or vermiculite, so it has better drainage. The plant roots will be able to absorb the moisture held in the soil, so they require less frequent watering. Some brands have slow-release fertilizers mixed in as well, so less fertilizing is required. The premium brands are more expensive than the all-purpose brands but are a good all-round potting mix.

Professional Potting Mix

These mixes are processed, which gives them a much better texture. They have a higher content of sphagnum peat moss, vermiculite, perlite, and composted bark. They require less attention than the other mixes because they have better drainage capabilities and are already fertilized. With these added benefits, they are also pricier than the above two options.

Specialty Potting Mixes

For specific plants, usually flowers such as orchids, cactus, and African violets, there are mixes specially formulated for their nutritional and water requirements. These mixes are usually more expensive and are not used for growing veggies or herbs.

All container soils need to be light enough to allow good air circulation for the vegetable plants to get the oxygen and nutrients needed for strong growth. Another function of soil in containers is to give plant roots something to hold on to so plants will stay upright. If you have a windy location (for example, if you are growing on a roof top of a high-rise building), your containers will need more soil and your planters will need to be heavier than if you were growing the same plants at ground level.

ESSENTIAL

Vegetables in containers need six to eight hours of sunlight; eight is better. If it is necessary for you to move your containers around to follow the sun, choose pots that you can easily move.

What to Put in the Container

When planning your container-garden layout, make a note of which vegetables can be planted early and which will do well later in the season; make sure the size of container will work for both types. A good rule to remember when growing vegetables in containers: When you take a plant out of your container, put another vegetable in its place. This way you will have a continuous supply of wonderful vegetables to harvest and enjoy.

The following are suitable vegetables to grow in containers:

- Beans
- Beets
- Broccoli
- Carrots
- Cucumber
- Lettuce
- Peas
- Peppers
- Radishes
- Spinach
- Tomatoes

To grow lettuce, spinach, salad greens, radishes, and green onions, you need a container approximately 8 to 10 inches wide and at least 6 inches deep. In this size container you could grow two or three of your leafy greens and up to a dozen radishes or green onions. For growing carrots, beets, peas, and beans—just remember your peas and beans will produce a better harvest if they are grown on a trellis or supported in some way—the best size container is approximately 12 to 16 inches wide and at least 10 inches deep. If you choose a rectangular container, you could make great use of the space by growing your peas and beans in the back and planting your root crops in front of them.

Larger vegetables, such as tomatoes, cucumbers, cabbages, broccoli, peppers, potatoes, or dwarf corn, need a container at least 16 inches wide and with at least 18 inches of soil to grow well. For best results, use transplants when growing these vegetables (except for potatoes and corn). Grow only one of these plants in each container. To fill up the pot and make it look more attractive, plant lettuce or herbs around the base of the larger plant.

ALERT

There are some plants, such as mint, comfrey, and borage, that you may like to have in your garden. However, these plants can quickly become invasive, so plant them into a pot and sink the pot into the ground. Keep the rim of the pot a few inches above ground level.

Consider the following tips in order to create a successful container garden.

Choose Dwarf Varieties

When choosing to grow in containers, look for dwarf varieties. These are vegetable plants that are smaller in size and therefore need less space to grow. Usually the root system needs less space as well, making these vegetables a great option for containers. There are many more dwarf varieties becoming available as the importance of growing some of your own food is becoming fashionable, and, for some, a necessity, especially those living in cities where space is limited. Check seed catalogs—often available for free at garden centers in your area.

Grow Vertical

If you want to grow a lot of vegetables on your balcony or patio, emphasize your vertical space by using trellises or fences. Grow vegetables that can be trained to grow upright such as snow peas, shelling peas, pole beans, cucumbers, and tomatoes. Choose attractive materials like bamboo, metal, or wood to make trellises or stakes for your plants.

Grow Early and Late Veggies in the Same Pot

Some vegetable plants grow better in the cool of spring or fall, whereas others are best planted when the weather is warmer. Vegetables will mature and be harvested at different times of the year, depending on how long they take to grow to maturity and how long they take to form ripe fruit or pods for you to eat. To make the most of your container: plant a crop of early maturing veggies such as radishes or baby salad greens in the early spring; then after they have been harvested, take out the old plants, add a little more soil mix, and plant your tomatoes or peppers with a few herbs like basil and parsley around them.

Planting a Container

Here are eight easy steps for planting your containers.

1. Select an appropriate-sized container that has drainage holes for the plants you are growing.
2. Fill the container with potting soil to within an inch of the top of the container.
3. Moisten the soil and let it absorb the water before planting (lukewarm water will be absorbed faster than cold water).
4. You can plant several plants in the same pot (except very large ones like tomatoes or squash). They can be crowded in a bit, as about ten small plants will fit into an 18-inch pot.
5. Set taller plants in the center of the pot and insert stakes prior to planting any other plants around the larger one. If you will be trellising plants, the larger ones can be placed at the back of the container so they will climb on the trellis, and others can be planted in front.

6. Water once the plants are in the soil; this will help to settle the soil, and the roots will get established more quickly.
7. Add more soil, if needed, after watering.
8. Keep the container moist and well fertilized.

Watering

Container plants need regular watering. How much you need to water will depend on the size of container, the type of plant, and the weather; *all* determine how often and how much you need to water. When your vegetable plants are young, they need to be watered more often because the soil will dry out from the top down. Since your young plants do not have a deep root system yet, they need the water nearer the top of the container. As your vegetable plants mature, the roots go deeper and therefore need less frequent watering.

ESSENTIAL

Make a pond in a pot to add a beautiful addition to any small-space garden. Choose a container that will hold a minimum of 20 liters or 5 gallons. A dark-colored interior will discourage algae, help disguise the organisms when present, and give the illusion of greater depth. A fountain could be added if you have access to electricity.

How Much Water Is Needed?

So how do you know how much water to give your containers? A good way to check to see if your container needs to be watered is to stick your index finger into the soil up to the knuckle—if you can feel moisture, do not water. If the soil feels dry, give the container a good drink. The container has had enough water if, after you have given it a good drink and the water has had a few minutes to settle, you can feel the moisture 2 to 3 inches from the top. If the container is quite dry, the water will drain quickly out the bottom, leaving very little water to be absorbed in the soil. If this is the case, keep giving the container a drink every few minutes until the water stops draining from the bottom. Over-watering is as big of a problem as under-watering, so make sure you check your containers regularly—at least once a day or two times—if the pots are small, and it is a hot day. To help keep the moisture from evaporating from your container, mulch can be used. Mulching the top of the soil with moss, leaves, grass clippings, or even shredded newspaper can prevent the moisture from evaporating too quickly, especially in hot weather. Mulching also works well when you are growing vegetable plants that prefer a cooler soil like spinach, lettuce, and Brassicas because it will keep the soil a bit cooler as well. If you are going away on vacation, especially for an extended period during the summer months, make sure you have someone water your containers while you are gone. Using a drip system on a timer is an option if you are going to be gone for a short period of time. Just make sure the hoses are secured in the containers so they get watered properly. If you only have a few pots, try cutting off the bottom of a pop bottle or plastic milk carton and placing the top of the bottle securely into the soil. Then fill the container with water. If the container is well moistened to begin with, the water will slowly be released as it is needed. This is a great option if you are gone for only a day or two. Do not use a sprinkler when watering your containers as the container often does not get enough water in it to be effective.

Fertilizing

Plants in pots depend on the gardener for nutrients. The roots cannot grow deep enough to access other nutrients from the earth in the same way that plants grown in a garden bed can. Your container plants need a good supply of nutrients in order to produce the fruit and pods you eat, but fertilizing is an important step that is often forgotten. Gardeners think that buying a good commercial soil mix will be enough to sustain the needs of their vegetable plants all season; however, this is incorrect. Veggie plants need a little boost during the season. Fruit and berry plants usually need a good fertilizing with manure or an all-purpose fertilizer in the early spring and once they start fruiting.

About a month after planting, start fertilizing your containers; continue to do so every ten days. There are some great organic fertilizers available. One option is to use a combination of liquid kelp and liquid fish fertilizer; the labels will tell you how often and the amounts they recommend for different sizes of containers. Choose organic fertilizers as they are better for your vegetables and for you. If you want to save some money, make fertilizer teas from compost or manures.

FACT

There are fewer disease and insect problems in container gardens. Plants grown in containers will avoid soil-borne pathogens, and slugs are less of a problem.

For a quick and easy fertilizer tea, fill a bucket half full of compost or hot animal manure and then fill it with water. Let the bucket sit for a day or two (overnight if you are in a hurry) and then pour out the dark brown liquid. Mix it with water in a one-to-two ratio. Use this liquid to water the plants in your containers. Fill the pail with water again and keep using the liquid until it starts becoming lighter in color; then throw the sludge into your compost and start over, making a new batch.

CHAPTER 7

From Lawn to Garden

Do you have a front or back lawn? With a little information, planning, and some sweat equity, this could be a perfect spot to grow some of your own veggies. This chapter explains the benefits of turning that lawn into a garden. You'll learn the best ways to get started, and discover information and suggestions on how to produce a productive food garden for you and your family. You will also find tips on choosing the best plants for your area and how to keep it looking good for your neighbors.

Benefits to Front Yard Gardening

Most suburban homes and some townhouses have a lawn area of some form. This is often the sunniest and one of the most unused spaces on the property—a perfect spot for a garden. Keeping a lawn looking good, green, and weed-free can take hours of your time. You may worry about water conservation, and reduce your watering in the summer—then the lawn turns brown and quite unattractive. You could spend money on fertilizing, reseeding, spreading weed control products, or a small fortune having someone else do all this for you. Why not start a veggie garden? You can utilize the space to grow your own food, which will ultimately save you money on your grocery bill as well as the money you would have spent on lawn maintenance.

A manicured front lawn can be a status symbol, and in some areas there are restrictions as to what you can or cannot do in the front yard of your home. It is, however, in most areas, becoming more acceptable to replace all or part of a front lawn with vegetables, herbs, and flowers. If you find there are concerns where you live, check with your neighbors or local government to see what you can do.

FACT

Most of us are dependent upon the import of food. In the event an emergency or a natural disaster prevents this import, communities in British Columbia, Canada, would run out of food in an estimated two to three days ("Making the Connection—Food Security and Public Health," Public Health Association of British Columbia by the Community Nutritionists Council of BC, 2004).

More urban areas are creating and supporting community green spaces. If you and your neighbors are too busy to create your own gardens, make it a block event. Get a few households together to create one garden on the block where everyone can share in the work and the harvest. It can be fun project, great for your community, and a great way to get your neighborhood working together. You can bet once one front lawn is turned into a productive food garden, others will follow.

For most of us, it is important to feed our families and ourselves healthy foods. Growing some of your own veggies, fruit, berries, and herbs is an excellent way to do this. With so many disasters happening around the world, it is important to think about what you would do if something happened in your area. One benefit of turning your front lawn into a food garden is reducing your reliance on imported foods. If you can provide even some of your own food in an emergency, it can help to increase local and community emergency preparedness. Now is the time to start a food garden.

Save Money and the Planet

Groceries are becoming more and more expensive and people are looking for ways to save some money on their grocery bills. Growing your own vegetables can be cheaper than purchasing them in the grocery store. You know how they were grown, and they are often more nutritious and definitely tastier. Planting a few seeds in a container or in your front yard will yield you delicious, healthier food to enjoy at any meal.

People are also becoming more concerned about the environmental cost of the food miles associated with our food system. In most of the United States and Canada, the food travels over 3,000 miles before it even gets to the grocery store. Then we spend more time and miles to get it home. That is a lot of fuel being used. Due to the travel time, foods are most often picked before they have ripened completely, which compromises the flavor and taste for the consumer. Then we wonder why we do not eat more veggies. Growing your own vegetables is a great way to add more variety to your meals, save some money, and protect our planet in the process.

Conserving Water

Water conservation can generate environmental benefits and more local governments are trying to support people in reducing the amount of water they use. Reducing the amount of pollution will reduce pollutants getting into lakes and rivers, and that in turn reduces the amount of water that needs to be treated. This reduction helps to protect our drinking water and our aquatic ecosystems. You will save water by growing vegetables rather than having a green lawn.

Starting a garden in your front yard does not have to be a daunting process. With a little planning and some time it can be a fun and easy project for the whole family. Start small. Map out an area that gets lots of sunlight and is near the water tap. Start planning what you want to grow, and then start putting seeds into the ground. Easy.

A single lawn sprinkler spraying 5 gallons per minute uses more water in just one hour than a combination of ten toilet flushes, two five-minute showers, two dishwasher loads, or a full load of clothes in the washer (source: Environment Canada at *www.ec.gc.ca*).

Problems You May Face

There are some things to consider before turning your front lawn into a garden. The most common concerns are your neighbors, government restrictions, poor soil, and exhaust fumes. All can be worked out for everyone concerned with a little planning and commitment on your part.

If you are worried about what your neighbors or community will say, take the time to tell them what you are planning to do. Have a neighborhood party and show your plans and the reason for turning your front lawn into a veggie garden. Check into local zoning laws to make sure there are no restrictions, and if there are, go to the town or neighborhood committee for permission. Growing your own food is important (often necessary for some families), and has become fashionable as well, so you should not have any problem creating a beautiful and productive food garden in your front yard.

If your neighbors are still concerned about what you are doing, the best course of action is to draw up a plan so they can see what you want to do. Use raised beds, as they will make it easier to keep the area looking tidy and well kept, which is often the biggest concern for most people. Take the time to make sure your garden looks as good as it can. Some people need to be shown that vegetables can be just as beautiful as flowers or grass. If all else fails, share your harvest. Your generosity will ensure the neighbors taste the benefits and perhaps you will even convert them to doing the same in their front yard.

Exhaust Fumes

Do you live near a busy road? Are you concerned about all the exhaust fumes that are in the air from all those cars? There has been no research done on the effects that type of pollution has on your veggies; however, growing vegetables in your front lawn can make a space more compatible with an overall healthier lifestyle. The benefits will outweigh any small effect the fumes may have on the crop. If you still have concerns, one solution is planting as far away from the road as possible; another is erecting a traditional fence or living fence with shrubs to help protect you, and your plants from the exhaust. These barriers can help to reduce the traffic noise as well.

A living fence can have the same effect as a traditional wood one and can be made with fast-growing shrubs such as laurel or cedar if those are available in your area. Shrubs may be a cheaper option, especially if you can get some free from neighbors, friends, or demolition sites. Either way, fencing will help to protect your garden from any predators as well as the fumes and noise. Having a fabulous garden in your front yard may have drivers slowing down to take a look—a positive for everyone.

Poor Soil

Often, the soil in a front lawn area is not the most fertile. The soil can be quite sandy as traditionally that is what is used as filler when homes are built. If the soil is not ideal right now, do not get disenchanted, as every garden has to start somewhere. No matter what kind of soil you have, it can be amended with organic fertilizers and organic matter such as compost and animal manures to make a great veggie garden.

QUESTION

What is the difference between organic and synthetic fertilizers?
Basically, the difference is that synthetic ones feed only the plant, whereas organic fertilizers feed the soil. Both methods can be used to grow plants. However, if you do not feed the soil, it will become depleted, which will weaken and destroy life-sustaining organisms and make it less likely to be able to support healthy veggies.

One solution to combating the problem of having poor soil is building raised beds. The disadvantage is you will have to spend some money upfront to build them as well as money on soil to fill the beds. However, raised beds are an excellent place to start if you find the soil your have is not going to work. Raised beds help to contain the garden soil so it will not spill on to the driveway or street, and raised beds can help make your front yard a very attractive garden.

How to Get Started

Choosing to turn your front lawn into a food garden can be a large or small project, depending on the size of your front area and what you want to accomplish. Taking the time to do a garden layout is important. The layout is a visual plan of what you want your garden to look like; it can be as simple as a few boxes drawn on a piece of paper or a design made by a landscape designer. The layout of your garden site is used to mark where your beds will go, the pathways, and what you plan to grow in each area.

What Is Your Garden Style?

Let us first investigate what you would like your vegetable garden to look like. Vegetable gardening takes time, energy, and money so planning ahead and knowing your goals will save time and money overall. When planning a vegetable garden, especially if you are a first time gardener, it is important to take a look at your garden style so you can get a clear idea of what your goals are for your garden site. Not sure what your style is? Go to your local bookstore or library and flip through books and magazines. What jumps out at you? Is it the formal-looking garden where all the vegetables are contained within specific areas and everything looks tidy? Is it the more natural-looking garden, which is more lush and full, with a variety of different vegetables and flowers? Do you like garden structures and lovely, meandering pathways? Do you like stone or bark mulch? A formal garden has orderly rows and structural elements such as raised beds and clear boundaries for where the garden begins and ends. Everything has its place and the garden looks manicured most of the time, which can work well if your neighborhood is quite formal. A natural or rustic garden has a more naturalized look where wild plants and vegetables grow in harmony, the boundaries are less clearly defined, and structures are often made from wooden posts, driftwood, and boulders.

These two styles are fairly extreme, and often one may appeal more than the other. Most people garden in between these two extremes, so try to envision what you would like your garden to look like. If you are not sure of how to begin, it is okay to ask for advice. Talk to other gardeners, check out local community centers for gardening classes, join a gardening club, or if you have the money, hire a landscape designer. Any of these sources can give you great tips and help you get started. Remember, gardens are a work in progress and can take several years to get to a final goal. It is good to know where you want to start and end. Desires and needs may change over time, so allow yourself some flexibility. That is also a big part of having fun while gardening.

ESSENTIAL

When choosing garden soil for your new raised beds, take the time to check out the soil before you purchase it. Pick up a handful, moisten it with a little water, and then rub a small amount between your thumb and forefinger. If it feels mostly gritty, it contains mostly sand; if it molds into a ball, it has too much clay. You want a balanced combination of the two, soil that is dark, rich-smelling, and that easily crumbles.

Be realistic with the amount of time you have to spend working in your garden. If you like the formal garden and only have two hours a week to put toward your garden, it probably will not look and produce the way you expect. A rustic garden also needs work in order to keep weeds from taking over, so start small and add to the veggie garden each year as you have the space and time.

Steps to Making Your Garden Beds

There are two ways to go about turning your front lawn into a fabulous food garden. The easiest is to build raised beds and place them on top of the sod. The raised beds are then filled with soil, which will kill the sod under it over time. The advantage to doing this is that it is a quick and fairly easy way to get started. Raised beds can be very attractive and your garden will be easy to maintain and look good for you and your neighbors. The main disadvantage is the cost of building the boxes and the cost of purchasing the soil. In this case the grass will still need to be mowed or mulched between the beds, so make sure your pathways will accommodate the width of your lawn mower.

The other option is to remove the sod. This option is time-consuming hard work, and when you remove the sod you are also removing some valuable soil. Not afraid of manual labor? Removing the sod is definitely your best option if you are planning to do row gardening or even if you are planning to put in raised beds. Removing the sod first will make maintaining the area even easier. You can use mulch between the beds rather than having to mow the grass, which can save time and some headaches later on.

ALERT

Keep your flat-edged shovel in good shape while removing sod. To sharpen your shovel, smoothly draw a flat file down the blade from top to bottom. Do not go back and forth; just move the file in one direction. File the blade until all the nicks are smoothed out. When the blade is sharp to the touch, move the file over the back edge to remove any buildup on that edge.

If you have decided to remove the sod to make your new veggie garden, there are three ways to do it. All take some effort, but the time and energy will be worthwhile once you start harvesting and eating your fresh tasty veggies. So get started.

Power It Out

You can remove the sod using a sod cutter. This can be extremely hard work, so be prepared for a workout. A gas-powered sod cutter is not as fast or as easy as claims make out, but it is worth a try if you want to remove the sod from a large area. Sod cutters usually can be rented at an equipment-rental store. Another option is to rent a rototiller to turn the sod and weeds under. One disadvantage of this method is that the grass and weed roots remain and may grow back, making weeding a problem later on.

Muscle It Up

A flat-edged shovel is the best tool you can use to remove the sod manually. Slice out an 8-inch by 8-inch square, slide the blade under it, and lift the chunks up by hand. The grass can be turned over and left in the ground; however, the weeds may continue to grow. The best option is to shake off as much of the dirt as you can and then remove the sod completely by putting into your compost, or starting a compost pile with it. In a few months the decomposed sod will make a great amendment to add back into your garden beds.

Smother It Down

The layer method smothers rather than removes the sod from your front yard. This option takes patience as it will take time, materials, and some energy to make fertile soil. Layering is also not the prettiest way of making a garden while it is in progress. The layered method prevents the grass from getting any sunlight, so the grass slowly decomposes over time without any effort on your part to remove it.

Choosing the Correct Plants

Plants need sunlight, reasonably good soil, water, and good drainage to grow well. Most front yards will provide all of these, although each yard will have varying degrees of these basics. You can always bring in soil or amend what you have; water can be piped in if needed, and soil drainage can be improved by adding in organic matter or by installing drainage pipes. Sunlight is the one necessity you have little control over, so choosing plants that fit with the amount of sunlight your garden gets is something to consider when deciding what to plant.

VEGETABLES THAT DO WELL WITH FOUR TO SIX HOURS OF SUNLIGHT:

- Carrots
- Lettuce
- Kale
- Peas
- Swiss chard

VEGETABLES THAT NEED MORE SUNLIGHT (AT LEAST SIX TO EIGHT HOURS):

- Cucumber
- Eggplant
- Peppers
- Squash
- Tomatoes

No matter how large or small your garden space, the best advice is to grow what you love to eat. If you love cabbage, grow what you can in your space—versus something that your family will not eat.

Keep It Looking Good

Now that you have a great veggie garden growing where your front lawn used to be, you are saving time by not having to mow and water it. However, now you want to make a good impression for your neighbors. How will you keep it all looking fabulous? Weeds have a tendency to get out of control very quickly. The trick is to pull them before they go to seed; that way they will not spread. When they do spread, thousands of little weed seeds are in your garden, which will mean you are weeding for many years to come (all from that one plant). So set aside a few minutes each day or an hour a week, depending on the size of your garden, just to do some weeding. If you do a little at a time, is does not seem so overwhelming.

Healthy, disease-free vegetable plants look the best. Taking the time to observe your vegetable garden and the plants you are growing is a way to catch any diseases or pests before they can spread and compromise other plants. Remove any diseased plants by placing them in a garbage bag immediately rather than carrying them through your garden. Investigate any pest problems you may have and find organic methods to remove or control them.

Take time every day or at least every few days to walk around the garden and look at the plants. Do you see any damage? Are there any holes in the leaves? Are plants dying or looking yellowish or sickly? These are all classic signs that there may be a problem of some sort. If you have any concerns, try to find out what is happening. Are there any pests that you can see? Do the plants need some added nutrients, or are they getting enough water?

Keep debris in your garden to a minimum to prevent any unwanted insects or pests from having a home. Healthy garden soil and keeping your garden clean are two of the best ways to ensure a productive harvest and keep problems with pests and diseases to a minimum. Both practices will make for a more attractive garden.

FACT

In the United States, the average family of four can use 400 gallons of water per day. Generally, about 30 percent of that is for outdoor uses. More than half of that outdoor water is used for watering gardens and lawns. Nationwide, landscape irrigation totals over 7 billion gallons of water per day—almost one-third of all residential water use. (*www.epa.gov*)

Over- or under-watering are two of the most common causes of problems in your vegetable garden patch. Proper watering of your vegetable garden will help to ensure you have the abundant harvest for you and your family to enjoy. One inch of water a week is a good rule of thumb. Too much or too little water will place stress on the vegetable plants, which will cause them not to produce as well as they could.

The Rain Barrel System

If you live in a climate that gets a fair amount of rain, install a rain barrel. A rain barrel is a closed container where water is collected from roof gutters. The water from the gutter is directed to the barrel by having the downspout enter the top of the rain barrel. It is best to have a barrel with a spigot at the bottom of the barrel; that way you can easily pour the water into your watering can to use in the garden.

▲   Rain barrel system with spout

There are a variety of types and sizes of rain barrels that can be purchased at your local hardware store or garden center. They can fill up fairly quickly in a heavy rainfall, so find one that works for your area. They are usually not difficult to install, but a professional landscaper could install one for you if you are unable to do it yourself. Collecting rain water to water your plants, rather than using your tap water, is an easy way to conserve your overall water usage. During the summer months a lot of areas have water restrictions, so collecting rainwater will allow you to have more than enough to keep your vegetable plants happy.

CHAPTER 8

Backyard Gardens

Many urban homes like townhouses or row house apartments have a small backyard space that can make a perfect spot for a small veggie garden. In this chapter you will find information and suggestions to help you get started with turning your backyard space into a food garden. You will find instructions on making raised beds and tips on choosing the best plants to grow in them. You will also find a garden design that you can use or modify it to fit your small-space needs.

How to Get Started

A backyard often has a similar landscape to a front yard, as they are both often covered in grass; however, front yards are usually exposed to the street and neighbors, whereas the backyard is more private. While the front yard is often seen as a status symbol and may have restrictions on what can be done, the backyard is usually used quite differently. It is used to play, to barbecue, have parties, and to relax. Creating a food garden here can have different challenges than having one in the front yard.

The first step to getting started with creating a veggie garden is to check out your site. How much sun does the area get? Most veggies need six to eight hours of direct sunlight. What is the soil like? Vegetables like a rich, fertile, loamy soil. However, this is often not available right in the beginning. But you can fertilize and amend to reach this ideal. Does water sit in the area or is it dry all season long? Either condition will have benefits and disadvantages, but most problems can be solved by creating proper drainage and having an accessible water source close by.

Once you feel the space will work for growing some of your own food, it is time to decide what you want the area to look like. Is the space already used for other activities like outdoor eating and relaxation, and do you want to keep doing those things? If so, how can you best include both a garden space and space for other activities? Taking the time to measure the area and then making a sketch on a piece of graph paper can help to mark out where everything could go. It is much easier to change and move things on a piece of paper than physically moving a garden bed.

QUESTION

What is a hybrid vegetable?
A hybrid is the result of crossing two or more species or cultivators of a plant to create a new one. Hybrids can carry on the strengths of both parents, but they seldom breed true.

Once you have a design in mind, what kind of garden beds do you want to make? The options are most likely the same as discussed in the chapter on front yards: digging up an area and making rows, building raised beds, or using containers where you can utilize the square foot method, vertical growing, or making a lasagna garden.

Are Raised Beds the Best Option?

If you are starting with poor soil or even no soil, one of the biggest benefits of growing your vegetables in raised beds is bringing better soil to fill them. It can take several years of hard work to make poor soil more fertile, so purchasing soil from a garden center or landscape company can be the easiest thing to do. There is a cost involved in building and filling your raised beds; however in the long run you will save yourself time and disappointment.

For small-space gardeners, the amount of space you have to grow in is often one of the main issues you face. A raised bed is easy to build if you have a long narrow spot, an oddly configured area, or issues with bending or kneeling. If you have funny angles to contend with, make your beds a triangle shape. A raised bed can be of any shape or height; all you have to do is design according to your needs.

▲ Raised wooden garden bed

Some issues to consider when deciding the size of a raised bed include the height and width of the bed. The higher the four sides, the more soil you will need to fill the garden. However, if you have difficulty bending, making a bed waist height is well worth the cost of extra soil. When planning the size of your raised beds, use the length of your arm as a guide. A width of 4 feet is probably the maximum you would want, as that is a comfortable width for most people to reach easily into the center of the bed. This feature is very important even if you can access all sides of the bed because you want to be able to reach your plants in the center with ease. If you only have access from one side of your bed, make sure you can reach all the way across. Gardening is much more enjoyable if you do not have to strain to reach the areas you are planting or weeding.

FACT

When you garden, it is important to take the time to stretch every fifteen to twenty minutes. Often you are bending, lifting, hoeing, or digging while gardening, and therefore using muscles that you may not use on a regular basis. Remembering to stretch or change positions while performing these tasks, and it will save you from having sore muscles at the end of the day.

The raised bed is an easy way to define where the bed and pathways are, which helps you to keep from walking on your garden soil. Other benefits to growing in raised beds are that moisture will drain away more quickly than with other arrangements, and the soil temperature will warm up faster in the spring. Both of these advantages will allow you to get your vegetables planted earlier in the spring. This is definitely a plus if you live in a rainy, cool climate or your garden site has poor drainage.

If a tidy and attractive vegetable garden is important to you, use raised beds, as they make a garden look neater and give definition and structure to a garden site. Different shapes can add interest if you have a particular look in mind. Raised beds can be used effectively to detract or enhance a certain spot in your garden. The material used to make the beds keeps the soil contained, leaving the pathways easier to mow or mulch and preventing weeds or grass from growing into your vegetable beds. This all contributes to a cleaner-looking garden.

Building a Raised Bed

Wood, stones, bricks, and cement are the most common materials used when making raised beds. Wood is easy to find, to build with, and often is not that expensive. When building your beds with wood, you want to choose wood that will not rot easily. If you can, choose wood such as cedar or redwood, as both these are more resistant to rot because of their natural oils. Stay away from pressure-treated wood or wood covered in creosote, as these products have heavy metals and poisons such as arsenic, copper, and chrome. These chemicals can leach into your garden soil and ultimately into your food.

ESSENTIAL

If you are considering hiring a landscape contractor, ask to see work that is at least a couple of years old to gauge how well it is holding up. Structures can be costly, and something built with quality materials and excellent workmanship will be worth the money if done well.

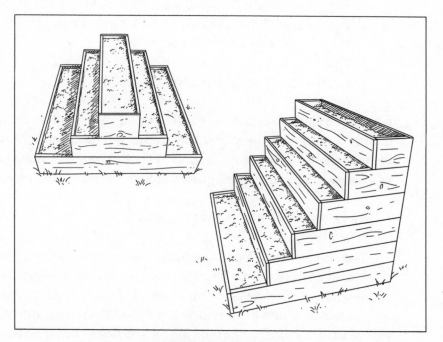

▲ Terraced garden layouts

If wood is not the look you want, rocks are often easy to find and can be very attractive. One disadvantage to using rock is that it does not have the same barrier from weeds and grass as solid wood sides; however, using cement to fill in the crevices and cracks between the rocks will make for a more solid barrier.

If you want a more defined raised bed but do not want to use wood or stone, try using cement blocks, standard masonry bricks, or larger interlocking bricks. They come in various colors and sizes and can be easily stacked to increase the height of your raised bed if height is a concern. For a more involved and a permanent option, make your raised beds with cement.

This design is for a 4-foot wide, 8-foot long, 12-inch high--wood raised bed. The first thing you want to do is decide exactly where you want your raised bed to be, as you want to build it on that same spot.

Here is your list of materials for one raised bed:

- ❏ Three (8-foot long by 12-inch wide by 2-inch thick) boards (wood made from cedar or redwood)
- ❏ One 4-foot length of (2-inch thick by 4-inch wide) board. Cut this into four 1-foot length (2-inch thick by 4-inch wide) boards (two by fours)
- ❏ Twenty-four (4-inch) wood screws for full dimension wood or (3-inch) wood screws for planed wood
- ❏ Drill
- ❏ Screw driver to match the wood screw heads

Most building supply stores will cut the pieces of wood for a minimal charge, saving you time. You now have two (8-foot by 2-foot by 12-inch) pieces and two (4-foot by 2-inch by 12-inch) boards to make your rectangular box; you also have four pieces of 1-foot lengths of two by fours.

HERE ARE THE STEPS TO FOLLOW:

Step 1: Lay each 8-foot length on the ground; place a piece of two by four at each end and using three screws on each, attach the two by four length to each flat end of the board. Drilling a hole not quite the length of the screw into the wood first will make screwing the pieces together easier. Attaching the two by four to the board will give the sides of your raised bed more support.

Step 2: These eight-foot boards will be used as the sides of your box. The 4-foot lengths are the ends of your rectangular box. Attach each 4-foot length to the two by fours using three screws on each corner. You now have a four-sided raised bed.

ESSENTIAL

If straw bales are plentiful in your area, they can be used as edging for a raised bed. The height would mean a large amount of soil would be needed but would also allow you to sit on the bale while planting or weeding the garden.

Choosing Your Plants

When deciding what you want to grow, there are several things to consider. The most important are what you like to eat and what you want to grow. Then look at your climate and the amount of sunlight your garden plot will get. If you get full sun all day, some plants will grow better than if the area only gets a few hours of sunlight. Some common veggies that need full sun are tomatoes, cucumbers, peppers, and squash; whereas lettuce, spinach, root crops, and plants in the cabbage family can do with a bit less sunlight (all still need at least 6 hours of sunlight).

The simplest way to start is to list the vegetables you are planning to grow and organize them into these four categories:

- **Root vegetables**—carrots, potatoes, parsnips, beets
- **Cabbage family**—broccoli, cabbage, Brussels sprouts, cauliflower, turnip, rutabaga, radish, kale
- **Heat-loving veggies**—corn, peppers, squash, tomatoes, cucumbers
- **Everything else**—lettuce, onion, peas, spinach, Swiss chard, beans

Make a note beside each vegetable on your list of the amount of space they need to grow to maturity. Using your list of vegetables sorted into the four categories, start placing the vegetables from the first category into the first section; then continue with the second category of vegetables, placing them into the second section, and so on. When marking where each vegetable will go, remember to use the correct spacing for each and put the taller plants to the north side so they do not shade out the sun for the smaller ones.

ALERT

If you have chosen to make a garden that you will be walking through, use plank boards as pathways. Lay a 12-inch wide board at whatever length you need to cross your garden. This will enable you to make a permanent pathway so the soil is not compacted and will allow you to walk in your garden without getting muddy feet.

By using a pencil you can easily erase and move items around your garden layout. By going through this process first, you can really see how planning will save money, time, and energy when it comes to actually planting your seed or transplants.

Vegetable Rotation

Different vegetable plants require different amounts of nutrients from the soil to grow well. You should add in organic matter and fertilizer to your soil each year; however, it is also important to move your plants around each year so as not to deplete these nutrients. One year you may grow a vegetable that uses a lot of nitrogen, and the following year you may plant a crop that uses more phosphorus. By rotating your vegetable layout the soil can have time to rebuild the nitrogen in that area.

Another benefit to moving your vegetables to different areas of your garden each year is to cut down on the pests and diseases in your garden. A few of these little guys can wreak havoc on your vegetable patch, so try to keep them out. Some vegetable plants will attract certain pests and diseases, which often live in the soil where the plant is growing. By moving this vegetable plant to another area of the garden, the pests or diseases have nothing to feed on and therefore will not survive. Different plants will repel certain pests and diseases, which will also help to keep them at bay.

Vegetable rotation is a process used to ensure certain vegetables or a family of vegetables is not planted in the same spot in successive years. You can keep your soil more fertile, reduce the amount of pests and diseases in your garden, and ultimately have a healthier and more productive vegetable harvest by moving your vegetables to a new spot each year.

ALERT

Kneel to weed rather than bending. If weeds are stubborn, do not yank on them as this motion can strain your neck, upper back, and shoulders. Loosen the weeds with a shovel, garden fork, or a trowel. Stretching exercises before gardening can also help to prevent problems.

Here is a simple and straightforward way to understand and plan your rotation. First divide your garden site into four fairly equal areas (five if you are planning to grow some perennial vegetables like asparagus or artichokes). You will plant a certain family of vegetables in each spot one year and move it clockwise to the next spot the year after. This will give you a four-year crop rotation. It is important to write down or draw a sketch of your garden so you have something to refer back to when planning for next season.

PLANT THE FOLLOWING VEGETABLES INTO YOUR FOUR AREAS:

- ❏ **In plot one, plant your cabbage family**—this includes broccoli, cauliflower, cabbage, Brussels sprouts, oriental greens, and kale.
- ❏ **In plot two, plant your heat-loving veggies**—these include tomatoes, cucumber, peppers, eggplants, okra, and squashes.
- ❏ **In plot three, plant your root vegetables**—these include carrots, potatoes, beets, radishes, turnip, and rutabagas.
- ❏ **In plot four, plant all the other vegetables**—these include lettuce, peas, beans, and Swiss chard.

If you are only planting a few vegetables or have a very tiny garden space, it is still important to jot down where you planted each veggie this season so as not to put them into the same area again for a few years. If you are growing your veggies in containers, it is important either to wash the container and change the soil each year or to plant the veggie in a different pot each year. This will help to keep your vegetables grown in containers healthier.

▼ **TABLE 8-1: FOUR-YEAR VEGETABLE ROTATION**

	Year 1	Year 2	Year 3	Year 4
Bed One	Cabbage family	Heat-loving veggies	Root vegetables	Everything else
Bed Two	Heat-loving veggies	Root vegetables	Everything else	Cabbage family
Bed Three	Root vegetables	Everything else	Cabbage family	Heat-loving veggies
Bed Four	Everything else	Cabbage family	Heat-loving veggies	Root vegetables

Backyard Garden Design

Let's look at a 32-square foot raised-bed vegetable garden. The following table shows you how many of each vegetable to plant across in the 4-foot-wide bed. The number of inches is the width of each row or the total space needed for the plant to grow to maturity. The bed is also divided into four equal sections (24 inches for each) based on the vegetable rotation discussed previously in this chapter.

▼ **TABLE 8-2: VEGETABLE GARDEN DESIGN**

Garden Bed	
2 cabbages; 2 broccoli	16-inch row
4 marigolds	8-inch row
2 cucumbers and 1 tomato	18-inch row
6 basil	6-inch row
16 radishes	6-inch row
16 carrots	6-inch row
8 beets	6-inch row
8 turnips	6-inch row
16 peas	6-inch row
16 beans	6-inch row
3 lettuce; 3 spinach	12-inch row

The above design lists vegetable plantings that can be used as-is, or you can modify the design to your needs. Vegetables need a certain amount of room in order to grow to maturity and, the plan above notes the amount of space the plants need. To make it easier for you to modify the above plan, the following chart lists vegetables and the number of plants that can be grown in a certain space so you can easily mix and match what you want to grow in your own garden.

▼ **TABLE 8-3: VEGETABLE EXCHANGE LIST**

| Vegetable Family | Space Needed |
List of Vegetables in Each Family	Number of Plants
Cabbage family	16-inch square area
Broccoli	1
Cabbage	1
Cauliflower	1
Brussels sprouts	1
Kale	1
Heat-loving veggies	18-inch square area
Tomato	1
Pepper	2
Eggplant	2
Cucumber	1
Basil	6
Root vegetables	12-inch square area
Carrots	4
Beets	2
Turnip	2
Radish	2
Onions	1
Leeks	1
Garlic	1
Everything else	12-inch square area
Lettuce	1
Oriental greens	1
Spinach	1
Swiss chard	1
Mesclun mix (broadcasted)	1
Annual herbs such as basil, parsley, cilantro	2

Vegetable Family	Space Needed
List of Vegetables in Each Family	**Number of Plants**
Vegetable exceptions	24-inch square area
Corn	6
Squash	1
Potato	1
Perennial veggies & herbs	24-inch square area
Asparagus	2
Artichoke	2
Perennial herbs such as sage, thyme, oregano, tarragon	1

The above chart is divided by vegetable rotation as well for your convenience.

Now you can start planting a garden in your backyard!

CHAPTER 9

Reused and Renewed Spaces

Almost any kind of item that will hold soil or any area with a little earth can be turned into a productive vegetable garden. Even in a concrete jungle there are lots of opportunities to start growing some of your own food. In this chapter you will find suggestions on how to reinvent spaces that may already exist. There are step-by-step instructions on how to make a straw-bale garden, and you will discover how to plant a garden using recycled items that can be found around your home or yard.

Reclaim an Old Garden

Perhaps you have a neglected garden and now have time to give it some attention. Or you may have just moved into a new home where the garden is a bit overgrown. Both circumstances offer great opportunities for growing your own food. The first thing is not to get overwhelmed by the project; take it one day at a time. If the area is new to you, find out what you can about the garden before you start cutting back and chopping things down. Ask the neighbors. Look through old newspapers, property records, or photographs to see what the space may have looked like in the past. If the area is just a little bit neglected and you know what has been grown in the past, take some time to reassess the situation and plan what you want to do before starting to clean up.

Once you are ready to start clearing the area, work on one section at a time, unless you have to rent equipment such as a chainsaw by the hour or day to clear the area. Clearing one area at a time will give you a greater sense of accomplishment. Take your time so you do not cut back more plants and vegetation than is necessary.

ALERT

If your garden is overrun with poison ivy, rake it out. Use a sturdy rake and carefully tug at the ivy. Most of it will come right up, roots and all. When you are done, rinse the rake to get rid of any plant oils. Wash your hands well, especially if they have come into contact with the ivy or the bottom of the rake. If you used gloves, throw them into the laundry so as not to spread any residue to other areas of your garden.

Once you have gotten to the bare bones of the garden, decide on a garden style. Choose a style you like based on the architecture of your home, or what the original garden may have looked like. This is a great time for drawing up a design on paper so you can decide what it is you want and whether or not it will fit in the area. Use as much of the existing structures as you can both to save money and to stay true to the time period of your home. Now start planting, relaxing, and enjoying your renewed space.

Reinvent Your Flower Bed

The side of a house, along a sidewalk, or any area you are growing flowers in may be the perfect spot to plant a few veggies or herbs. Veggies and herbs have similar soil and light requirements as many flowers; they make great companions for attracting beneficial insects and repelling unwanted pests, and help make your garden pest-free and healthy.

There are some very attractive vegetable plants that can make your flower bed even more attractive by adding different colors, textures, and height to the area. The following list of vegetable plants can be a beautiful addition to any space.

DECORATIVE VEGETABLE PLANTS

- ❏ Artichoke
- ❏ Asparagus
- ❏ Carrot
- ❏ Eggplant
- ❏ Jerusalem artichoke
- ❏ Kale (Russian red variety is the loveliest in color)
- ❏ Lettuce (many different green and red colors)
- ❏ Mustard greens
- ❏ Oriental greens
- ❏ Peppers
- ❏ Squash (Be careful; they can take up a lot of space)
- ❏ Swiss chard (Bright Lights variety has rainbow-colored stems)

Herbs can also be popped into any empty spot in the flower bed. They are easy to grow and do not need a lot of attention once established. Choose perennial plants such as sage, rosemary, thyme, oregano, and marjoram that are easy to grow and can be used for several years without much maintenance. Annual herbs like basil, chive, and parsley will add some great fragrance to your flower garden and are great for using in summer barbecue recipes. None of these herbs are expensive, and all can be easily pulled and renewed each year.

FACT

Nasturtiums are a garden snack food. Just pull the flower or leaves off and chew them for a wonderful peppery flavor. For best flavor, pick the blooms and leaves in early morning when their water content is highest. Store flowers in a plastic bag in the refrigerator and use them in salads, sandwiches, or as a garnish.

If you have a shady flower bed and want to grow some veggies, there are some that will grow well for you. Most veggies need at least six hours of sunlight; however, there are a few that can handle a little less sunlight.

SHADE-TOLERANT VEGETABLES

❑ Lettuce
❑ Spinach
❑ Cabbage
❑ Peas
❑ Salad greens

Flower Bed Design

If you want to redo your flower bed or want to start a new one, here are some options to try.

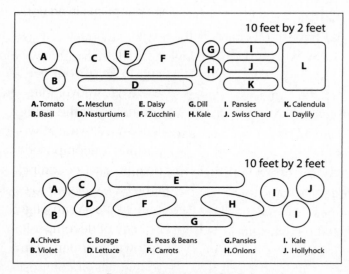

▲ Design to revamp your flower bed

Straw-Bale Gardens

Straw-bale gardening is a method of gardening where plants and seeds are grown in straw bales rather than soil. Because it is a method using very little, if any soil, it is sometimes considered a form of hydroponic gardening. It is a great way to grow annual vegetables, herbs, or flowers in an area where there is little soil available or an area that has very poor soil. A bale garden can be placed on a patio or balcony where there is no soil in sight, making it a great option for a small urban garden. Since the bale is a couple of feet in height, you will be growing your plants a few feet above the ground, which makes gardening easier for disabled or older gardeners, or for those gardeners who suffer from aches and pains when bending or kneeling.

Wheat straw is recommended; however, oat straw will work just as well. Avoid pine and hay bales. Hay bales have grass seed, which can cause a weed problem in your garden. Straw is the stem of the grain that is separated, then baled; a hay bale is the entire plant including the stem, leaves and seed heads. It is best to use a bale that is bound by synthetic twine so the twine will not rot as quickly, keeping the bale intact longer.

FACT

If you have a sunny wall that is rot-proof (cement, for example), plant tomatoes or cucumbers and grow them vertically. Place your straw bale against the wall and position a trellis behind the bale or attach it to the wall to support growing your plants in an upright position.

Place the bale where you want to grow your garden, as it will get very heavy once wet and will not be easy to move. Place the bale so that the string runs around the bale; you do not want the string to come into contact with the ground. To cure the bale, you will want to wet it thoroughly (if you can find a bale that is already partially decomposed you will be ahead in the process). The wet bale will heat up as it decomposes. This process will take a week to ten days and then the bale will start to cool down. To quicken this process, you can wrap the bale in plastic and lightly sprinkle 5 ounces of ammonium nitrate on the fourth day of decomposition.

Once the bale starts to cool down, you can plant your veggies. If you want to start with seeds, lay 2 or 3 inches of compost, potting soil, or peat moss on top of the bale as if you were icing a cake. You can plant your seeds directly into the soil and the plant roots will grow into the straw. If you are planting transplants, you can put them directly into the bale rather than adding soil. To transplant, take a sharp trowel and thrust it into the bale. Lever the trowel, forcing the bale to come apart. Pop in the transplant and let the bale spring back to the original shape. In both cases, direct seeding and planting transplants, you will need to water the bale thoroughly.

A straw-bale garden will last one or two seasons. It is important to keep the bale moist throughout the season. Since there is little or no soil for the plants to access, nutrients are important. Fertilize your bale garden weekly (if you want it to last one season), or every second week (to have it last two years). Use compost tea or an organic, multipurpose fertilizer to keep your plants growing and producing an abundant harvest. You can add worms to the bale as well, if you only want to use the bale for one season. Adding worms and feeding the bale will increase the decomposition process of the bale.

FACT

Garden centers and nurseries may sell bales of straw, as gardeners use the straw for mulch. If not, they may be able to help you find a source. If you have an animal breeding farm or a horse stable in your area, this would be another place to check.

PLANT A STRAW-BALE GARDEN

- Six cucumber plants
- Three each of squash, zucchini, or melon plants
- Two tomato plants (smaller varieties)
- Four pepper plants
- Twelve to fifteen bean or pea plants
- Twelve to sixteen lettuce, Swiss chard, and annual herb plants

Tall vegetables such as corn, pole beans, or large tomatoes are not necessarily the best plants to grow in a straw-bale garden, as it is difficult to put stakes into the bale and the plant may topple if it gets top heavy. Root crops are not recommended in this type of garden as the straw will compress their roots rather than allow them to grow to maturity.

You can use one bale to make your garden or position several to make an even more interesting raised-bed area. After one or two years of growing veggies in the straw bale, it can then be added to your compost or used as mulch for other garden beds.

The Tire Garden

Making a garden bed by stacking two or three used tires is another option for a small-space garden in which to grow potatoes, tomatoes, melons, or cucumbers. The soil in black-tire beds will become very hot, too warm for most plants, especially if the beds are placed in a sunny location. Choosing to grow heat-loving plants is the best option for this type of bed. If the area is shady or you live in a colder climate, the heat absorbed by the tire garden can be beneficial even for other veggies.

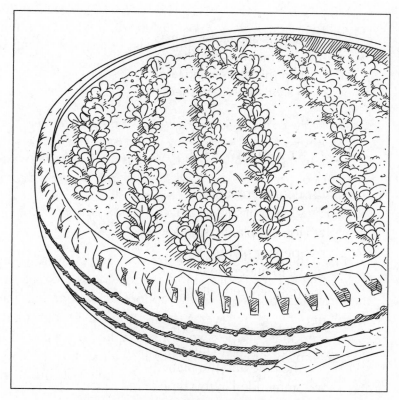

▲ Possible planting scheme for a tire garden

There is some debate as to whether or not used tires are safe for growing vegetables. Since synthetics are used to manufacture tires, when the rubber slowly degrades, it releases zinc and carcinogenic PAHs (polycyclic aromatic hydrocarbons) and other compounds into your soil. The amounts released are extremely small, and happen over a long period of time. This action may be a concern if you want to grow organic veggies. There is no evidence that these by products are harmful to the plants or the soil; however, some individuals are very concerned about any release of potentially harmful substances when growing food. Some gardeners suggest using the tire bed for growing flowers or shrubs rather than edible plants.

The Bag Garden

A bag garden will work on a patio, or in any small-space garden where very little soil area is available. There are a few options that can be used to make a bagged garden. The simplest is buying a bag of potting soil and using it as your garden bed. This type of garden will not be more than 6 inches deep, so growing lettuce, salad greens, Swiss chard, kale, peas, beans or cucumbers is a better option than growing root crops.

ESSENTIAL

Use a plastic gallon jug for a watering device. Remove the cap, cut out the bottom, turn it upside down, and force the neck into the ground close to the base of the plant. When the plant needs water, just use your hose to fill the jug. You can put fertilizer or even compost into the jug, and the water will carry it to the plant's roots.

Place the bag of soil in the area where you want your garden to grow. Poke some holes (about six) into the topside of the bag, then turn it over so the new drain holes are on the bottom. Now cut a flap into the bag. If you are planning to grow several smaller vegetables, cut the flap large enough to accommodate all the plants or seeds. If you are planning to plant one or two larger plants, make the flap smaller. Make sure the flap is cut only in the top area of the bag so the sides remain intact, as they are needed to hold the soil together. Water the garden bag and plant your seeds or transplants. It's simple! Fertilizing every few weeks with compost tea or an all-purpose, organic fertilizer will help your plants grow to maturity.

Another option for a bagged garden is using a sturdy, plastic grocery bag. Poke a few holes in the bottom for drainage and then fill the bag with soil. Plant some lettuce or herbs and this will make an interesting and attractive minigarden that can be easily moved around to catch the sun rays.

Burlap Sack Garden

Using a recycled burlap sack is yet another option for a bagged garden. Burlap sacks can be found for free or purchased from coffee shops that roast their own beans. This will make a deep garden, which will work well for tomato plants, potatoes, root crops like carrots or beets, and cabbage family vegetables.

▲ A burlap sack garden

You will need:

- ❑ Burlap sack
- ❑ Large empty coffee can, both ends removed
- ❑ Pebbles
- ❑ Potting soil
- ❑ Veggie plants or seeds

Place the sack where you want to grow your veggies. Roll down the sack; place a can (6 inches across with top and bottom removed) in the center of the sack and fill the can with pebbles. Place potting soil or compost around the can and firmly pat it down. Pull out the can; now you will have a center of rocks surrounded by soil. Roll the sack up a bit more, place the can in the center again, and add more rocks and soil. Continue this process until the sack is full. Place three stakes equal distance apart into the sack, pushing them into the soil as far as you can; this will support the sack in remaining upright.

If you want to grow more plants than just from the top, you can cut holes around the outside of the sack (just make sure they are not directly above each other) and plant smaller plants into the soil through the holes. Water the burlap sack on a regular basis and enjoy your funky food-producing garden.

Truck Garden

What about filling the back of a pickup truck with soil and planting your veggies? There are two filmmakers, Curt Ellis and Ian Cheney, doing exactly this. They are based in Red Hook, Brooklyn, and are using the garden to promote urban agriculture and get research for their new film. They planted arugula, lettuce, tomatoes, and hot peppers in their truck garden. How cool is that? You may not want to plant in a vehicle you want to drive or commute with; however, if there is an old vehicle that is no longer running and has become an eyesore, perhaps it can become a reinvented garden. Anything can become beautiful if you want it to be by using a little ingenuity and some work.

▲ A truck bed garden

Bathtub Garden

An old bathtub would make an attractive and very functional veggie garden. It would be deep enough to grow several different vegetables including root crops and tomatoes. The drain hole is already there, and the tub would be large enough to grow a surprising amount of food. The tub would be classed as a container, so you want to use light potting soil or compost to fill it rather than regular soil, which would become compact and too heavy for the plants. Placing rocks or broken tiles on the bottom will make for better drainage for the soil and plants. As there is only a limited amount of nutrients in the soil, fertilizing every few weeks will help to keep the plants happy and healthy.

ALERT

Use a pail of clean, dry sand as a storage place for small garden tools. Brush or wipe any dirt from your tools and then push them into the sand when you are not using them. The sand will help to keep the tools from becoming rusty.

An old bathroom sink, washtub, half barrel, large pail, a large pot, or large earthen bowl would make a smaller container garden for lettuces or herbs and would look attractive among your other garden beds, on porch steps, or on a balcony. With any container, make sure there is some kind of drainage hole in the bottom so the plant roots will not get waterlogged.

CHAPTER 10

Gardening High Up

Do you live in a condo or a high-rise apartment in the middle of a city with only a patio or balcony for your outdoor space? Even if all you have is a windowsill, there are still several options for growing some of your own herbs and veggies. In this chapter there are suggestion on how to grow herbs, veggies, and some fruits in some very tight spaces. You will also find tips on growing on rooftops and perhaps making a green roof, if that is an option for you.

Balcony and Patio Gardening

When space is tight, it is best to concentrate on growing small quantities of several different crops and choosing smaller or dwarf varieties of larger plants. Growing some veggies, herbs, and even some small fruit or berry bushes will add an interesting choice to your dinner table as well as something beautiful and fragrant to enjoy. Planting in pots is probably the easiest and most common way for growing food on a balcony or patio, as there is usually no earth space available. Edible crops also appreciate the shelter and warmth a balcony or patio can give them.

When planning your space, checking out how much sunlight the area gets is the first step. Most veggies, herbs, and fruit or berry bushes need at least six hours of sun, so take the time to check this out. If you get fewer than the six hours, there are fewer options, but you can still grow some things. Second, you will need to decide what you want to grow, list what you like to eat, and see what are the best options to grow in your space. The third step in planning your container garden is choosing the proper-sized container in which to grow the veggies. You will want to give your plants enough space so they can grow to maturity. Most herb and veggie plants need a pot with at least a depth of 1 foot of soil to grow their best.

FACT

A bubbling fountain is an attractive and safe alternative to a pond in a small space. Water is pumped up through the center of an object or pipe, then trickles down over pebbles to make a very calming and relaxing sound for your patio or balcony.

Regular watering, feeding, and properly supporting your plants is important so they will stay healthy and produce food for you. In a location where weight is an important consideration, use plastic or fiberglass containers and fill them with Styrofoam pieces and lightweight potting soil.

Another option is growing your herbs and veggies in a bagged garden. You can get a shallow plastic container and place the bag of potting mix into it. Make sure you poke a few drain holes in the bag, then turn it over and cut a flap into the top of the bag to expose the soil for planting. The plastic container will hold moisture as well as keep the area clean; it will act the same as a tray under a container. Just make sure there is no water sitting in the plastic container, as most plants do not like their roots to be too wet—they can start to rot.

Some easy-to-grow veggies on a balcony or patio are climbing varieties of peas and beans. Trellising them will save space and make them easier to harvest. Some crops that are great looking as well as edible are golden zucchini, red-stemmed Swiss chard, red-leafed beet, and lettuce, which comes in various shades of green or red and will be lovely for a small space. Some root crops such as carrots, turnips, beetroot, and radishes that can be harvested as baby veggies are also good options for container gardens.

Fruits and berries can also be easily grown in pots on a balcony or patio. Grapes can be trained to climb up a wall or trellis. Dwarf fruit trees can be grown in a traditional wooden container, or larger ceramic or plastic containers can be used. Berry bushes such as blueberries and raspberries will make another great addition to a container garden, as will strawberries grown in a hanging, bagged garden or clay strawberry pot. Kumquats or lemons are the hardiest of citrus plants, and though they do not survive outdoors except in very mild areas, they can be grown in large pots on a patio in the summer and brought indoors or sheltered when the weather gets cold. There are many options to make your small space a mini food-producing garden.

Window Boxes

Even without a balcony or patio to puts some pots on, most people have a sunny windowsill that may work just as well. The best option would be to hang a window box outside a window that opens; the plants will get more natural light and you can easily reach to water and fertilize the plants. If opening a window is not an option, you can grow a few pots of herbs indoors near a sunny window.

Window boxes come in terra-cotta, wood, galvanized steel, plastic, and cast stone, giving you many options to choose from. Window boxes can be made of guttering and offer an inexpensive recycled option. They can be potted like any other container with a deep layer of potting mix. Or they can be used as a holding station for small pots. The boxes can sit on windowsills, or can be hung on brackets, or from straps or chains. Guttering is available at hardware stores and can easily be cut to whatever length you may want. End caps can also be purchased to give you closed container. Use waterproof caulking to seal leaks at the seams and end caps. Guttering comes in various colors, making it a decorative and creative container.

Most window boxes are approximately 2 to 3 feet in length and 6 to 8 inches deep, although there are many different sizes to choose from. If you do not have a sturdy window ledge to support the box, a lightweight option is probably best. There are some great hooks and hangers for supporting a window box over a balcony rail or on the windowsill.

ALERT

Containers, bagged gardens, and window boxes will need watering every day, especially if the area gets full sun, so check your planters regularly. Have a hose stored under your sink so you have easy access for watering your balcony or patio garden.

A window box is not usually very large, so the options are more limited; however, you can still grow some of your own food. Some plants that will grow well in a window box are lettuce, Swiss chard, parsley, chives, basil, peas, and beans (if they can be trellised in some way). When planting your window box, choose plants that will work best for your location. If the area is not too hot, lettuce or spinach will grow in a shallow window box; however, if the area gets a lot of heat, some annual herbs such as basil, parsley, and chives could a better option for you.

▲ Window box with mixed herbs

A Hanging Garden

There is a huge range of hanging baskets and hanging garden bags available. Like any containers, if cared for properly, they can be reused year after year simply by replacing the potting soil and plants each year. The traditional hanging wire–framed basket must be lined before placing soil into it. Moss, coco fiber, or felt are the most common options when purchasing liners; however, burlap, landscape fabric, newspaper, or a recycled wool sweater will work just a well, giving you some other options and inexpensive price ranges to choose from. These materials all work well, as they will hold the soil in place and will also allow water to drain. Solid plastic baskets do not need liners and often have a drip tray attached to them that helps to prevent water from draining out too quickly. Hanging garden bags can be purchased at garden centers, hardware stores, and online.

Unusual containers for hanging plants can be created out of almost any waterproof fabric like old plastic shower curtains, oilcloth, colorful vinyl bags, and heavy-duty plastic kitchen bags. The only tools you will need to make these attractive instant planters are a pair of scissors, a grommet setter, and grommets. Cut the fabric you are using in a square, circle, or any other shape you may want. Insert the grommets, spacing them evenly around the upper edge of the fabric. Attach S-hooks and hanging chain; then pot up your "nonpot" as you would any container. Your planter is ready to hang.

FACT

A compact bush or trailing variety of tomato such as "Tumbler" makes for an attractive and productive hanging basket. Adding parsley or basil as a filler can make the basket even more lush and beautiful.

Hanging baskets can be used on balconies or in pergolas, or half baskets can be hung on walls to make a living wall. One advantage to hanging baskets is you can move them around the garden or patio to access sun, shade, or protections, depending on the weather. Baskets attached to a wall will benefit from added warmth and protection from winds if you are planting some fall or winter veggies or herbs. Hanging baskets can be very attractive, helping to add beauty as well as grow food in your small space.

Make sure the brackets you are hanging the baskets on are securely attached to a structure. It is important to hang your baskets so they can be easily reached to water, fertilize, rotate, and maintain. Hanging baskets can sometimes be difficult to maintain as they are exposed to wind, rain, and often hot temperatures. The heat may require the baskets to be watered at least once a day. To help store water in the basket, add a saucer or pie plate to the bottom of the container before putting in the soil; the saucer will act as a reservoir for the water to sit so the plant can soak it up.

Herbs are good plants for hanging baskets as they are naturally quite drought tolerant. An herb-hanging basket filled with yellow mimulus, parsley, golden marjoram, oregano, and lemon thyme makes a colorful and edible basket. Another planting combination in an herb basket is nasturtiums with variegated pineapple mint and a silvery curry plant. Thyme, when it flowers, will attract bees and butterflies and will do well in a container or hanging basket also.

ALERT

If the soil in your container or hanging basket becomes so dry that the water just runs off, add a couple of drops of a mild dishwashing liquid to your full watering can to help the water to penetrate the dry surface.

A great way to water and fertilize hanging baskets is to use a long-handled spray gun attached to your hose. There are also pulley systems you can purchase to raise or lower your basket to a height that works best for you. When watering baskets or window box gardens, water may drain out the bottom of the container, so be conscious of who or what may be below when watering them.

The Green Roof

A green roof is the roof of a building that is partially or completely covered with a growing medium, and plants are growing on it. A contemporary approach to greening buildings is to integrate plants and support structures in the construction of the building itself. Green roofs can be constructed on any building, no matter how big or small. They can be purely aesthetic and integrate a building into its surroundings. Green roofs are definitely beneficial for the environment. There are two types of green roofs—extensive and intensive. They'll be discussed later in this section.

FACT

Green roofs do not have to be only on large buildings in large cities. You can easily make a small-scale green roof on a gardening shed or gazebos in your backyard. The roof will add an attractive feature to your garden and give your neighbors something to talk about.

A green roof can reduce the temperature of a rooftop by absorbing heat and rainwater, which can help to insulate a building, thus making the building more energy efficient as well as making if more fireproof and soundproof. Growing plants on a rooftop cleans the air, makes a beautiful green space to enjoy, attracts wildlife, and is attractive to look at from windows of neighboring buildings or when flying overhead. So there are many benefits to turning an unusual area into a garden space.

A green-roof garden usually requires the same maintenance and inputs as a garden grown at ground level. Soil depth is about 6 inches and a lightweight-growing medium rather than regular soil is used on the rooftop. This type of green–roof garden can support a wide range of plants such as vegetables, herbs, flowers, and small trees. These roofs need to be accessible to people and usually need to look good.

Extensive green roofs are not usually made for regular human usage. They are usually regarded as more ecological or sustainable, as they require fewer resources such as water than a traditional or intensive roof garden. The depth of the soil is often less, and plants require less maintenance: usually grasses, low-growing ground-cover plants, and plants that are more drought-resistant. Extensive gardens are also less expensive to construct.

A properly constructed green roof consists of several layers needed to protect the existing roof structure, while retaining adequate soil and moisture for the plants to grow. Before you start, it is important get a professional to give you advice on weight restrictions and other concerns regarding the rooftop you want to use as a garden. Check with your city or town regarding zoning restrictions and with your insurance company about insurance coverage related to installing a green-roof garden. It can be an expensive undertaking to turn a roof, especially a larger one, into a garden. Do your research beforehand.

FACT

CitySoil, a Canadian company, has created an eco-friendly, ultra-lightweight soil engineered for weight-restricted rooftop gardens and green-roof installations. The soil is made from only natural and recycled components; it's also fully recyclable and features high wind resistance along with porosity and permeability.

A properly designed green roof consists of five layers. The base layer is the most important element. Its function is to prevent water from leaking through and to prevent root penetration into the existing roof structure. Often the existing roof surface will be enough but check with a qualified professional. The second layer is the drainage system. The pitch of your roof will determine what type of system you will need. Systems vary from simple fabric to more extensive drainage troughs. Effective drainage is needed so excess water will be directed to gutters and downspouts, keeping your plants from getting waterlogged and the existing roof from being damaged.

The third layer is the growing medium. This is usually a lightweight soil that will contain nutrients, retain moisture, and allow the plant roots to grow. A 6-inch depth is needed to grow most common vegetables, herbs, and flowers. The fourth layer is a root-permeable filter layer used to prevent the growing medium from washing away and causing problems for your drainage system. If you have a sloped roof, supports may be needed to hold the growing medium in place; this can usually be easily done with wood framing.

The final layer is the planting. Use plants that are low growing and not too deep-rooted such as salad greens, lettuce, peas, beans, squashes, and cucumbers. Tall plants have a tendency to dry out more quickly, and can become a fire hazard if not maintained properly.

Rooftop Gardening

Rooftop gardens are becoming more popular as more people begin wanting to grow food, herbs, and flowers, and there is less and less green space available, especially in large cities. Rooftops on large high-rise apartment or office buildings are unused spaces that can easily become productive food-producing gardens. Rooftops get ample sunlight and rain, and most buildings are built to accommodate the weight of soil and the plants growing in it.

Make sure everyone has official access to the roof by either a stairwell or elevator. Access is extremely important in any roof-top garden as materials need to be transported and the garden beds need to be easily maintained. You also want people to use and enjoy the space for relaxation. Water is another important consideration. Check to see if a tap could be installed on the rooftop, or if the roof structure can carry the weight of a water reservoir in which you can collect rainwater. You will also want access to electricity as well as an area where you can store tools and gardening supplies so everything is easily available when needed.

ALERT

It is always important to check the load bearing capacity of a balcony or rooftop before creating a garden on it. If you want to grow more than a few containers on your balcony or plant a rooftop garden, hire an engineer to check out the area so you have the proper information before getting started.

Creating a rooftop garden is different from making a green roof and it can be done in various ways. Most gardeners utilize containers for growing plants; however, with proper waterproofing, drainage, and growing medium, the soil can be placed directly on the roof (similar to green roofs), making the garden a more traditional garden. Sunlight is one of the essentials in growing food-producing plants, and as most roofs are elevated, they will get more sunlight than most ground areas especially in an urban environment. Depending on what you are growing and the temperature on the roof, some shade may be required. So, when designing your garden, incorporate a shade wall, trellis, pergola, or taller plants to shade smaller ones.

Wind is another concern on any rooftop garden as wind is usually stronger up high than at ground level. Strong winds can damage plants. It is important to study the direction of winds at different times of the year so you can protect your plants. Planning vertical walls, structures, or temporary covers is recommended. When building structures, make sure they are securely attached to the roof or building.

If you are interested in starting a garden on the top of your apartment or office building, it can be a very worthwhile project. Just make sure you do your research. Get proper plans and authorization from the city and building owners before you start any work. All the legwork in the beginning will give you years of enjoying and eating from a beautiful garden.

CHAPTER 11

Urban Gardening

Over 60 percent of the world's population lives in urban areas. Even if only a few people wanted to grow some of their own food, a lot space would be needed for planting. Now you'll learn about various garden concepts such as community gardens, collective gardens, the SPIN garden, and community-shared agriculture as urban options for growing some of your own veggies. Read on to discover spaces such as school yards or grassy areas on the street that may have potential in becoming productive urban gardens.

Community Gardens

A community garden is a space set aside within a neighborhood where a group of people can grow vegetables. Community gardens have been set up in empty parking lots in the center of the city, in local parks, or on private property that has been leased or donated to the neighborhood for planting gardens. The main purpose of such a garden is to offer space to those urban dwellers who want to grow food but who do not have the space or opportunity where they actually reside.

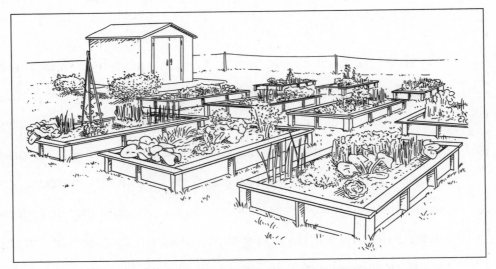

▲   A typical layout of community garden beds

The community garden is divided into garden plots of equal size that are managed by individual growers. Some gardens have individual, raised boxes for each person; others just use plots of ground designated for each gardener. There is usually a nominal fee and each gardener is responsible for maintaining his specified area. Local governments, community services, or profit or nonprofit groups may fund these gardens, and there usually is a committee to oversee the common garden areas.

One benefit to this type of garden is autonomy for gardeners. People can use the plot for as long as they want, they can garden whenever they like, and they can purchase materials and supplies as a group to save money. Other benefits are city water or reservoirs for storing rainwater that are available for everyone to use, as well as shared gardening tools to save each person from having to purchase everything. The disadvantages are the regulations that are set, including restrictions on what can be done in the garden area, and there is often a waiting list for a plot.

Collective Garden

In a collective garden, a group of people come together to garden in a specific area. The harvest is usually divided according to the gardeners' needs and often part of the harvest is donated to other community groups such as meals on wheels, soup kitchens, and food banks. In this type of garden there is a leader: someone who takes charge, organizes events, and teaches others how to garden.

Here are five good reasons to shop at local farmers' markets: eat the freshest and tastiest vegetables, support family farms, nourish yourself with less-processed foods, get to know where your food comes from, and use the market to connect with your community for social interaction.

The advantage to this type of gardening group is that it creates a feeling of solidarity, offers a strong feeling of belonging to a group and sharing in the work, and it links people to their community. This type of gardening can offer leadership to groups in need, such as young people needing something constructive to do, or therapeutic gardening for senior citizens, or those with mental and physical challenges. The disadvantages are finding a space to garden, lack of continuity as the group changes, fixed times to do the work, and the complicated setup and maintenance.

SPIN Gardening

SPIN stands for "small plot intensive." It is a farming system taught through specific courses. The basis of this type of gardening is connecting individuals who have land that is not being used to persons who want to grow vegetables for making a profit. The person wanting to grow makes an agreement with the owner of the property (with the garden space such as a backyard) to use the area, usually in exchange for some of the harvest.

The advantages to this type of gardening are numerous. You do not need land or capital to get started, it can be used in either a city backyard or a rural community, and it enables a person who wants to grow vegetables to do so. The main disadvantage is that you are putting time and energy into a space that you do not own and that may not be a long-term option. If you want to make a profit growing and selling vegetables, you may need several areas to grow enough produce, all of which can be time-consuming and difficult to manage.

ESSENTIAL

When choosing crops to grow, make sure you choose varieties that are resistant to disease. If possible, choose a range of vegetables that will produce in succession and over a period of time so you can enjoy veggies all season long.

The SPIN method of gardening is mainly used for growers who want to make a profit from growing vegetables. However, for an individual who lives in a condo or apartment where there is no outdoor space available, this may be an option to consider. Connecting with a friend or someone in your community who has a backyard and is unable to use it, or does not want to, but is willing to have someone come in and grow some veggies in exchange for some of the harvest, could be a win-win for both parties.

Community Shared Agriculture

A community shared agriculture (CSA) garden is usually started by a local farmer who decides to grow vegetables and sells them to a committed group of people who are willing to sign up and pay in advance for a certain amount of food each week during the growing season. This allows the farmer to receive money in the spring when it is needed to get everything started up, and gives the individual or family fresh produce, usually organically grown food, on a regular basis.

Being a member of a CSA does not mean you grow the veggies your-self. But often part of the agreement is volunteering on the farm helping to plant, weed, and harvest some of the vegetables so you are involved in some aspect of producing the food you are eating. This is a great way for people in urban areas to learn about where their food is coming from and help sup-port others in growing our food. Even if you have a tiny garden of your own already, this is a great way for you and your family to get more fresh local veggies and to support another grower. The website *www.localharvest.org/csa* allows you to find participating farms in your area.

The School Yard

Schools are beginning to recognize the important role school-based food gardens can play in a student's learning and social development. Developing and maintaining a food garden gives students the opportunity to learn about nutrition and environmental issues, increases their access to healthy food, and promotes social and emotional development by greening the school grounds and making green spaces for the local neighborhood. School-based gardens allow the integration of fresh food into cafeteria meals and school meal or snack programs.

ESSENTIAL

Most loose-leaf lettuce can be grown successfully without thinning; however, most head lettuce or butter head varieties need thinning for good head development. Pull some of the young plants after their second leaves appear, leaving the remaining plants at the spacing recommended on the seed packet, usually about 6 to 12 inches apart.

For the urban dweller, and especially if you have children, the school yard garden is a way to become involved in your community as well as grow veggies that can be used in the school or potentially sold to raise money for your school. If the garden is large enough, the produce could be distributed during the summer months to garden volunteers or families in need, allow-ing our children to have fresh healthy food available to them.

Sidewalk Gardening

The tiny strip of soil between the sidewalk and the street or your own sidewalk and your driveway is often wasted on a little grass or weeds, so why not use it for growing some veggies, herbs, and flowers? You could set up an attractive raised bed, fill it with compost or a good soil mix, and plant lettuce interplanted with parsley and some dusty miller. Another option is to plant other salad greens, flowers, and even some root crops that could be harvested as baby veggies, making it a very attractive area.

A raised bed will contain the soil, look tidier, and be more attractive. Make the raised bed out of cedar or redwood, at the width of the area to whatever length works (6 feet is a good length) and 3 inches high. Before you start going ahead and setting up a garden area that is not on your property, get permission from your local city authorities. Some areas have regulations as to what these strips of ground can be used for as they often belong to the city.

The soil in these areas is often lacking in nutrients and organic matter, so breaking up the soil before placing it in a raised bed is recommended. Make sure you use a healthy soil to start with; then keeping the area tidy, weed-free, and well watered will make it more attractive for the neighbors or city officials. Any area near a roadway can become dusty, so regularly spraying the veggies will help to keep them healthier.

ESSENTIAL

If you want to use a plastic planter-box liner in your cedar window or garden box, buy the liner first and then determine the size you will need to build your box. The advantage to using a liner is you can lift it out of the box to change soil or plantings, which is a definite benefit especially if the planter is in a difficult to reach area.

The space along the edge of steps of your porch is a great place to put some containers filled with veggies and herbs. Pots need to be watered often, daily in hot weather, and you want to make sure the pot you are using is large enough to sustain the plant's root system when it grows to maturity. Foliage will turn yellow if there is a lack of nutrients, often a sign the pot is too small. Pots of peppers, tomatoes, and eggplants along with some pots filled with colorful flowers can make a very attractive entrance to your home.

CHAPTER 12

Companion Planting

Companion planting will work well in small-space gardens, especially if you can do a few small beds throughout your front or backyard. You could also try growing several different plants in your containers on a balcony or rooftop. In this chapter you'll learn the basics of companion planting and gain some tips to help you along the way. You'll also find a list of plants that work well together and a few garden designs to get any gardener started.

Fundamentals of Companion Planting

Companion planting is growing a variety of vegetable plants, herbs, and flowers in the same area to influence a healthier, more productive garden. Planting certain plants close to each other can create support for the plants, utilize space and soil nutrients more efficiently, help prevent pests and disease, and create a habitat for beneficial insects.

Companion Planting Can "Lend a Hand"

By planting certain plants together, they can give each other the physical support they may need. Corn or sunflowers are both plants that grow with tall, strong stalks. These are great for supporting beans or cucumbers. Another example of a plant that can help another is to plant a row of corn on the south side of your lettuce. The corn will give the lettuce shade from the summer heat—shade that the lettuce needs, allowing you to harvest the lettuce longer.

Better Use of Space and Nutrients

You can use your space and soil nutrients more efficiently using companion plantings, especially if you have a limited area in which to grow. For example, after your spring crop of radishes and spinach has finished in July, get your bed ready for your fall planting of cabbages by adding in manure and compost. Place out your cabbage transplants; then in September or October plant your garlic bulbs around the cabbage. The cabbage will be harvested in the early winter, leaving nutrients and space for the garlic to grow in late winter and early spring.

FACT

Blanching is a technique of mounding soil or other materials around the base of a plant to prevent the light from reaching it. This practice makes the stalk whitish in color like, for example, celery or leeks. The lighter color is often more preferable when selling these products.

Another example is to plant your basil around the base of your tomato plant, just making sure that your tomato plant will be supported so enough light will reach the basil. The basil and tomato plants like the same grow-ing conditions, have similar water requirements, and are good companion plants. Or, plant your celery and leeks near each other; they both have sim-ilar growing requirements and grow best when blanched. These are just some examples of ways companion planting will maximize a small-space garden and help you use time efficiently.

Helps to Prevent Pests

Planting a diverse range of plants in your garden can mask or hide a crop from certain pests. The diversity is one way companion planting seems to work. Insects can be repelled or attracted by the odor of certain veggies, herbs, or flowers. Knowledge about particular plants can be used to draw a certain pest to one plant (the sacrificial plant) rather than to another. Plant-ing mustard greens near your cabbage, for instance, will attract the flea bee-tle to the mustard rather than the cabbage plant. Planting onions or chives in your carrot bed will help to prevent carrot fly from reaching the carrot root. Dill will attract aphids rather than having them get into your broccoli heads. These are just some examples of how one plant can be beneficial to another if they are grown near each other.

Attract Beneficial Insects

Creating a habitat and providing food for beneficial insects is another principle of companion planting. The tansy flower is a great example, as ladybugs love this flower. The ladybug is your garden friend, so using plants to attract or keep it in your garden is one of the best ways to prevent unwanted insects like aphids. Ladybugs feed heavily on aphids. Rather than immediately pulling spent plants, letting some of your veggie plants go to flower is an easy way of attracting insects and birds to your garden. They will be attracted by the smell and food that is available in these flowers.

Companion planting is one of the oldest traditions when it comes to plant-ing a garden. Historical records show the ancient Romans utilized a variety of plants in their garden designs to prevent pests. The Native Americans grew what is known as the "three sisters." Corn, beans, and squash were planted together to save on space and prevent pests, and because they supported each other while growing (the corn stalks supported the beans and squash to grow vertically). Many gardeners swear by companion planting; however, since there is no scientific proof that growing certain plants together makes for healthier ones, there are some people who dismiss companion planting as an old wives' tale. Give some of these suggestions a try in your own garden and make your own case for the benefits of companion planting.

ALERT

When planting a diverse garden with a variety of vegetables, herbs, and flowers, it is important to label your plants (especially when young) so you remember where things are planted. Another important tip: make sure your pathways are obvious so no plants will be trod on accidentally.

How It Works

If you are a gardener wanting to switch from growing with pesticides to organic methods, it can be frustrating when you first start. Healthy soil produces healthy plants; however, if you have been using chemical fertilizers or pesticides in your garden, your soil may not be as healthy as you think. Chemical fertilizers feed the plant, not the soil, so when transitioning to using organic methods you may experience an increase of pests in your garden until you can get your soil fertility back. Using companion planting may be one way of making the transition a little less painful.

FACT

Dandelions may seem like a curse, but they can really be a blessing. Dandelion roots penetrate deep into the earth, absorbing some important nutrients that regular vegetable plants never get to. When you cut or pull out the dandelion, do this before it flowers and especially before it goes to seed. Either add it to your compost or work it back into your garden bed. It will add these hard-to-reach nutrients into your soil.

Nature will take care of herself, but most traditional gardens are not anywhere near a natural environment. We usually grow our veggies in monocrops, with veggies grown in straight rows—something that does not occur in nature. Instead, nature has a diverse variety of plants growing amongst each other. This variety is what companion planting is all about. A selection of plants grouped together usually will grow better than when grown in monocrops.

When designing your companion garden, you want to think of natural woodlands where plants and animals coexist and are part of a thriving system. Use organic materials such as mulch to add humus to your beds, thereby attracting earthworms. Grow a variety of tall and short plants together, and intermix flowers and herbs among your vegetable plants to help create a diverse garden space. These diverse plantings will mimic nature and create a natural life chain for plants, insects, and animals to live harmoniously, which is what Mother Nature is all about.

The Companion List

Growing certain plants together will help them to grow healthier by attracting or repelling insects, better utilizing your small garden space, and helping keep your soil more fertile. Here is a list of common plants that work well together and those that are better planted apart from each other.

▼ TABLE 12-1: COMPANION PLANTING CHART

Vegetable	Positive Effect	Negative Effect
Asparagus	Parsley, tomato	Onion
Bean	Beet, borage, cabbage, carrot, cauliflower, corn, marigold, squash, tomato, strawberry	Chive, fennel, garlic, leek
Beet	Cabbage, kohlrabi	Runner bean
Broccoli	Bean, celery, dill, onion, oregano, potato, sage, rosemary, nasturtium	Lettuce, strawberry, tomato
Brussels sprouts	Bean, celery, dill, nasturtium, potato, sage, rosemary	Strawberry
Cabbage	Bean, beet, celery, dill, nasturtium, onion, oregano, potato, sage, rosemary	Grape, strawberry, tomato
Carrot	Bean, leek, onion, pea, radish, rosemary, sage, tomato	Dill

Vegetable	Positive Effect	Negative Effect
Cauliflower	Bean, beet, celery, dill, nasturtium, onion, oregano, potato, sage, radish	Strawberry, tomato
Celery	Bean, cabbage, leek, onion, tomato	
Corn	Bean, melon, pea, squash	
Cucumber	Bean, broccoli, celery, Chinese cabbage, lettuce, pea, radish, tomato	Sage, rue
Eggplant	Pea, tarragon, thyme	
Kohlrabi	Beet, onion	Bean, pepper, tomato
Leek	Carrot, celery	Broad bean, broccoli
Lettuce	Beet, cabbage, clover, pea, radish, strawberry	
Onion	Beet, cabbage, carrot, lettuce, potato, strawberry, tomato	Bean, pea
Pea	Carrot, corn, cucumber, eggplant, lettuce, radish, spinach, tomato, turnip	
Pepper	Basil, carrot, lovage, marjoram, onion, oregano	Fennel, kohlrabi
Potato	bean, cabbage, corn, lettuce, onion, petunia, marigold, radish	Apple, pumpkin, tomato
Pumpkin	Bean, corn, nasturtium, radish	Potato
Radish	bean, cabbage, cauliflower, cucumber, lettuce, pea, squash, tomato	Grape, hyssop
Spinach	Cabbage, celery, eggplant, onion, pea, strawberry	
Squash	Bean, corn, mint, nasturtium, radish	
Summer squash	Bean, corn, mint, nasturtium, radish	Potato
Tomato	Asparagus, basil, cabbage, carrot, onion, parsley, pea, sage	Fennel, potato
Turnip	Pea	
Zucchini	Bean, corn, mint, nasturtium, radish	Potato

Planting Your Companion Garden

Most people are often either short on space or time when it comes to gardening, so it is important to grow what you love to eat! If your family loves to eat something that you spend a small fortune on, perhaps this is one of the items you can grow. If you have never tried growing that certain vegetable before, it can be fun to experiment with trying to grow something new. If you have never grown *anything* before, be brave and plant the first seed; you will be wonderfully surprised and pleased when it actually produces food for you. Knowing your garden conditions is another important aspect when planning a food garden.

If you have an existing garden and want to try something new, or if you are having specific pest problems in your garden, companion planting can be a fun way to experiment with some new ideas and perhaps help to turn what is now a problem into something more positive.

FACT

Herbs are grown for their leaves, seeds, buds, bark, fruits, and even their roots. They have been grown for centuries for their flavoring in cooking and canning, for their medicinal use, and now as companion plants for their ability to repel or attract insects to your garden.

Companion planting can seem daunting at first; however, it is not all that difficult when you get started. Once you have your list of what you want to grow, the next step is to divide the veggies into different families: either the botanical family, feeding family, performance family, or the pest fighting family. Choosing which family to base your planting on will depend on what your needs are, how detailed you want to get, and how much time and energy you want to put into our companion garden. Here is more information on each.

Botanical Family

The botanical name is also called the scientific, proper, or Latin name, and every plant known to man, however rare, has one. The first way you can divide up your garden is by botanical family name (see table below). This can seem quite difficult at first glance. The reason you may want to grow this way is each vegetable in a specific family requires similar growing conditions and maintenance. The plants will also have similar pest problems. You can group some of the families together as well to make it even easier.

▼ **TABLE 12-2: BOTANICAL/FAMILY CHART**

Botanical/Family Name	Vegetable
Alliaceae/Onion Family	Onions, leeks, garlic
Apiaceae/Carrot Family	Carrot, celery, parsnips
Asparagaceae/Asparagus Family	Asparagus
Asteraceae/Daisy Family	Endive, chicory, lettuces
Brassicaceae/Mustard Family	Kale, radishes, cabbage, Brussels sprouts, broccoli, cauliflower, turnips, rutabaga
Chenopodiaceae/Goosefoot	Beets, spinach, Swiss chard
Curcurbitaceae/Gourd Family	Cucumber, squash, melons
Papilionoideae/Pea and Bean Family	Peas, beans
Poaceae/Grass Family	Corn, rye, wheat
Polygonaceae/Buckwheat Family	Buckwheat
Solanaceae/Nightshade Family	Peppers, eggplants, potato, tomato

When planning companion gardening using the botanical family, it is easy to provide care as the growing requirements are similar within each family.

Feeding Family

Some veggie plants require more of a certain nutrient than others do; therefore, some need a more fertile soil. Others can grow very well in an average soil. Here is a listing of the nutrient demands of some common vegetables.

▼ **TABLE 12-3: VEGETABLES GROUPED BY NUTRIENT DEMANDS**

Heavy Feeders	Moderate Feeders	Light Feeders	Cleaners & Builders
Celery	Broccoli	Beets	Beans
Corn	Brussels sprouts	Carrots	Peas
Cucumbers	Cabbage	Garlic	

Heavy Feeders	Moderate Feeders	Light Feeders	Cleaners & Builders
Eggplant	Cauliflower	Leeks	
Melons	Chinese cabbage	Onions	
Peppers	Kale	Potatoes	
Pumpkins	Lettuce	Radishes	
Squash	Parsley	Turnips	
Tomatoes	Salad greens		
	Spinach		
	Swiss chard		

Grouping plants using this method is one of the simplest ways to start companion planting and works well in small spaces, especially if you are just starting a new garden, working in an area that does not have that fertile soil, or do not have a lot of money to spend on amending and fertilizing your whole garden. You can amend and fertilize one bed at a time, utilizing it to plant the high feeders; the other plants can go into the less fertile part of your garden. Then each year you can enrich another area of the garden.

Performance Family

In this method you divide the vegetables you want to grow into groups that will support other plants either by giving shade or protection of some sort. For example, growing a tall plant, such as corn, sunflowers, pole beans, or cucumbers, on a trellis on the south side of your lettuce or spinach will give it the shade it needs to grow well. Or, growing beans or peas up a tee-pee, with lettuce and spinach growing inside it, will offer the leafy vegetables the shade and cooler temperature that they love.

By using the performance family as a way to organize, you make use of limited space since you can grow several different plants in one area usually by utilizing vertical space. This method can also help in pest prevention because a variety of plants grown together can confuse pests. Your soil will stay more fertile because monocrops can quickly deplete certain nutrients in the your garden soil.

There are some wonderful easy-to-grow flowers and fruits that grow on trellises, offering shade for the veggies that like less heat or for a chair for the gardener to relax in. Jasmine, honeysuckle, and clematis are some beautiful fragrant perennial flowering plants that work well on a trellis; or for an edible trellis, try growing figs, grapes, or peaches.

The three sisters method is one good example of performance-family growing where corn, beans, and squashes are planted together. The corn helps the beans and squash to grow upright; the pods and fruit remain healthier and easier to harvest when they are upright versus lying on the ground.

Pest-Fighting Family

If your garden is overrun by certain pests, you could utilize this method of dividing your plants to help fight the little creatures. There is no guarantee that growing plants together will rid your garden of pest problems, but there have been gardeners who have accomplished small miracles with companion planting. It does not hurt to give it a try, especially if you want to grow organically, which means not using any chemicals or pesticides in your garden to fight problem pests or insects.

▼ **TABLE 12-4: PEST PROBLEM? FIND THE PLANT TO HELP.**

Companion Plant	Pests Repelled	Planting Instructions
Basil	Aphids, asparagus beetle, mite, mosquitoes, tomato hornworm	Plant among tomatoes, eggplants, and asparagus. Brush against it to release aromatic oils.
Borage	Tomato hornworm	Plant near tomato or let self-sow throughout the garden to attract beneficial insects.
Calendula	Asparagus beetle	Plant throughout garden as the flower attracts beneficial insects.
Catnip	Aphids, asparagus beetle, Colorado potato beetle, squash bugs	Plant in pots and place in the ground near peppers, potatoes, and tomatoes.

Companion Plant	Pests Repelled	Planting Instructions
Chives	Aphids, Japanese beetle	Plant among raspberries and grapevines.
Garlic	Japanese beetle	Plant around roses and other flowers. Mix with water to make a mixture to spray on infected plants.
Geraniums	Japanese beetle	White-flowered ones can be used to trap the beetle.
Horseradish	Colorado potato beetle	Is a spreading perennial so plant among other permanent plants like asparagus raspberries, strawberries, and rhubarb.
Hyssop	Cabbage moth	Plant among broccoli, Brussels sprouts, cabbage, and cauliflower.
Marigolds	Mexican bean beetle, root-knot nematodes, root-lesion nematodes	Plant a solid block in an area that is a nematode infested area. Once the plant flowers, chop the plants down and till them into the soil.
Mint	Aphids, cabbage moth	Plant in pots and place into the ground as it is very invasive.
Nasturtiums	Aphids, Colorado potato beetle, Mexican bean beetle, squash bug	Have a pretty edible flower and can be grown as a mulch to protect ground beetles and spiders.
Onions	Carrot-rust fly	Plant with carrots in either alternating rows or in clusters to repel the carrot flies.
Parsley	Asparagus beetle	Plant on the edges of asparagus beds. Leave over winter and let some go to flower to attract beneficial insects.
Radishes	Cucumber beetle	Plant a few seeds among cucumbers, squash, and pumpkins.
Rosemary	Cabbage moths, carrot-rust fly, Mexican bean beetle	Plant among cabbage family plants, lettuce, and carrots.
Rue	Japanese beetle	Can be a growth inhibitor for most plants so only plant near perennials.
Sage	Cabbage moth, carrot-rust fly	Plant among perennial flowers and other herbs.
Savory	Mexican bean beetle	Plant near tomatoes and beans.
Tansy	Colorado potato beetle, squash bugs	Plant to attract beneficial insects.

Companion Plant	Pests Repelled	Planting Instructions
Thyme	Cabbage moth	Plant near cabbage family plants or in permanent areas of your garden. Creeping thyme it an excellent ground cover.
Wormwood	Flea beetles, mosquitoes	Plant in perennial beds and near where people may be. Rub the plant on skin to repel mosquitoes.

Many of these recommendations are based on tradition or folklore, so they may or may not work in your garden. Again, using companion planting is worth trying, especially if you have specific pest problems. Start with dividing the veggies you want to plant into one of the above families, then add in your herbs and annuals that make good friends with the veggies.

The Garden Plan

The following garden plan is divided into three of the families previously discussed:, botanical families (tomato family, cabbage family, and squash family), performance families (perennial bed, pole beans, and lettuce), and feeding/pest families (onions, carrots). The plan has six beds that can be as small or large as you have space; if all you have is a few square feet or some containers on a patio, just plant one of each of the plants including the herbs or flowers, which are good companion plants. These plantings could be used in a larger row garden or in raised beds as well.

Bed One
Perennial herbs like sage and thyme
Strawberries with bachelor buttons
Asparagus with hollyhocks or basil along edge
Bed Two
Tomatoes with clover, basil
Parsley, cilantro, lemon balm

Bed Three
Winter squash with nasturtiums
Summer squash/zucchini with calendulas and marigolds
Bed Four
Broccoli with zinnias
Brussels sprouts with cosmos & dill
Cauliflower/Cabbage with chrysanthemums
Bed Five
Potatoes/beans with dill
Peppers with strawflowers and alyssum
Bed Six
Pole beans/lettuce
Carrots/onions
Swiss chard, kale, beets with tansy and chives

It is important to rotate your crops each year to help prevent pests and to help keep your soil healthy.

ESSENTIAL

Pathways allow easy access to your garden beds; they are needed so your plants are not trampled. Use the pathways to walk through your garden while observing your plants, to have easy access for weeding, and to have access for watering your plants. Keep the pathways well mulched so they are easy to see and maintain.

CROP ROTATION FOR THE SECOND YEAR:

- Bed one remains in the same place as these are perennial plants.
- Bed two plants go into bed three
- Bed three plants go into bed four
- Bed four plants go into bed five
- Bed five plants go into bed six
- Bed six plants go into bed two

In companion gardens, plants are usually planted close together, similar to square-foot gardens. By planting the veggies, herbs and flowers close together, the plants will produce a green canopy. The cover, which can help to keep the soil moist as well as reduce weed growth, will make your garden a low maintenance garden.

Companion Garden Tips

There are many variables that can affect how a garden will grow. Some are out of your control, like the amount of sunlight or rain you may get. You can always use grow lights, give protection from too much rain, or give your plants water when it does not rain enough. But there is still no guarantee your plants will do well. Pests or diseases sometimes seem out of your control as well, and options are sometimes limited, especially when you are committed to using only organic methods. Here are a few tips that might make your gardening experience more enjoyable.

These are the best companion flowers to grow with your veggies:

- **Geraniums**—try them in a corner of the bed near the cabbage family veggies, as they help to repel the white cabbage butterfly.
- **Lupine**—is good for most veggie plants and can stimulate the growth of corn.
- **Marigolds**—control destructive nematodes, making the marigold a good companion for root crops.
- **Nasturtiums**—plant near squash, tomatoes, and members of the cabbage family, as they will trap slugs and snails and will repel aphids, cucumber beetles, and white flies.
- **Petunias**—good companion to beans, potatoes, tomatoes, and members of the cabbage family, as they repel bean beetles, potato beetles, and squash beetles.
- **Sunflowers**—are a host plant for beneficial insects such as the predatory wasp and will attract bees to your garden.

Here are more tips, to ensure your companion planting is successful:

- For perennial plants like asparagus, it is more practical to plant tomatoes around the bed rather than interplanting, so as not to disturb the asparagus roots.
- Borage and other wildflowers can self-seed and start looking untidy; however, before you pull these plants out, check to make sure they are not providing much needed shelter for beneficial critters such as praying mantis.
- Flowers such as marigold need to be intermixed to do their job well, not just planted at the end of a bed.
- Grow ground covers such as clover or alfalfa between your rows of veggies. This helps keep weeds down, prevents soil erosion, and helps the soil to retain water longer.
- Plant some lettuce, Swiss chard, and basil in your flower bed. They make a beautiful and tasty addition to the beds and your dinner plate.
- Plant lettuces or spinach under a bean teepee; just make sure you can easily reach to harvest them. In the center area that you cannot easily reach, plant flowers that will attract beneficial insects.
- Carrot family herbs and flowers such as caraway, lovage, fennel, and angelica have beautiful lacy flowers and attract beneficial insects like ladybugs and parasitic wasps.
- To supply water for insects at ground level, just fill a clay saucer or an aluminum tin with a few pebbles and then add enough water to just cover the pebbles.
- Beneficial insects need protection during winter months, so take time to mulch your garden with straw or dried shredded leaves.
- There are dozens of cover crops you can use in your garden. The four most common in the companion garden are alfalfa, buckwheat, annual rye grass, and white clover. They give protection to insects during the winter, and when tilled under in the spring, add organic matter to the soil.
- When weeding, take the time to identify some goldenrod, cosmos, borage, Queen Anne's lace, wild daisy, and wild aster. Leave some of them to flower, as they will attract beneficial insects.
- Plant mint and catnip into pots sunk into the soil so they do not spread and overtake your garden.

Growing your own food can be fun and relaxing (unless you are a commercial grower; then that is a whole different book) so try not to stress too much about how things are doing in the garden. Get to know your garden conditions, be willing to experiment, try new ways to do things, and try to learn something from your so-called mistakes. As Janet Kilburn Phillips said, "There are no gardening mistakes, only experiments."

CHAPTER 13

Veggies in Small Spaces

No matter what size of garden space you may have, you can grow a productive vegetable garden. In this chapter you will learn how to grow lettuce and other greens, root crops, cabbage family crops, peas and beans, and heat loving veggies. You'll discover which types are best for a tiny garden spot or a container garden. Read on for easy-to-follow information and tips on how to plant, care for, and harvest specific vegetables, so you can grow a fabulous small-space veggie garden.

Lettuce and Salad Greens

Lettuce and salad green mixes are some of the easiest vegetables to grow in a small-space garden. There are several types and varieties of lettuce you can choose from, each offering differently textured leaves and unusual colors. Loose-leaf types are preferable in a small-space or container garden because the outer leaves can be picked, leaving the center of the plant to produce new growth.

Other salad greens that are easy to grow are arugula (sometimes called rocket), corn salad, curly cress, sorrel, endive, and dandelion (sometimes called chicory). The seeds of these leafy greens are usually sown by broadcasting to a garden bed and are cut as individual leaves when they are 2 to 3 inches high. You can also allow the plant to mature and cut as a whole. Usually you can purchase these as transplants, making it easier to plant them in a container garden. Plant several different varieties of lettuce, salad greens, spinach, and Swiss chard in your small-space garden; that way you can enjoy tasty and colorful salads.

FACT

If you live in a mild climate, plant some lettuce seeds before mid-August for a fall/winter harvest. Try planting cold-hardy, butter-head types that will provide a lettuce harvest through November.

QUICK TIPS FOR GROWING LETTUCE AND SALAD GREENS

- **Botanical Name:** Asteraceae
- **Family Name:** Daisy family
- **Edible Parts:** Leaves and stems
- **Location:** Shady area with cool temperature. Lettuce grows well in raised beds and containers.
- **Best Soil:** Loose, rich, well drained, pH 6.0–6.8
- **When to plant:** Transplants are usually available from early March to mid-July, or direct seed as soon as you can work your soil. Plant a few seeds every few weeks.

- **Companion planting:** For a positive effect, plant with beets, cabbage, peas, clover, and radish. There are no plants that have a negative effect on lettuce plants.
- **Weeding:** Keep the area around the plant well weeded.
- **Watering:** Drip irrigation or overhead sprinkling will work well. Plants need 1 to 2 inches each week and may require more if the weather is hot. Sprinkling the leaves in the early morning will help to keep the plant cooler during the hot part of the day.
- **Care:** Provide some shade in the heat of the summer. A floating-row cover works well.
- **Fertilizing:** Add compost tea or fish fertilizer around the base of the plant every two to three weeks after planting. If planted in a container, add fertilizer every ten days.
- **Pests and Diseases:** Use crop rotation as prevention. Some common pests and diseases are slugs, aphids, cabbage looper, flea beetle, downy mildew, and Fusarium wilt.
- **Harvesting:** Cut off outer leaves on leaf lettuce and salad greens. For head lettuce varieties, harvest when the head is firm using a sharp knife to cut off at the base of the plant.
- **Storage:** Wash leaves, dry them in a salad spinner, and then place them into a sealed plastic bag or container. They will store well for up to a week in the refrigerator.

Spinach

Spinach is easy to grow in the ground or in containers; the only consideration is that it bolts easily in warm weather (70°F or 24°C) so it is best grown either early or late in the season. It needs a rich soil, so prepare your garden bed with several inches of compost or aged animal manure. Spinach does best in full sun, which is one of the reasons it is best grown early in the season when the sun is not too hot. Make sure the garden bed is well drained, especially if you live in a wet climate. Spinach has one of the darkest-colored leaves of all the vegetables, and because of this, offers a wealth of vitamins and minerals.

QUICK TIPS FOR GROWING SPINACH

- **Botanical Name:** Chenopodiaceae
- **Family Name:** Goosefoot
- **Edible Parts:** Leaves and stems
- **Location:** Full sun, low temperature season
- **Best Soil:** Rich soil abundant in nitrogen, pH 6.2–6.9
- **When to Plant:** Transplants are usually available March to July; or direct seed as soon as the soil can be worked.
- **Companion Plants:** For a positive effect, plant with cabbage, celery, eggplant, onions, peas, and strawberries. There are no plants that have a negative effect on spinach.
- **Weeding:** Keep beds well weeded.
- **Watering:** Keep soil moist; sprinkling will keep the leaves cooler in warm weather.
- **Care:** May need a little shade if the weather gets warm. A floating-row cover works well.
- **Fertilizing:** Both in the ground or in containers give spinach plants a nitrogen-rich fertilizer once they are one-third grown, or approximately once every ten to fourteen days.
- **Pests and Diseases:** Aphids, slugs, cabbageworm, and leaf miner are common.
- **Harvesting:** Can be harvested at any size from baby leaves, by cutting outer leaves, to maturity by cutting at the base of a mature plant.
- **Storage:** Spinach does not store well. Wash leaves, dry them in a salad spinner, and then place them into a sealed plastic bag or container. Leaves will keep in the refrigerator only for a few days.

Swiss Chard

Swiss chard is easy to grow in the ground or in containers, and is one of the best plants for a beginner as very little can go wrong. It can be harvested for several weeks. Swiss chard is related to the beet family but is grown for its leaves and stems, not for its roots. Like most other greens, Swiss chard likes a nitrogen-rich, well-drained soil. It will grow well in spring, summer, and in the fall. Just a few plants will last you all spring and summer, if you keep harvesting the outer leaves and let the center grow.

FACT

Swiss chard is a power food with twelve of the main nutrients for a healthy diet. The best way to maximize the many nutrients in Swiss chard is to steam the leaves for two to three minutes. A quick steaming will also retain the bright color of this vegetable.

Swiss chard is one of the most colorful vegetables. It comes in a rainbow of colors—red, yellow, orange, green, and white. As well as being a tasty, nutritious vegetable, it can make a lovely addition to your flower garden or containers garden.

QUICK TIPS FOR GROWING SWISS CHARD

- **Botanical Name:** Chenopodiaceae
- **Family Name:** Goosefoot.
- **Edible Parts:** Leaves and stems
- **Location:** Sunny, well drained
- **Best Soil:** Rich, loamy soil, pH 6.5–6.8
- **When to Plant:** Transplants are available starting in March, or sow direct as soon as your soil can be worked.
- **Companion Plants:** Plant with cabbage, celery, eggplant, onion, pea, and strawberry for a positive effect. There are no plants that have a negative effect on Swiss chard.
- **Weeding:** Keep area well weeded.
- **Watering:** Keep soil moist. Drip irrigation or hand watering are recommended over sprinkling. As the leaves get larger they will impede overhead water from reaching the plant roots.
- **Fertilizing:** In either the ground or in containers, use a nitrogen-rich fertilizer two to three weeks after transplanting, or once the plants reach about 6 inches high and then every ten days.
- **Pests and Diseases:** Use crop rotation as prevention for cabbageworm, aphids, flea beetle, and leaf spot.
- **Harvesting:** Outer leaves can be eaten at any size; baby leaves are often used in salads. Break the outer leaves off or cut them with a sharp knife.

- **Storage:** Swiss chard will not store long. Wash leaves, dry them in a salad spinner, and then place them into a sealed plastic bag or container. Chard will keep in the refrigerator for a few days.

Root Crops

Root vegetables are grown for their edible roots and are easy to grow in containers and other small spaces. Some types you may want to try are beets, carrots, rutabaga, radish, potatoes, garlic, and onions.

Carrots, Beets, Rutabaga, and Radish

Carrots are one of the most popular vegetables eaten, whereas beets, rutabagas, and turnips are usually love or hate vegetables; either you eat them on a regular basis or have no desire to eat them at all. The small, red radish is usually available only in the spring. It is a quick-growing vegetable that is great for a kid's garden or to intermix with other root crops. When you pull the radishes, you are making more room for the other plants to grow.

More fruits and vegetables are available to us today than at any time in history, but they do not pack the same nutritional punch as they did sixty years ago. So are the findings of a study published in the *Journal of the American College of Nutrition*. Researchers call it the dilution effect. Farmers are feeling the pressure to grow crops bigger and faster, which sacrifices the amount of nutrients the plant is able to absorb.

Root crops are easy to grow, have a long harvest, take up a small space in your garden, and can be stored, so they are a great addition to any home garden. The roots can be harvested small and can taste sweeter than the mature plant. The young leaves of the beet plant are sought after and make a great addition to salad. Depending on your space, try planting several seeds of each type so you can harvest some young leaves as well as let some plants mature. If you choose to eat the vegetables small, you can replant that area with more seeds or even another vegetable to extend your harvest and to maximize your space. All of these veggies will grow well in a container so long as it is deep enough (at least 12 inches) and you use a light soil mixture.

QUICK TIPS FOR GROWING CARROTS, BEETS, RUTABAGA, AND RADISH

- **Botanical Name:** carrot—Apiaceae; beets—Chenopodiaceae; rutabaga—Brassica napobrassica; radish—Brassicaceae
- **Family Name:** Carrot—Carrot family; Beets—Goosefoot family; Rutabaga—Brassicaceae family; Radish—Mustard family
- **Edible Parts:** Roots on all of them; tops on beets and rutabaga
- **Location:** Sunny, open area
- **Best Soil:** Fertile, well-drained, clean bed, pH 5.5–to 6.8
- **When to Plant:** Sow April to mid-July for a continuous harvest
- **Companion Plants:** Cabbage has a positive effect on beets so try to plant them near each other. Avoid planting beets near your beans as the beets can have a negative effect on how the beans grow.
- **Weeding:** Keep well weeded, especially when the plants are small.
- **Watering:** Soil needs to be kept moist when seeds are first planted and then need regular watering after they have sprouted. If you are using an overhead sprinkler, make sure you leave it on long enough for the water to penetrate several inches into the soil in order to reach the roots (carrots do not like their tops to get wet).
- **Fertilizing:** Dig in compost or aged animal manure and a balanced fertilizer when preparing the beds. If grown in containers, fertilize with fish fertilizer or compost tea every ten days.
- **Harvesting:** Beet or Rutabaga leaves can be cut when they are about 3 inches high. Start harvesting carrots when they reach finger size, beets and rutabaga when they are the size of golf balls, and radishes when they are marble size. Gently tug the plant from the ground.
- **Storage:** Store the root vegetables in a plastic bag and keep them in the refrigerator for up to three weeks. If you have a large amount to store, the root vegetables can be packed in a box filled with peat moss and stored in a root cellar.

Potatoes

Potatoes are the most-used vegetable in the world. They are easy to grow in the ground or in large containers, and are a good vegetable for storage. They are nutritious and can be cooked in many different ways. Potatoes need a long growing season (approximately four months) with continuous cool weather for best production.

Plant your potatoes as early as you can get into your garden. They are grown from stem cuttings, which are also called seed pieces or seed eyes; the eye is where the new sprout will grow. A potato plant can take up a lot of room, and several plants will be needed for a small family to eat fresh, more if you want to store them for use during the winter months. But if it is a veggie you love to eat, make room for at least a few plants. Potatoes can be grown in containers. Just make sure the containers are large and deep; a stack of three or four old tires will do the job.

FACT

Early varieties of potatoes take up less space and only form a clump about 17 inches wide. They have attractive flowers in shades of white, pink, mauve, lavender, violet, and purple and can add an ornamental value to your garden or container.

If you live in a mild climate, potatoes are hardy enough that they can remain in the garden all winter, if well mulched, and can be harvested as you need them. They need a fair amount of space as the roots can grow quite large.

QUICK TIPS FOR GROWING POTATOES

- **Botanical Name:** Solanaceae
- **Family Name:** Nightshade family
- **Edible Parts:** Tubers
- **Location:** Sunny, well-drained but moist area. Potatoes thrive in cool weather.
- **Best Soil:** Fertile, slightly acidic, sandy loam soil, pH 4.8–6.0

- **When to Plant:** Seed them as soon as you can work your garden bed in the spring.
- **Companion Plants:** For positive effects, plant with bean, cabbage, corn, lettuce, onion, marigold, and radish. Do not plant near pumpkin or tomatoes, which can both have a negative effect on your potato plants.
- **Weeding:** Keep well weeded when the plant is small.
- **Watering:** Water regularly from the time the vine first emerges above ground until the plant flowers. After flowering, the plant needs less water with normal rainfall usually being sufficient if the plants are mulched.
- **Care:** Keep mounding (hilling) soil up around the vine as it grows; this helps to keep the potatoes covered.
- **Fertilizing:** Fertilize with compost tea once the flowers start to emerge.
- **Pests and Diseases:** Wire worm, Colorado beetle, scab, aphids, and flea beetles are some common pests and diseases.
- **Harvesting:** New or small potatoes can be harvested once the plant has flowered by digging around under the vine and pulling out a few tubers. When the vine turns brown and dies back, the tubers are fully mature. Then the whole plant can be pulled; use a garden fork to dig up the larger tubers gently.
- **Storage:** Potatoes are a great vegetable for storing and will keep for several months if stored properly. Make sure they are dry before storing them in a cool dark area.

Garlic

Garlic is a cool-season crop grown mainly for its bulb; however. the flower stem is also edible and very tasty. Garlic is a fairly foolproof vegetable and is easy to grow in the ground or in containers. It needs a sunny, well-drained area and is usually planted in the fall, either in October, or at the latest, early November, and then harvested the following June.

Choose the biggest cloves to plant and mulch the beds after they are planted. Garlic will grow slowly over the winter, and all of a sudden in January and February, once the days start to get longer, they will shoot up quickly. In the spring, keep the plants well weeded and give them more mulch and regular watering if you do not get any rain. In early spring the garlic plants will produce flower stalks which are called garlic scapes. These can be eaten and cooked the same way the cloves are used. Removing the flowering stem before it fully flowers will allow the plant to put more energy into producing a larger bulb.

FACT

For centuries, garlic has been known for its powerful medicinal qualities. In ancient Egypt there are hieroglyphs engraved on the pyramid Giza that show garlic was used to protect the builders. Doctors in ancient Greece and Rome believed garlic was a cure-all for many ailments and diseases.

When the garlic tops start to turn brown and die back, it means the garlic bulbs are ready to be harvested. To harvest your garlic, use a garden fork to loosen the soil so the bulbs do not break. Garlic needs to be dried in order for it to keep properly; leave the bulbs in the sun for up to three weeks to cure. Protect them from the rain by covering them or bringing them indoors if the weather is bad.

QUICK TIPS FOR GROWING GARLIC

- **Botanical Name:** Alliaceae
- **Family Name:** Onion family
- **Edible Parts:** Bulb (cloves) and flower stem
- **Location:** Sunny, dry, well-drained area
- **Best Soil:** Rich, pH 6.0–to 6.8
- **When to Plant:** Plant bulbs in the fall or in the early spring if you live in an extremely cold climate. Plant the cloves with the pointed end up.
- **Companion Plants:** For a positive effect, plant near carrots and tomatoes. Beans, peas, and strawberries can have a negative effect, so avoid planting near each other.
- **Weeding:** Needs to be kept well weeded.
- **Watering:** Will need regular watering in the spring if there is very little rainfall.

- **Care:** Mulch with straw or hay in the fall and again in the spring when the plants are a foot high; this will help prevent weeds and keep the soil from drying out.
- **Fertilizing:** Fertilize with compost tea or fish fertilizer after the flower stalks have started to form.
- **Pests and Diseases:** Using crop rotation will prevent most pests and disease. Aphids and thrips can be a problem.
- **Harvesting:** A sign the bulbs are ready to be harvested is when the tops start to turn brown and die back. Loosen the soil around your plants with a garden fork and then gently pull out the bulbs, trying to keep the stem and bulb intact. The bulb will dry better if it is not broken off.
- **Storage:** If dried and stored properly garlic will keep for several months. After curing in the sun for a few weeks, clean off any dirt remaining on the bulbs and store them in a paper bag or box in a cool, dry storage area. Garlic can be braided and hung in a cool dark area as well.

Onions

Onions grown for their bulbs can be temperamental, as they like cool temperatures when they first start growing and then need the heat in order to produce their bulbs. Green onions are much easier to grow and are great for container gardens. Both varieties require a rich well-drained soil that is free of debris.

FACT

To keep water and liquid fertilizers from being wasted, place your containers directly under your hanging baskets when watering them. Any overflow from the basket will drip into the containers below.

Once the tops start to turn brown, your onions bulbs are getting near to maturity. When the tops start to fall over, take a garden rake and gently bend all the browning tops over so they all are lying down. Leave them this way for a few weeks, and then start to pull onions as you need them. If it is coming to the end of your season and they all need to be pulled, make sure you allow them to dry so they will store well. You can place the onions on news-paper, on a screen, or drape them over the edge of a pail with the green end hanging inside. Leave the bulbs in a sunny, dry spot for about ten days so they are thoroughly dry before storing them.

QUICK TIPS FOR GROWING ONIONS

- **Botanical Name:** Alliaceae
- **Family Name:** Onion family
- **Edible Parts:** Bulbs and leaves
- **Location:** Sunny, moist but well-drained area
- **Best Soil:** Rich, well-drained, light soil free of debris, pH 5.6–6.5
- **When to Plant:** Transplants are usually available in early spring; onions can also be started from seed indoors and then transplanted outdoors.
- **Companion Plants:** For a positive effect, plant with beets, cabbage, carrots, lettuce, potatoes, and tomatoes. Beans and peas have a nega-tive effect, so avoid planting near each other.
- **Weeding:** Need to be kept well weeded
- **Watering:** In the early stages of growth onions need lots of water, so keep the soil moist. Stop watering once the leaves start to turn brown.
- **Care:** Onions like rich soil, so when preparing the garden bed make sure you add in several inches of compost or aged manure.
- **Fertilizing:** Side dress with compost (place around the base of the plant) when the bulb first starts to swell, and again when the leaves are about 1 foot tall.
- **Pests and Diseases:** Very few pests or diseases are found in onions, and the best way to prevent them is to use crop rotation.
- **Harvesting:** When growing sets for green onions, harvest once the greens are about 12 inches tall. For the bulb, pull it up once the leaves have turned brown and died back.
- **Storage:** Onions will store for several months if dried properly. Once they are harvested, lay the onions on newspaper or a mesh screen in a sunny dry area. Let them dry for a week to ten days, turning them a few times each day. Make sure they are protected from any moisture or dampness.

The Cabbage Family

These vegetables are also known as cole crops or the Brassica family, and include broccoli, Brussels sprouts, cabbage, cauliflower, and kale. They are cold-hardy vegetables that produce a lot of food for the space they use and will grow in most types of soil. Cole crops also do well in containers so long as the container is large and deep enough (at least 16 inches of soil is recommended).

Most broccoli varieties will produce one large head averaging about 6 to 8 inches in diameter. Once this head is cut off, the plant will continue to produce side branches with smaller heads. Keep cutting these before they flower and you will be harvesting broccoli from one plant for several weeks.

Brussels sprouts are probably the most peculiar-looking vegetable plant. They look like little palm trees with lumps growing from the plant stem or trunk. The bumps, which are usually 1 to 2 inches in diameter, are the Brussels sprouts. They are often called baby cabbages, as the sprouts look like a miniature cabbage. Each plant should produce between fifty and 100 sprouts! This is a cool-season vegetable that is harvested in the late fall. The taste of this vegetable is improved by a light frost.

FACT

For harvesting winter vegetables, plant Brussels sprouts, kale, spinach, and sprouting broccoli in July and August. Transplants are available in the summer, making it easy to fill an empty spot in your garden or container with a new plant.

The mature cabbage forms a head from a rosette of thickened leaves. The cabbage head can be round, pointy, or flattened, depending on the variety, and can have richly colored and textured leaves. There are red varieties with purplish red leaves, green varieties, and a savoy cabbage that has crinkly leaves.

Cauliflower is said to be the most difficult vegetable in the Brassica family to grow. It is a cool-season vegetable; however, it is very sensitive to the frost as well as to heat. Sunlight will turn the white head a darkish-yellow color, which is not very appealing, so each head needs to be covered or blanched.

Kale has a high level of vitamin C and calcium, and has the highest levels of beta-carotene of all the green vegetables. Kale will survive over winter and the leaves are more tender and sweet once they have been touched by frost. But kale will easily go to seed and spread throughout your garden, so it is important to pull the plants out before the seeds spread if you want to contain it.

FACT

Make you own kneeling pad for the garden by stuffing an old hot water bottle with rags and pantyhose. Use just enough stuffing to give the water bottle a nice cushion effect.

QUICK TIPS FOR GROWING CABBAGE FAMILY VEGGIES

- **Botanical Name:** Brassicaceae
- **Family Name:** Mustard family
- **Edible Parts:** Flower buds, leaves on kale
- **Location:** Cool, well-drained area
- **Best Soil:** Rich, moist loamy soil, pH 6.0–6.8
- **When to Plant:** Transplants are available April to mid-July.
- **Companion Plants:** For a positive effect, plant with beans, onion, potato, oregano, dill, sage, and nasturtiums. Planting with tomatoes and lettuce will have a negative effect on broccoli.
- **Weeding:** Keep well weeded around base of the plant.
- **Watering:** Water deeply at least once a week around the base of the plant. Hand watering or drip irrigation is best, because if an overhead sprinkler is used, the water is blocked from reaching the roots by the large leaves.
- **Fertilizing:** Start to fertilize about three weeks after setting out the transplants, and again when the bud starts to form on the plant. If grown in containers fertilize with fish fertilizer or compost tea every ten days.
- **Pests and Diseases:** Root maggot, cabbageworm, and club root are common. Crop rotation is essential for prevention of pests and diseases.

- **Harvesting:** For broccoli and cauliflower, cut the head when it is about 5 to 6 inches in diameter or before the buds start to open. For cabbage, cut the head once it fills out and becomes firm, and with kale cut the outer leaves, leaving the center to produce more leaves. Broccoli will form side branches off the main stem. These branches will produce smaller heads, which need to be cut regularly or they will flower.
- **Storage:** Cabbage family veggies will stay for a few weeks in your refrigerator.

Peas and Beans

Beans are one of the easiest vegetables to grow. You sow the seeds directly into the garden or container. The seeds will germinate quickly in the right temperature, grow vigorously, and produce a significant harvest for the area they use in the garden. There are several different types of beans: bush beans (sometimes called snap beans), runner beans, pole beans, shell beans for drying, lima beans, soybeans, and fava beans (sometimes called a broad bean). Most varieties need warm soil to germinate, so they are usually planted in the late spring. One tip is if you can walk barefoot on the soil without it feeling cold, it is time to plant your beans. The exception to this rule is fava beans, which are a cool-weather bean and best planted in early spring.

FACT

When constructing a teepee stake to support your climbing beans, use a rubber band to hold the stakes in place temporarily. This will allow you to keep both hands free to easily tie the stakes together.

Peas are a cool-season crop and can be planted early in the spring. There are three common types of peas: shelling peas are grown for the seeds, snow peas have a flat edible pod, and snap pea pods and seeds are eaten together. Snow and snap varieties will need to be staked as they can grow up to 5 feet high; plan for a trellis if choosing to grow these types.

QUICK TIPS FOR GROWING BEANS AND PEAS

- **Botanical Name:** Papilionaceae
- **Family Name:** Pea and Bean family
- **Edible Parts:** Seeds and pods
- **Location:** Open, sunny area
- **Best Soil:** Sandy, loamy, neutral pH
- **When to Plant:** Bean seeds need a temperature of 70° to 90°F, or 21° to 32°C, so are usually not planted until late spring or early summer. Peas like cooler soil and can be planted as early as mid-March if the soil is dry enough.
- **Companion Plants:** For a positive effect, plant with beets, cabbage, carrot, corn, squash, and tomato. Plants that will have a negative effect are chive, fennel, garlic, and leek.
- **Weeding:** Keep well weeded, especially when plants are small.
- **Watering:** Do not water bean seeds until they are sprouted, then water regularly after that. Peas like a moist soil for best germination.
- **Care:** Set up stakes for pole or runner beans and snow or snap peas at the time of planting.
- **Fertilizing:** Fertilize with fish fertilizer or compost tea after the first heavy bloom and again when the pods are starting to form. Fertilize every ten days if grown in pots.
- **Pests and Diseases:** Aphids, leafhopper, Mexican beetle, mite, damping-off, and downy mildew are some common pests and diseases.
- **Harvesting:** For bush bean varieties, harvest when the pod is still small about 4 to 6 inches long. Runner or pole beans are harvested when the pod is 6 to 10 inches long and still flat. Dried varieties are harvested when the pod is fully mature. Shelling and snap peas should be picked once the pod is full, but snow peas can be harvested once the pod is about 3 inches long and before the peas form. When picking, gently tug the pod with one hand while holding the plant with the other hand so as not to pull the whole plant out.
- **Storage:** Fresh beans and peas will last for only a week or so in the refrigerator. They both can be frozen and will keep in the freezer for several months. Dried beans will store for several years if harvested and dried properly.

Heat-Loving Veggies

Heat-loving vegetables such a cucumbers, eggplant, peppers, and tomatoes are ideal plants for growing in containers. They can be placed in a sunny, hot location or can be easily moved around to follow the heat. They often require protection from the wind and rain, which is another great reason for growing them in containers—patios and balconies are naturally more sheltered than open areas.

Cucumbers

Because of their vines, cucumbers can be an attractive addition to a garden or patio. To save space, train the plants to grow upright. If grown in containers, cucumbers need plenty of soil, as they are heavy feeders. Choose a larger pot with a depth of at least 12 to 16 inches of soil for best results. The three most common types of cucumbers are the long English varieties, which have an edible peel; the slicing varieties, which have a harder peel that is usually not eaten; and small-sized ones used for pickling.

FACT

When mildew appears on the leaves of your cucumber and squash plants, spray a liberal amount of the following mixture: 1 quart water, 2 teaspoons baking soda, and a squirt of dishwashing liquid.

Cucumbers need to be pollinated, so when choosing a variety it is important to know if it is a hybrid or standard variety. Standard varieties have both male and female flowers on the same vine and insects or the wind will do the pollinating for you. The male flower comes out first and looks like a miniature cucumber. The female flower is identified as the swollen ovary just behind the male flower. Hybrid varieties have separate female and male plants; therefore, they will need to be pollinated by hand. If there is only a male or female flower, no fruit will form. Go to your garden center and purchase another plant that will pollinate the first one for you.

QUICK TIPS FOR GROWING CUCUMBERS

- **Botanical Name:** Cucurbitaceae
- **Family Name:** Gourd family
- **Edible Parts:** Fruits
- **Location:** Well-drained soil. Cucumbers are great veggies for growing in greenhouses or containers.
- **Best Soil:** Rich, warm sandy soil, pH 5.5–6.8
- **When to Plant:** Transplant or sow directly in the late spring once the soil temperature reaches 60°F or 16°C.
- **Companion Plants:** For a positive effect, plant with beans, broccoli, cabbage, lettuce, peas, radish, and tomatoes. Sage can have a negative effect on cucumber plants so keep them apart.
- **Weeding:** Keep well weeded especially when the plants are small.
- **Watering:** Cucumbers need lots of water. Deep watering at the roots is best rather than using a sprinkler. If the weather is warm, water the plants every second day, especially if they are growing in a greenhouse or container.
- **Care:** They are best grown on a trellis so the plant gets good air circulation and light, and saves space.
- **Fertilizing:** Fertilize with manure tea or fish fertilizer one week after the plant blooms and then again three weeks later. If plants are grown in containers, fertilize every ten days.
- **Pests and Diseases:** Aphids, cucumber beetle, flea beetle, mite, squash bugs, downy mildew, and powdery mildew can all affect the cucumber plant. If the plant is diseased make sure you do not compost it!
- **Harvesting:** Harvest the fruit when they are 6 to 12 inches long, this may vary depending on the variety you are growing. Cut the fruit from the plant rather than twisting or pulling it off, which can damage the plant. Pick the fruit regularly so that new fruit will keep forming.
- **Storage:** Cucumbers are best wrapped in plastic and stored in the refrigerator. They will keep for up to a week.

Eggplant

Eggplant needs hot weather and rich soil to grow its best. This vegetable is much more common in Europe than it is in North America; however, if you enjoy a great moussaka, try growing eggplant in your backyard or in a container on the patio. Eggplant is in the same family as tomatoes and peppers; therefore, if you plant them together in the same area, it is easier to do your vegetable rotation.

The most common eggplant variety produces a large, oval-shaped purple colored fruit. You can also find varieties that have yellow, green, and white-colored fruit and others that form rounded or cylinder-shaped fruit. These can all add color to your garden and are definitely fun to show off to your guests.

The American president Thomas Jefferson (1743–1826), an innovative horticulturist, is credited with introducing the edible eggplant to North America. Eggplant continues to be grown in his restored garden in Monticello, Virginia.

Eggplant needs full sun and abundant heat. It is, therefore, the ideal candidate for a greenhouse, a container on a patio, or a more sheltered but sunny spot in your garden. Each plant will produce from eight to ten fruits.

QUICK TIPS FOR GROWING EGGPLANTS

- **Botanical Name:** Solanaceae
- **Family Name:** Nightshade family
- **Edible Parts:** Fruit
- **Location:** Sunny and warm location
- **Best Soil:** Well drained, fertile with pH of 5.5–6.8
- **When to Plant:** Transplants are available late spring and best planted once the weather is hot.

- **Companion Plants:** For a positive result, plant with peas, thyme, and tarragon. There are no plants that have a negative effect on eggplant.
- **Weeding:** Keep weeded, especially when the plant is small.
- **Watering:** Keep soil moist. This is most important when the plants are young.
- **Fertilizing:** Fertilize with compost tea or fish fertilizer after the first bloom and again when the fruit starts to form. If grown in containers, fertilize every ten days.
- **Pests and Diseases:** Flea beetle, lace bug, aphids, Colorado flea beetle, and red spider are some common pests that affect the eggplant.
- **Harvesting:** Harvest when the fruit is firm to touch, is fully colored, and has a glossy look. Cut the fruit off with scissors, leaving a ½-inch stem on the fruit. Do not twist or break off the fruit as this may damage the plant. Harvest regularly so the plant will produce more fruit.
- **Storage:** Store eggplants in a plastic bag in the warmer section of your refrigerator. They will keep for up to five days.

Peppers

Peppers come in various shapes from chunky, long and skinny, round, and cone shaped in shades of green, red, and yellow. Their flavors range from mild and sweet to sizzling hot. Sweet peppers are also known as bell peppers because of the shape of the fruit. They can be harvested when green; however, if left on the plant to mature, they will turn either yellow or red, depending on the variety. Hot pepper plants grow taller and have narrower leaves than the bell varieties and their fruit can range in size from 1¼ inch to about 7 inches long.

ALERT

Choose a cloudy day or later in the day when the sun is not so hot to transplant your vegetables. The hot sun can wilt or scorch the young leaves, leaving them stressed. Make sure the transplants are moist before they are planted, and gently water them in after they have been placed in the ground.

Peppers are a very popular vegetable cooked by themselves or with other foods. They are also eaten raw in salads or as appetizers. When preparing to use your pepper, cut it in half; then remove the stem and rinse away the seeds. Fresh or dried hot peppers need to be handled carefully because the oils in the skin can burn your skin or eyes. It is suggested that you use rubber gloves and hold the hot pepper underwater when preparing it. Remove the seeds from a hot pepper as they can add to the hot taste.

QUICK TIPS FOR GROWING PEPPERS

- **Botanical Name:** Solanaceae
- **Family Name:** Nightshade family
- **Edible Parts:** Fruits
- **Location:** Very sunny, well-drained area
- **Best Soil:** Fertile soil that does not have an excess of nitrogen as a too-rich soil will form leaves but poor fruiting, pH 5.5–to 6.8
- **When to Plant:** Transplant is put out once the temperature is 65°F or 18°C.
- **Companion Plants:** For a positive effect plant with basil, carrots, onions, oregano, and marjoram. Fennel will have a negative effect on peppers so avoid planting them near each other.
- **Weeding:** Keep well weeded when plants are small.
- **Watering:** Water regularly and keep soil moist when the plant is flowering and fruiting.
- **Fertilizing:** Use fish fertilizer or compost tea after the first bloom and then after the fruit starts to form. If grown in containers, fertilize every ten days.
- **Pests and Diseases:** Aphids, armyworms, Colorado potato beetle, corn borer, mites, and cutworms are some common pests.
- **Harvesting:** Harvest sweet peppers when they are firm and full sized, either as green peppers or leave them to turn red or yellow. Harvest hot peppers when they are full size and have turned yellow, red, or dark green, depending on the variety. When picking, gently pull or cut the pepper from the plant leaving a stem ½ inch long.

- **Storage:** Fresh peppers will last one to two weeks in the refrigerator if not washed. Place in a sealed plastic bag. Peppers can be frozen, dried, and preserved by pickling or canning.

Squash

Squash is an easy vegetable to grow and each plant can produce a large number of fruits; however, they can take up a large amount of space. There are two types of squash: summer and winter. The main difference between these is the amount of time they take to mature and how well they will store once harvested. Summer squash is a warm-weather vegetable that is eaten before the fruit has fully matured. The skin and seeds are eaten as part of the whole fruit. The winter squashes take longer to mature and are usually harvested in the late summer or fall. They usually have a larger fruit than summer varieties and the skin is tough and inedible. The seeds are often removed before cooking as well. Some varieties, such as a pumpkin, produce lovely edible seeds that are delicious when roasted.

ALERT

To support container boxes, screw galvanized L-shaped brackets into the wall and then screw a bracket to each side of the window box. If the box hangs below the window, support it with brackets attached to the wall and base.

Squash plants require lots of water, and since the leaves become very large, it is best to water the plant by hand or with drip irrigation around the base of the plant so the water reaches the roots. Squash leaves are more susceptible to mildew if they get wet.

QUICK TIPS FOR GROWING SQUASH

- **Botanical Name:** Cucurbitaceae
- **Family Name:** Gourd family
- **Edible Parts:** Fruits and some seeds
- **Location:** Well-drained, sunny location

- **Best Soil:** Fertile, light soil. If you have clay soil, add lots of organic matter to lighten it, pH 5.5–6.8.
- **When to Plant:** Set out transplants or sow seeds directly when the soil temperature is 60°F or 16°C.
- **Companion Plants:** For a positive effect, plant with beans, corn, radish, mint, and nasturtium. Potatoes can have a negative effect, especially on summer squash varieties, so avoid planting them near each other.
- **Weeding:** Keep well weeded when the plant is young.
- **Watering:** Requires regular watering. Watering at the base of the plant rather than overhead watering is better for the plant.
- **Care:** Plants need a large amount of space to grow. If grown in a small space or large container, consider training them to grow on a sturdy trellis.
- **Fertilizing:** Give the plants fish fertilizer or compost tea once they have reached about a foot tall and are just starting to spread. If grown in containers, fertilize every ten days.
- **Pests and Diseases:** Aphids, cucumber beetles, mites, nematodes, squash bugs, squash vine borer, and powdery mildew can affect squash plants.
- **Harvesting:** For summer squash (zucchini), once the fruits start to form, pick every few days when the fruit is still fairly small (6 to 8 inches) as they are tastier when young. For winter squash, harvest when the skin is hard. Gently use your fingernail to pierce the skin. If your nail leaves a mark, the squash is not ready to be harvested; if there is no mark, it is ready for harvesting. When picking, cut from the plant, leaving a small stem on each fruit.
- **Storage:** Summer squash will store for up to a week in the refrigerator. Winter squash, if cured properly, will store for several months. Cure winter varieties by leaving the cut fruit in the sun for several days. Turn the fruit every few hours so all sides will get the sun. Cover them if they will be left out at night.

Tomatoes

Tomatoes offer more of a harvest per cubic inch of space than any other vegetable plant. There are dozens of varieties available so you can choose the variety you like. Cherry tomatoes are often a great choice for hanging baskets as they are fairly compact and do not need a lot of space to grow. Other varieties are also easy to grow in containers, so long as they are in a large enough pot to accommodate their large root system (use a minimum depth of 16 inches).

FACT

Determinate tomato plants are bush types that stop growing once they have reached 3 to 5 feet and the fruit ripens over a shorter period of time. Indeterminate plants have vines that keep growing until frost kills them. The plants can reach up to 12 feet in height and they produce larger crops over a longer period of time.

Often gardeners will give tomato plants either too much or too little water. When you first transplant a tomato plant, it will need to be watered every few days until it is well established. When grown in the ground, tomatoes usually only need a deep watering once a week; however, one sign that the plant is not getting enough water is when the fruit splits.

QUICK TIPS FOR GROWING TOMATOES

- **Botanical Name:** Solanaceae
- **Family Name:** Nightshade family
- **Edible Parts:** Fruit
- **Location:** Sunny and warm area
- **Best Soil:** Fertile, well drained, pH 5.5–6.8
- **When to Plant:** Set out transplants once the weather is warm, usually late spring or early summer.
- **Companion Plants:** For a positive effect, plant with asparagus, basil, cabbage, carrot, onion, parsley, peas, and sage. Potatoes and fennel can have a negative effect, so avoid planting close to tomatoes.
- **Weeding:** Keep well weeded, especially when the plant is young.
- **Watering:** Water deeply once a week.
- **Care:** In cooler climates tomatoes may need protection to grow their best. In the Northwest, the rain is also a concern because tomato

plants do not like their leaves to get wet. In that region it is best to grow the plants under a plastic or glass shelter. If it gets too hot (over 100°F or 38°C), the plant will stop producing fruit. So make sure there is good ventilation if the tomatoes are grown under cover.

- **Fertilizing:** Fertilize with fish fertilizer or compost tea two weeks before and again two weeks after the first picking. If grown in pots or hanging baskets, fertilize every ten days.
- **Pests and Diseases:** Aphids, cutworms, tomato hornworms, flea beetles, leaf miners, nematodes, whitefly, Fusarium wilt, verticillium wilt, and blossom-end rot can all affect your tomato plants.
- **Harvesting:** Harvest all your tomatoes, even the green ones, before the first frost. Green tomatoes will ripen if left in a warm area.
- **Storage:** Ripe tomatoes will not store for more than a few days. Green tomatoes will ripen indoors if left in a warm spot. Tomatoes can be frozen, canned as whole tomatoes or diced, and made into sauces or chutney to be enjoyed all winter long.

Everything Else

There are only a few perennial vegetable plants with asparagus, Jerusalem artichokes, and Rhubarb being the most common ones grown by home gardeners. They require an area where they will not be disturbed if you will be digging or tilling your garden. Once perennial plants are established, they need only a little maintenance to continue producing food.

Asparagus

Asparagus is a perennial vegetable that needs a permanent area to grow. It will not grow in containers. Once planted it will produce new shoots each spring and will continue to grow for fifteen to twenty years without too much work on your part. It is best to buy one-year-old crowns or rhizomes, as asparagus takes three years to grow from seed to harvest. In the first year of planting, resist cutting any of the spears so they can leaf out. The feathery foliage will nourish the roots, which in turn will give you more spears in the second year. In the second year you can harvest the first few spears, but stop harvesting once the spears start to look spindly or have a diameter less than

¼ inch. The third year and for many years after, you will be able to harvest over a much longer season.

When preparing an asparagus bed, you want to dig in generous amounts of compost or aged manure. This can be done by digging a trench 1 foot deep in your bed and then filling it with 3 to 4 inches of organic material. Mix this with the existing soil. Lay the crowns in the trench, covering them with 2 inches of soil—do not cover the tips of the shoots. As the plant grows you can add more soil around the plant.

FACT

If you live in a fairly mild climate where the ground does not freeze, it is okay to plant small fruits like blueberries, raspberries, grapes, and dormant fruit trees. You can find bargains on perennials at local nurseries in the fall and early winter months, so take advantage of them.

In the fall, cut back the fern-like foliage of the asparagus plant. This is also a great time to mulch the bed with aged manure as it will add nutrients to the soil as the manure decomposes over the winter. The mulch will add protection from the cold; however, avoid using sawdust as it is often too acidic for the plant.

QUICK TIPS FOR GROWING ASPARAGUS

- **Botanical Name:** Asparagaceae
- **Family Name:** Lily family
- **Edible Parts:** Young shoots called spears
- **Location:** Full sun
- **Best Soil:** Fertile, well-drained, sandy to clay loam, pH 6.0–6.7
- **When to Plant:** Set out plants in early spring when any danger of frost is passed.
- **Companion Plants:** There are no other plants that have a positive effect but avoid planting onions near your asparagus as the onions can have a negative effect.
- **Weeding:** Weed regularly.
- **Watering:** Keep well watered.

- **Care:** Cut back the foliage in the fall once it turns brown.
- **Fertilizing:** Apply a high-nitrogen fertilizer twice a year—once when the spears emerge and again at the end of harvest. If you have a soil that has a lower pH than 6.0, apply lime in the spring as well.
- **Pests and Diseases:** Aphids and asparagus beetle
- **Harvesting:** Do not harvest the spears produced from the first year of planting. From the second year onward, harvest the spears when they are about 3⅛ inches thick and 6 to 8 inches high. Stop harvesting once spears are thinner than 3⅛ inches or smaller than the diameter of a pencil. To harvest, cut the spear ½ inch below the soil.
- **Storage:** Asparagus is best eaten fresh. It will stay in the refrigerator for about a week.

CHAPTER 14

Herbs for Small Spaces

Herbs are a wonderful addition to any small-space garden. They can be intermixed among your veggies as they make great companion plants. They are attractive and fragrant, making them a great addition to any flower bed. Herbs are perfect for growing in containers, too. This chapter has some tips on how to grow, harvest, and preserve your herbs. You will also find a list of common culinary herbs with growing tips and suggested uses for all of them.

Growing Herbs

When planning your herb garden, first decide where you would like to locate the plants. Herbs can occupy any part of a garden. Traditionally they are put near the back or front door so the plants are easily accessible to the kitchen. They can be grown among your vegetable or flower gardens, or grown in pots on a balcony or deck. If you are starting from scratch, take the time to consider where you want to place your herbs, especially if you are planning to stay in this home for many years. Most common culinary herbs are perennials, so they will continue to grow for a long time. Choosing the proper site is important in keeping the plants healthy and free of any problems.

Your garden site needs to suit the herbs you are planning to grow. If your site it shady, choose the herbs that can tolerate a bit less sun, or if it is a bit wet, make sure the plants will take a little extra moisture at certain times of the year. If possible choose a level site that has good drainage and is easy to access. A hilly area will drain quicker than a flat one, making it more difficult to keep the plants well watered. If this is all the area you have, consider terracing your garden to make it more accessible and easier to work in.

Planting herbs can be useful in many ways, not just for culinary use. So deciding what you want to grow can depend on your garden site as well as what use you have for that specific herb. Many aromatics such a mint, parsley, sage, rosemary, and garlic repel certain insects and pests, so they are valuable growing in among your vegetables. Balm, dill, and thyme will attract beneficial insects such as bees, which are needed to help propagate your veggies and fruits. There are many medicinal uses for herbs as well.

FACT

The bay leaf we use in soups and stews is the dried leaf from the bay laurel tree. It is a good source of vitamins A, C, and B as well as having folic acid, calcium, and manganese.

Many herbs can be grown in pots indoors during the winter months. Place them in proper-sized containers and position them in a sunny window so you can enjoy using them all winter long. Grow perennials such as marjoram, chives, mint, and winter savory from divisions or cuttings taken in the fall. Basil, dill, and parsley are annuals and will need to be started from seed outdoors (in pots) in late summer and then transplanted into larger pots in the fall. When growing herbs indoors make sure you use a light, well-draining potting soil, and water as needed. Try not to let the plants dry out or be overwatered.

Harvesting Herbs

One of the first rules to remember when harvesting herbs is to pick them early in the morning. The best time is just after the dew has dried, but before the sun has hit the leaves. The reason for this timing is that the essential oils found in the herb leaves lose their quality of flavor and fragrance once the leaves are exposed to heat.

There is nothing wrong with the dew on the leaves; it just takes longer to dry the herbs' leaves if they are picked when wet. The best time to harvest is a cool, dry morning; however, if you are using the herb immediately, it does not matter when it is picked.

When harvesting from perennial herbs, it is important not to harvest too much of the plant in the first year of growth. If the plant is cut back too much, the root system will not be able to develop properly. A light trim will help to shape the plant and encourage bushiness. Once the plant has become established, you can harvest up to two-thirds of the plant each season.

FACT

To substitute fresh herbs for dried in a recipe, use 1½ to 2 tablespoons chopped fresh herb for each teaspoon of dried herb. To release the flavor of the whole fresh herb, crush it first in the palm of your hand before adding it to your recipe.

Most annual and biennial plants can be cut several times over the season, and a good rule of thumb is to cut the top half of the plant at each cutting. Just before the first frost, either pull the plant or cut it at ground level. The same is true when harvesting biennials such as parsley. If you are growing to save herb seeds, mark the plant early in the season and do not cut it so that it will produce a large amount of seeds. Biennials will not produce seeds until the second year.

Use a sharp scissors or knife when cutting your herbs or gently nip the stems of the softer herbs such as basil. When collecting leaves, cut the whole stem and then strip the leaves off the stem. Harvest the stems and leaves from the top of the plant, as new growth will come from the main stalk. If you are harvesting from herbs that grow from a central stem like parsley, harvest the outer leaves first. That way more growth will produce from the center of the plant. Herbs retain their best qualities if they are left unwashed until they are used.

Drying Herbs

Most herbs dry easily, and under the proper conditions will retain their aroma and flavor. You want to have a dark, cool, dry area with good ventilation to dry your herbs. Depending on your climate you may need fans or dehumidifiers because it is best to air-dry herbs in low humidity and with a soft breeze. Try to choose the best quality herbs you can for drying so that you get quality flavors to use in your recipes later.

ESSENTIAL

Pesto is another way of preserving fresh basil. Pesto is a sauce from the Mediterranean in which basil leaves are pounded or blended together with pine nuts, oil, and Parmesan cheese. Place the sauce into small bags or plastic containers and freeze for using later.

Bunches of herbs can be hung or screens can be placed in a dry attic, around a hot water heater, or on top of a refrigerator. You can also place screens of herbs covered with paper towel in your car and park it in a shady spot; the warmth in the car will quickly dry them. If the weather is not cooperating or you do not have time to let the herbs dry naturally, you can place them in a warm oven to speed up the drying process. Set the temperature to 80° to 100°F or 25° to 38°C. Make sure you monitor the process until the leaves are crispy dry. It will usually take three to six hours for them to dry completely. Food dehydrators will work for drying herbs using similar temperatures as for oven drying.

For drying in bunches it is best to use long-stemmed herbs such as your perennials. Tie the stems into 1 inch bunches; then tie the string to a clothes hanger and hang it in a dark, dry, cool place. If dust is a problem, place the bunch into a brown paper bag to protect the herb from collecting any dust. The hanging methods for drying can take up to two weeks for the herbs to become dry enough to store.

When saving herb seeds, snip the seed head once the seeds have turned brown. You will then have to blanch the seeds, making sure any insects or pests that may be in the seed will be killed. Wrap the seed in cheesecloth, tie it up, and then submerge the bag into boiling water for 1 minute. Another option is to place the herb seeds in a sieve and run hot water over them. Spread the washed seeds on paper or a fine-mesh screen to dry in the sun. If you are planning to sow the seeds rather than use them for flavoring your food, do not blanch the seeds.

Preserving Herbs

Fresh sprigs or chopped leaves of herbs can be wrapped in foil or plastic wrap and kept in the refrigerator for a week or so. To keep them for a longer period of time they will need to be frozen or dried. To keep freshly chopped herbs fresh, place them into cube trays, cover with water, and freeze. When you want to use them just remove a few cubes at a time and drop them into your soup or stew. Sprigs of herbs can be wrapped in plastic wrap or foil and frozen for several weeks.

Another method of storing fresh herbs is to mash or finely chop them and mix into softened butter. Spread the butter on a tray and allow it to harden in the refrigerator, then slice or cut into pieces. Place the pieces into a plastic bag and freeze. Herbed butter is great on breads or on barbecued meats.

Common Culinary Herbs

The gardening of herbs is as old as civilization. In almost every culture in history there are references to using herbs for preparing and preserving food, scenting the air, and treating illness and wounds. Most herbs are wild, tough plants that have not changed despite being cultivated for centuries. Almost all herbs grow best in sunny, well-drained, fertile soil; however, many will survive in less than ideal conditions.

The following alphabetical listing of some common culinary herbs gives you basic information on the growth patterns, size, growing conditions, propagation, common pests and diseases, and some suggested uses.

Quick Tips for Growing Basil

Basil is one of the most popular herbs grown. It is an attractive plant that can be stuck in any corner of your veggie or flower garden or in any container outdoors or indoors; just make sure it is a sunny, hot spot.

- **Type:** Annual
- **Growth habit and size:** Height 1–2 feet (30–60 cm); spreads to 1 foot (30 cm)
- **Growing conditions:** Sun, light rich soil, slightly acidic
- **Propagation:** From seeds, start indoors and plant outside in early summer.
- **Flowering times:** Continuous, beginning in mid-summer; remove flowers to encourage leaf growth.
- **Pests and Diseases:** Plant away from mint to prevent damage from plant bugs.
- **Harvesting:** For immediate use, pinch leaves from the base of branches; for storing larger amounts, cut the plant to 6 inches once or twice during the season.
- **Preserving and storing:** Dry leaves.
- **Suggested uses:** Great accompaniment for tomatoes, peas, squash, meats, eggs, tossed in salad, potatoes, and cheese.

ALERT

The tender leaves of basil are easily bruised, causing the fine tissue membranes to rupture and the essential oils to blacken. Cutting basil with a finely sharpened knife and slicing it into fine strips is a way to avoid blackening the leaves.

Quick Tips for Growing Bay Leaf

In zone nine or higher, these make attractive shrubs for your garden. Elsewhere they can be grown in pots and brought indoors in the winter.

- **Type:** Shrub
- **Growth habit and size:** Height 14 feet (4 m); 6 feet in pots (1.8 m)
- **Growing conditions:** Full sun or partial shade, in well-drained soil
- **Propagation:** From seed, if flowers are left on the plant, they will self-sow.
- **Flowering times:** Blooms in spring; plants will rarely flower if grown in pots.
- **Pests and diseases:** Watch for signs of scale insects and wash them off with alcohol wipes.
- **Harvesting:** Pick leaves as needed.
- **Preserving and storing:** Dry in the dark, spread leaves out between sheets of absorbent paper with a weight on top to keep them flat. For quick drying, use a warm oven.
- **Suggested uses:** Use in soups, tomato sauces, poached fish, and meat stews. Dried leaves placed in cupboards will repel storage pests.

Quick Tips for Growing Borage

Borage has a cucumber flavor and the drooping clusters of flowers attract bees. The plants can repel tomato worms and are good companions for strawberries and fruit orchards.

- **Type:** Hardy annual
- **Growth habit and size:** Height: 2–3 feet (60–90 cm); spreads to 16 inches (40 cm)
- **Growing conditions:** Full sun or partial shade, in well-drained soil
- **Propagation:** From seeds, if flowers are left on they will self-sow.
- **Flowering times:** Continuous from mid-summer
- **Pests and diseases:** Japanese beetle
- **Harvesting:** First leaves can be picked at about six weeks after seeds germinate. Pick flowers just before they open.

- **Preserving and storing:** No good way of preserving leaves; for candied flowers, dip in egg white, then sugar, and then dry them.
- **Suggested uses:** Use flowers in salads, eggs, and pickles. Cook leaves like spinach or use them fresh in fruit punch or lemonade.

Quick Tips for Growing Chervil

Chervil is a delicate herb popular in French cuisine. It can be planted to repel slugs in your garden.

- **Type:** Hardy annual
- **Growth habit and size:** Height 1–2 feet (30–60 cm); fern-like leaves resemble carrot tops
- **Growing conditions:** Partial shade, in moist well-drained soil
- **Propagation:** From seeds
- **Flowering times:** May to July
- **Pests and diseases:** Earwigs
- **Harvesting:** Leaves are ready six to eight weeks after sowing. Cut plant back to ground.
- **Preserving and storing:** Fresh leaves are best, but can be dried.
- **Suggested uses:** Great addition to consommés, beans, peas; combine with lemon balm for fish and egg dishes.

Quick Tips for Growing Chives

Chives make good companions for carrots, are attractive, and can be used as a border in flower gardens.

- **Type:** Hardy perennial
- **Growth habit and size:** Height 6–12 inches (15–30 cm)
- **Growing conditions:** Full sun or slight shade in rich well-drained soil, cool temperatures
- **Propagation:** Lift and divide clumps every three or four years.
- **Flowering times:** Bloom in June
- **Pests and diseases:** Avoid wet areas to prevent bulb disease.
- **Harvesting:** Cut leaves often, close to the ground.

- **Preserving and storing:** Does not preserve well, so grow fresh for winter use.
- **Suggested uses:** Great in salads or cooked with meats and stir-fry.

Quick Tips for Growing Cilantro (Coriander)

Cilantro is the parsley-like leaves and coriander is the seed.

- **Type:** Hardy annual
- **Growth habit and size:** Height 1–3 feet (30–90 cm)
- **Growing conditions:** Full sun, in soil with good drainage
- **Propagation:** From seed.
- **Flowering times:** Spring to late summer
- **Pests and diseases:** Usually free of pests and disease
- **Harvesting:** Pick young leaves as needed; cut seed heads when ripe.
- **Preserving and storing:** Dry seeds; leaves do not keep well.
- **Suggested uses:** Use leaves in rice dishes, curry sauce, soups, or salads. Use the ground seeds in rich meat soups and stews.

QUESTION

What is a bouquet garni?
A bouquet garni is a collection of herbs tied together and used to flavor soups, stews, or sauces. Traditionally the bouquet garni includes a bay leaf, thyme, and parsley or chervil, all bunched together and tied in cheesecloth. The string is attached to the pot handle and the cheesecloth is removed before eating.

Quick Tips for Growing Dill

Dill has attractive foliage and looks great in the background of a flower bed. It is a highly aromatic plant, a good companion for cabbage, and a negative companion for carrots.

- **Type:** Hardy annual
- **Growth habit and size:** Height 3 feet (90 cm)
- **Growing conditions:** Full sun, in moist well-drained soil

- **Propagation:** From seed
- **Flowering times:** Summer to fall
- **Pests and diseases:** Usually free of disease; may attract aphids if soil gets too dry
- **Harvesting:** For best flavor, pick leaves just as flowers open. Cut stems in dry weather as seeds ripen.
- **Preserving and storing:** Dry leaves slowly at about 100°F or 38°C. Hang mature flower heads in a warm, dry place with a tray beneath to catch seeds. Dry in sun or a slightly warm oven.
- **Suggested uses:** Great mixed in potato salad, cream cheese, and cottage cheese. Use with salmon, salad, and pickles or on fresh tomatoes. Cook whole with carrots or parsnips.

Quick Tips for Growing Fennel

A fennel plant resembles dill but is taller and coarser. In ancient times fennel was known as an all-purpose medicine.

- **Type:** Perennial
- **Growth habit and size:** Height 4 feet (1.2 m)
- **Growing conditions:** Full sun, in ordinary well-drained soil
- **Propagation:** From seeds every two to three years
- **Flowering times:** July to October
- **Pests and diseases:** Usually free of pests and diseases
- **Harvesting:** Pick leaves as needed; they are best just before the flowers bloom. To use stems, cut young flower stalks just before blooming. For seeds, cut stems in August and dry seeds.
- **Preserving and storing:** Dry and freeze leaves.
- **Suggested uses:** Can be used interchangeably with dill. Use with Brussels sprouts, or to flavor bread. The seeds can be used ground in lentil soup or with rice.

ESSENTIAL

Mint or lemon balm are the two main herbs used to make a tisane, which is a tea made from fresh or dried herbs steeped for a few minutes in boiling water.

Quick Tips for Growing Lovage

This is a shrub-sized perennial that looks and smells like celery but is larger. If you are unsuccessful in growing celery, try growing lovage instead. It works well as background planting in your garden.

- **Type:** Hardy perennial
- **Growth habit and size:** Height 6 feet (1.8 m); spreads 2–3 feet (60–80 cm)
- **Growing conditions:** Sun or partial shade in rich, deep, moist soil
- **Propagation:** From seeds or by root division in the spring
- **Flowering times:** June to July
- **Pests and diseases:** Leaf miner on leaves (prune away infested leaves)
- **Harvesting:** Pick young leaves as needed. Cut seed heads when ripe.
- **Preserving and storing:** Dry or freeze leaves. Hang mature flower heads in warm dry place with a tray underneath to catch seeds. Seeds can be dried in the sun or a warm oven.
- **Suggested uses:** The stems can be used in replacement of celery in any cooked dish. Lovage can also be used as a thickener.

Quick Tips for Growing Marjoram

Marjoram is grown for its fragrance and the flavor of the leaves. It is a good border plant.

- **Type:** Tender perennial
- **Growth habit and size:** Height 2 feet (60 cm); spreads 12–18 inches (30–40 cm)
- **Growing conditions:** Full sun, in rich, well-drained soil
- **Propagation:** From seeds or by root division in warm areas
- **Flowering times:** August to September
- **Pests and diseases:** Usually free from pests and diseases
- **Harvesting:** Encourage foliage by removing flowers as they appear. Pick leaves as needed. For drying, cut before flowers open in mid-July.
- **Preserving and storing:** Dry leaves.
- **Suggested uses:** Great with fish, soup, broccoli, cheese dishes, roast chicken, beef, pork and stuffing.

Quick Tips for Growing Mint

The most popular mints are apple mint, spearmint, and peppermint. Mint is a repellent to the white cabbage butterfly. Mint will grow well where water drips, such as near a faucet that is used in the summer time.

- **Type:** Perennial
- **Growth habit and size:** Height 2–3 feet (60–80 cm); spreads 12–18 inches (30–40 cm)
- **Growing conditions:** Partial shade, in rich moist, well-drained soil
- **Propagation:** Divide roots in fall or spring
- **Flowering times:** July to August
- **Pests and diseases:** Thin crowded lumps for good air circulation to prevent root and foliage diseases. Watch for aphids.
- **Harvesting:** Pick leaves as needed; for a double crop, cut plant to ground in mid-summer.
- **Preserving and storing:** Dry and freeze leaves.
- **Suggested uses:** Use in jelly, fruit juices, candy, frosting, cakes, pies, chocolate dishes, pork, potatoes, or peas.

ALERT

Mint will spread rapidly and take over your small-space garden if not contained. It is best to grow mint in a container that you can place in your garden or on a patio. The pot can be buried in the ground, leaving at least 2 inches of the pot above ground level so there is no possibility of the roots spreading.

Quick Tips for Growing Oregano

Oregano is also called wild marjoram, but it is more shrub-like and spreading. Leaves are darker and have a sharper flavor and fragrance.

- **Type:** Hardy perennial
- **Growth habit and size:** Height 12–30 inches (30–75 cm); spreads 18–24 inches (40–60 cm)
- **Growing conditions:** Full sun, in almost any well-drained soil

- **Propagation:** From seeds or division in mid-spring
- **Flowering times:** July to September
- **Pests and diseases:** Mites and aphids; needs good drainage to prevent root diseases
- **Harvesting:** Pick leaves as needed; for drying cut off the top 6 inches from the stem before flowers open.
- **Preserving and storing:** Dry leaves.
- **Suggested uses:** Use in tomato sauces, Greek salad, pork, pizza, green beans, salads, chili, lamb, and guacamole.

Quick Tips for Growing Parsley

Parsley can easily be grown in a pot on a balcony or windowsill. Interplant with roses and tomatoes to enhance the growth of both. Use as a breath freshener.

- **Type:** Biennial, grown as an annual
- **Growth habit and size:** Height 8–12 inches (20–30 cm); spreads 12 inches (30 cm)
- **Growing conditions:** Sun or partial shade, in rich, moist, deep soil
- **Propagation:** From seed as an annual. Plant will self-sow if allowed to flower in the second year.
- **Flowering times:** Early spring to second year
- **Pests and diseases:** Rarely bothered by pests; needs good air circulation to remain healthy.
- **Harvesting:** Cut stems as needed—no more than two or three at a time from one plant. Harvest leaves before flowering.
- **Preserving and storing:** Freeze or dry by dipping in boiling water and placing on a pan in very hot oven for about one minute.
- **Suggested uses:** Can be used with almost every meal. Put in stews, soups, sandwiches, sauces, stuffing, eggs, cheese or just use as a garnish.

QUESTION

Which herbs will tolerate dryer soil?
Burdock, catnip, chicory, marjoram, oregano, savory (winter), and thyme are some of the herbs that will grow well in a dryer climate.

Quick Tips for Growing Rosemary

Rosemary is a repellent to cabbage butterflies, carrot flies, and mosquitoes.

- **Type:** Tender perennial
- **Growth habit and size:** Height 2–6 feet (60–180 cm); spreads 2–6 feet (60–180 cm)
- **Growing conditions:** Full sun or partial shade in light well-drained soil
- **Propagation:** By hardwood cuttings in fall or spring
- **Flowering times:** June to September
- **Pests and diseases:** Usually free of pests and disease.
- **Harvesting:** Cut sprigs as needed.
- **Preserving and storing:** Dry or freeze leaves.
- **Suggested uses:** Use in poultry stuffing, with cauliflower, fish, or in herb breads. Add to water when boiling potatoes that are intended to be mashed.

Quick Tips for Growing Sage

Sage repels cabbage white butterfly, carrot flies, and ticks.

- **Type:** Hardy perennial
- **Growth habit and size:** Height 1–2 feet (30–60 cm); spreads 18 inches (40cm)
- **Growing conditions:** Full sin, in almost any soil. Fairly drought resistant so avoid overwatering.
- **Propagation:** Divide the plant in spring every four to five years.
- **Flowering times:** Spring
- **Pests and diseases:** Slugs but rarely any disease
- **Harvesting:** Pick leaves as needed. For drying cut the top 6 inches of stalks before flowing in early summer.
- **Preserving and storing:** Dry leaves.
- **Suggested uses:** Use with poultry, sausages, fish, pork roast, hamburgers, peas, and herb bread. Mix with cream cheese.

ESSENTIAL

Rosemary is best grown in a container, as a border plant, in rock garden, or even in a hanging basket. The upright form of the plant can also be trained as topiary. The benefit to growing in a container is that the plant can easily be brought indoors in cold weather.

Quick Tips for Growing Savory

This herb is attractive to bees and will make flavorful honey. Interplant with beans and onions to increase their yield. Savory has a lovely peppery taste.

- **Type:** Annual
- **Growth habit and size:** Height 6–12 inches (15–30 cm); spreads 6–12 inches (15–30 cm)
- **Growing conditions:** Full sun, in rich, light, well-drained soil
- **Propagation:** From seeds
- **Flowering times:** June
- **Pests and diseases:** Usually free of pests and disease.
- **Harvesting:** Leaves are most flavorful before the flowers bloom in mid-summer. Cut plant partially back for a second crop.
- **Preserving and storing:** Dry leaves.
- **Suggested uses:** Use with eggs, salads, beans, peas, meats, chicken, soups, and stuffing.

Quick Tips for Growing Tarragon

Tarragon has a slight licorice flavor and is very useful in any kitchen.

- **Type:** Hardy perennial
- **Growth habit and size:** Height 2 feet (60 cm); spreads 15 inches (20 cm)
- **Growing conditions:** Full sun, in dry, not too rich, well-drained soil
- **Propagation:** Divide roots of established plants in the spring.
- **Flowering times:** July to September

- **Pests and diseases:** Usually free of diseases and pests. Aphids may be a problem in some northern climates.
- **Harvesting:** Pick leaves as needed. Cut plant to the ground in the fall.
- **Preserving and storing:** Dry or freeze leaves.
- **Suggested uses:** Use in fish or meat sauces, with shellfish, eggs, cheese dishes, green salads, pickles, and tomatoes. Tarragon makes great herb vinegars.

Quick Tips for Growing Thyme

Thyme is a repellent to the cabbage butterfly.

- **Type:** Hardy perennial
- **Growth habit and size:** Height 6–15 inches (15–38 cm); spreads 9–12 inches (18–30 cm)
- **Growing conditions:** Full sun, in almost any well-drained soil
- **Propagation:** Divide established plants every three to four years.
- **Flowering times:** Mid-summer
- **Pests and diseases:** Needs well-drained soil to prevent root and stem disease.
- **Harvesting:** Pick leaves as needed. For drying cut plant just before flowers open in early summer.
- **Preserving and storing:** Dry leaves.
- **Suggested uses:** Use with beef, pork, fish, turkey, eggs, cheese, in stuffing, beans, and vegetable soup.

All herbs lose flavor quickly when heated, so add them to recipes at the end. Dried herbs have a more intense concentrated flavor than fresh herbs, so when substituting them in a recipe use dried herbs for fresh herbs at a ratio of 1 to 3.

CHAPTER 15

Fruits and Berries
for Small Spaces

You can always find room for growing fruits and berries in a small-space garden. You can grow bushes, canes, vines, or dwarf trees either trained against a wall, fence, grown in containers, or in an open area. In this chapter you will learn how to grow fruits and berries. You will find specific information and instructions on how to grow strawberries, raspberries, blueberries, and some common fruit trees such as cherries, apricots, apples, peaches, plums, pears, and apples.

Is There Room to Grow Fruit?

In a time when house lots are getting smaller and becoming more costly, it is important to maximize your space as efficiently as possible. In Europe, where space is at a premium, fruit trees and berries are grown in every available space and corner of a garden. It also makes good sense to grow some of your own fruits and berries, especially when you want to ensure what you are eating is free of pesticides and chemicals. You can grow berries or dwarf trees in place of ornamental trees and shrubs as they look lovely in the spring when the blossoms are out and then in the fall when the fruit is plentiful and ripening.

Walls and fences are a great place to train dwarf fruits trees and berry bushes to maximize your small space. They can also be grown in the open, surrounded by lawn, or you can incorporate a flower garden using shade-loving plants such as hostas, pansies, periwinkle, or alyssum to make a beautiful complement. Some berries such as gooseberries or currants can take a little shade and can be grown around the base of a fruit tree.

Trees are a tall element in a garden. When planting around the base make sure you leave access so you can easily maintain the tree. Consider the size of your mature tree when planning your garden so that large trees do not shade your vegetable garden as they grow to maturity.

FACT

For centuries the Chinese have considered the beauty of fruit-tree blossoms as essential in a landscape.

There is pleasure in picking and then eating your own fruits and berries. In contrast to fruits bought from the grocery store, which are picked still unripe, fruits picked fresh from a tree or bush in your garden are sweeter and tastier because they are picked at their prime.

Fruit Growing Basics

Most fruits are put into two categories: small fruits and tree fruits. Among the small fruits are strawberries, raspberries, blueberries, currants, blackberries, and gooseberries. Some fruit trees that are usually grown in home gardens are apples, cherries, peaches, pears, and plums. Grapes are grown on a vine so they are a little different.

Small fruits are usually grown on either bushes or canes, except strawberries, which are a low-growing, bedding plant. Bushes have permanent spreading branches that grow to about 4 feet high and about as wide. Blueberries and currants grow on bushes. If you have a small space, these can be trained to grow as espalier along a fence or wall.

Canes are slender shrubs that have stems starting at ground level. They need to be controlled by being trained along a stake and wire or string and they need to be cut back each year after fruiting so there is room for new growth to develop. Raspberries and blackberries grow on canes.

ESSENTIAL

Dwarf trees can be grown in a traditional square wooden tub. The tubs can be placed on a patio or balcony and will make a very attractive feature to your small-space garden.

The fruit trees that are most suitable for home gardens are dwarf stock, which can be grown as individual trees or as a horizontal cordon or fan espalier. Espalier is a lattice made of wood or wire on which to train fruit trees by selecting lateral branches to grow horizontally on each side of a main stem. Training fruit trees to grow on an espalier is one of the best tree forms for a small-space garden. The tree will have a single stem with no major spreading branches. It will take up little space, be easy to manage, and have a high yield for a small tree. Espaliered trees need to be supported with wires and need careful pruning and training. The most popular dwarf trees are apples and pears.

Pollination

Most flowers need to be pollinated to develop into fruit. The wind or insects usually transfer the pollen from one plant to another. Most fruit trees have both a male and a female organ but are not self-fertile (fertilized by their own pollen). Some need to be grown with another variety that flowers at the same time so they can pollinate each other.

Before deciding on what tree to put in your garden, find out what the pollination needs are by asking at your local nursery, or do thorough research if you are purchasing through a catalog. Small fruits, except for blueberries, can be fertilized by their own plant.

Pruning

Pruning of fruit trees and bushes is done in two different stages. The young tree or bush needs to be trained to the shape you want. Once the main framework is established, they need to be pruned annually. The main reason for pruning is to regulate the crop, to improve the quality of the fruit, as well as to keep the tree healthy. Pruning for most fruit trees is similar to that used for an apple tree; however, some shaping will depend on the growth habit of your tree.

ALERT

When purchasing a tree, choose one that is one or two years old. Older trees will be too hard to reestablish. In the first year, only the main stem grows; in the second season the side shoots (branches) grow from the main stem. In the third year, the side shoots grow from the first branches, and so on.

Pruning is generally done in late fall or late winter as there is more of a chance of disease entering the wood if done in the early fall. Grapes are an exception and need to be pruned in the spring as they produce fruit on the current season's wood. Shoots that bore fruit previously need to be cut out.

Planting Your Tree

Most trees or shrubs are bought in containers and are best planted between mid-fall and early spring. Fruits do not like waterlogged soil so make sure the area where you will be planting is well drained. You also want to make sure the soil is not frozen. When you are ready to plant, dig a hole wide enough so you can spread the plant's roots outward and deep enough so the roots will be covered by 3 or 4 inches of soil.

Place a stake as deeply and firmly in the center of the hole. You want the stake to be tall enough to reach the point where the stems begins to branch. Place 4 to 6 inches of aged manure or compost into the hole and work this into the existing soil. If the tree roots are dry, soak them in water for a couple of hours. Plant the tree no deeper than it was in the container, which is indicated by the soil mark around the stem. Fill the hole with topsoil, shaking the tree a few times to settle the soil around the roots. Once the roots are covered, firm the soil around the base of the tree by gently treading on it. Tie the tree to the stake.

It is best not to grow grass around your tree for two or three years.

ESSENTIAL

Branches heavily laden with fruits may need to be supported so they do not break. This can be done by placing loops of rope around the branches that are tied to the top of a central stake (which is tied to the tree stem). Branches can also be propped up with a fork stake. With both methods, use padding between the branch and stake or rope to prevent chafing.

If you are planning to grow your tree as an espalier, make sure you erect the trellis or supporting wires before you plant your tree. If planting the tree against a structure, set the stem at least 6 inches from the wall or fence and lean it slightly toward the structure to make it easier to tie and train.

Berry Patch

Berries are generally easy to grow so long as they get enough sunlight and moisture. To ensure a good crop, separate the older fruit bearing canes from the new growth. One way of doing this is tying the new growth together or tagging it so you can easily identify what is new and old growth. Once the fruit has finished on the older stalks they can be cut back. This practice allows light to reach the new growth and provides room for new growth.

Berries such as blueberries or blackberries can be grown successfully against a wall or fence to maximize your small space.

Blackberries

Blackberries can be grown either erect or trailing.

- **Botanical name:** Rubus fruitcosus
- **Family name:** Rosaceae
- **Growing characteristics:** Best grown in a sunny location but will take partial shade.
- **Soil:** Well-drained soil with a pH of about 5.5 is best.
- **Water and fertilizer:** Require adequate moisture all season. A month or so before new growth starts in the spring, apply 10–10–10 fertilizer (½ pound per 10 foot row).
- **When to plant:** Canes are best planted in early fall, although if the ground does not freeze they can be planted up until early spring.
- **Care:** Disease and insects are kept at bay by planting your bush in an area that has been cultivated for several years. Choose disease-resistant varieties. Remove old canes after harvest and keep plants free of weeds and fallen leaves.
- **Harvest:** Berries start producing in August.

Blueberries

Check with your local nursery for the best varieties to grow in your area.

- **Botanical name:** Vaccinium corymbosum
- **Family name:** Ericaceae
- **Growing characteristics:** Blueberries do best in a sunny location but will grow in partial shade.
- **Soil:** They need an acid soil with a pH 5.0–6.0; if you have an alkaline soil, plant your blueberries in pots. Blueberries are not completely self-fertile, so plant two varieties together to ensure good pollination.
- **Water and fertilizer:** Like water-retentive soil. In the spring, apply a high-nitrogen fertilizer (½–1 ounce per square yard). If you have sandy soil, do a second application a month later.
- **When to plant:** Plant in the fall or spring with plants 3 to 4 feet apart.

- **Care:** In northern climates bushes should be protected from the cold winds. In summer mulch your plants with well-rotted manure, compost, or peat. You may need to protect your bushes from birds with netting.
- **Harvest:** June or July

The evergreen salal berry grows larger in the shade (about 5 feet) than when grown in a sunny spot (about 2 feet). It is hardy in zones six to nine, has gorgeous lily of the valley–type flowers, which are followed by sweet, juicy, dark purple berries. The green growth is attractive in the garden and used in flower arrangements.

Currants and Gooseberries

Currants and gooseberries can be grown in most areas. Red currants do best in cooler, humid regions. Black currents are not as popular.

- **Botanical name:** Ribes
- **Family name:** Rosaceae
- **Growing characteristics:** Currants and gooseberries grow on a bush. They will grow well in either a sunny location or in partial shade. They flower early in the year, so choose an area that will be less likely to get a heavy frost.
- **Soil:** They like water-retaining but well-drained soil.
- **Water and fertilizer:** Water only during prolonged dry spells and fertilize in late winter or early spring. Use a complete fertilizer and place around the base of the bush.
- **When to plant:** Plant early spring or in the fall
- **Care:** Take out any suckers that grow from the main stem or the roots. Control weeds by mulching. Birds are a common problem and placing netting over your bushes will help.
- **Harvest:** Pick when fully ripe.

Raspberries

The best way to grow raspberries is in a row, with the canes trained between stakes and wires.

- **Botanical name:** Rubus idaeus
- **Family name:** Rosaceae
- **Growing characteristics:** Raspberries generally do best in full sun but can be grown in partial shade.
- **Soil:** They like a soil that is slightly acidic and well drained but with moisture retention. Raspberries do not do well on slopes, especially if the soil drains quickly. Try placing them where they will have some protection from wind or cold. Canes that have produced fruit die and are replaced every year by new canes that grow from the roots.
- **Water and fertilizer:** Water well in warm or dry spells. Mulch with manure, compost, or peat to help retain moisture. Apply horse manure in the fall and fertilize approximately one month before the new growth starts in the spring.
- **When to plant:** Plant one-year-old canes in the fall.
- **Care:** Keep well weeded; hand weeding is best as hoeing between the canes can damage the shallow root system. Canes need to be supported, and you can do this by placing posts at either end of your row and stringing wire between them on either side of the canes.
- **Harvest:** Some varieties bear fruit mid-summer on the previous season's shoots; others fruit in early or mid-fall on the current growth.

Strawberries

There are two different kinds of strawberries. One kind produces only one crop of fruit, and the second is an ever-bearing kind that produces one crop in early summer and then another one in mid-fall. Ever-bearing strawberries are usually less hardy and do not store fresh for long.

- **Botanical name:** Fragaria
- **Family name:** Rosaceae
- **Growing characteristics:** Strawberries like a sunny location.

- **Soil:** They like fertile, well-drained soil that is slightly acidic with a pH 5.5–6. The soil should have enough organic matter in it that it will retain moisture.
- **Water and fertilizer:** Water regularly in dry weather, especially when ripening begins, and during the first few weeks after planting new plants. Apply a complete fertilizer in late winter.
- **When to plant:** Plant in either spring or fall. Ever-bearing varieties are best planted in the spring.
- **Care:** In the first season remove the blooms from one-crop varieties that were planted in the fall or spring. On ever-bearing varieties, remove flowers in early spring to encourage more and better berries later in the season. Runners will freely grow once the plants are actively growing and these can be cut off to make sure more energy goes to producing more fruit.

A three-year cycle is the usual method for strawberries. The young plants are set out in the spring, for harvesting the next summer. The next year these plants will produce less and should be removed right after fruiting. To get a bumper crop of strawberries you want to be setting out new plants each year.

Once berries start to form, tuck dry straw under the berries to keep them from touching the ground, which will make them less susceptible to rotting. In the fall cut off any runners that have grown (this conserves the plant's energy). Control weeds with shallow hoeing.

- **Harvest:** To ensure good flavor, pick strawberries with their stems attached and when the berries are fully ripened all around. They bruise easily so avoid excessive handling.

Grape Arbor

Grapes are grown to be eaten fresh, dried into raisins, and made into juice or wine. Grapes are one of the most amenable plants that you can train. Grapes and kiwi are vigorous climbers and love a sunny wall or pergola to grow on.

- **Botanical name:** Vitis
- **Family name:** Vitaceae
- **Growing characteristics:** The main stem of a grape vine is called a trunk. The trunk sends off laterals, which if left alone will develop arms, spurs, and canes. It is the canes that bear the fruit. Vines can be trained to have one, two, or three trunks, depending on the variety and how they are allowed to grow. Vines must have full sunlight if you want fruit to be sweet enough for fresh eating and making wine.
- **Soil:** Grapes like a soil with good drainage and that is moderately fertile.
- **Water and fertilizer:** Grapes require a lot of moisture and good drainage. Fertilize at least once every year as the plants use up nutrients quickly.
- **When to plant:** Plant in early spring or fall. Plant the vines in rows.
- **Care:** Mulch early spring with well-rotted manure mixed with straw.
- **Harvest:** Tasting is the best test for maturity. If grapes are sweet and flavorful they are ready to be picked. The next best guide is color. Green varieties turn whitish or yellowish when they are ripe. Black and red varieties take on an added depth in their color.

FACT

One of the most cold-hardy, shade-loving fruits is the Asian kiwi, which will thrive in light to moderate shade. The variety "Arctic Beauty" bears grape-size, smooth, and tasty kiwis. The vines need some pampering to get started but once established, they can produce up to 100 pounds of fruit in a season.

Both grapes and kiwi need a long growing season free of frost in the spring to produce good fruit. If you live in a cool climate you may need to delay the growth by cutting back the plant in the spring, especially if there is a chance of frost. You may need to restrict root growth as well so the plant receives enough moisture for the fruits to ripen. Thin the large bunches of the plant early (when fruit is pea size) so larger bunches can form. Pollination of the flowers is often improved if done manually; a small paintbrush will work well for this.

Common Fruit Trees

When choosing your fruit trees the top priorities are appropriate size for your space and the hardiness and suitability for your climate.

Apples

Apples account for more than half of the world's entire production of tree fruits. They have a variety of tastes, textures, colors, crunchiness, and sweetness. They are the last fruit to ripen in the season.

- **Botanical name:** Malus
- **Family name:** Rosaceae
- **Growth characteristics:** Apple trees need deep, rich, slightly alkaline soil to grow well and can start bearing fruit from two to ten years after planting. The best time to plant young trees is in the fall; in cold climates plant only in the spring. Some varieties will grow up to 30 feet whereas others can be grown in a small space such as at the corner of a building.
- **Hardiness:** Zone six or higher. Crab apples can be grown in very cold areas. They are not suitable for fresh eating but can be canned, juiced, and made into applesauce.
- **Pollination:** Apple trees need to be pollinated. Two trees of different cultivars or species that are blooming at the same time are needed for pollination to occur. After pollination, the fruit size is determined largely by the weather during the three or four weeks following blossom drop, when cell division occurs in the developing fruit. Warm, sunny weather will produce larger fruits than cloudy, cool weather.
- **Watering:** Regular watering is required; for young trees make sure the soil is kept moist. An inch of water is needed each week until at least midsummer if there is no rainfall. A prolonged period of dryness will prevent fruit from reaching its full size. Fertilize trees in late winter. Sprinkle the fertilizer over the soil covering an area slightly larger than the spread of the tree's branches and let it penetrate naturally.
- **Pruning:** Pruning a young tree (first four years) will create a strong, regular framework of healthy branches. After that, the first aim is to keep the tree open to light and good air circulation: the second is

to maintain the right balance of growth and fruit production. Winter pruning (late fall to late winter) will promote direct energy to go to fruit bud growth. Summer pruning (mid- to late summer) reduces foliage and promotes the formation of more fruit buds.

- **Care:** Avoid hoeing or forking around the base of the tree as this can damage shallow roots. Thin fruit to two per cluster.
- **Harvest:** Most varieties ripen in October and November: a few will ripen earlier. To test to see if a fruit is ready, gently lift one in the palm of your hand and twist gently. It is ready if it parts easily from the tree with the stalk remaining on the tree.
- **Grown in containers:** Dwarf stock will grow well in pots.

Cherry

A cherry tree is the largest and is often called the loveliest of all fruit trees. They are slightly harder than peaches and less hardy than apples. Only a fan-trained tree is suitable for a small-space garden; even then they take up a lot of wall space.

- **Botanical name:** Prunus
- **Family name:** Rosaceae
- **Growth characteristics:** Cherries blossom in April after a frost. Fruit will develop on the bases of year-old shoots and from spurs on the side of two- or three-year-old branches. The blossoms open to produce one to three flowers and fruits per piece. Cherry trees need deep, well-drained soil with a pH of 6.5.
- **Hardiness:** Zone six or warmer; if you live in a colder zone, try growing sour cherries. The tree will be prone to damage if temperatures go below 10°F or 23°C.
- **Pollination:** No varieties are completely self-fertile so growing at least two varieties is best; however, check with your nursery as newer self-pollinating varieties may become available.
- **Water and fertilizer:** Regular watering is required when young.
- **Pruning:** Do in early spring once the cold weather has passed.
- **Care:** Birds are one of the main problems (in early summer cover the whole tree with netting).
- **Harvest:** July (earliest fruit to be harvested)

- **Grown in containers:** Usually too large for containers (tart cherry trees come in dwarf stock); can be grown as an espalier against a wall or fence.

ESSENTIAL

There are other great ways to pollinate your apple and peach trees. If a neighbor has a tree within 100 feet of your tree, your neighbor's tree should work well for pollination. Another option is to graft a branch from a second variety onto the first tree. Or fill a pail of water beside a tree whose buds are about to open and fill it with almost-blooming branches of wild apple, crab apple, or domestic apple tree that needs a little pruning.

Peach and Nectarine

Peaches and nectarines are excellent homegrown fruits as they are decorative and usually problem-free. The trees will bear fruit soon after planting, grow quickly, be easy to prune, and are good candidates for growing espalier. Nectarines are simply peaches without the fuzz and are usually less productive and produce smaller fruits than peaches.

- **Botanical name:** Prunus
- **Family name:** Rosaceae
- **Growth characteristics:** Plant them in a sunny location that is sheltered from the wind in deep, well-drained soil; wet feet will lead to winter damage, fungus, disease, and eventual death. Both peaches and nectarines are very tender, so choose a cultivar for the hardiness of your climate.
- **Hardiness:** Zone seven or higher. Flowers will die if winter temperatures are below 13°F or minus 25°C.
- **Pollination:** They are self-fertile (each flower fertilizes itself) so only one tree is needed.
- **Water and fertilizer:** Consistent watering is necessary when climate is dry. Nectarines need more frequent watering and a little more fertilizer than peaches while the fruit is swelling.

- **Pruning:** Fruit forms on new wood; prune in June. When peaches are the size of marbles, start thinning them out and reduce clusters to a single fruit.
- **Care:** Mulching around the base of the tree with straw or leaves will help to protect the plant root.
- **Harvest:** Late August to September; peaches and nectarines ripen after cherries. They are ready to pick when the flesh around the stalk yields to gentle pressure from the fingers.
- **Grown in containers:** Small cultivars can be grown in pots or can be trained as espaliers.

Pears

Pears are the second most popular tree crop in the world. You can wait as long as ten years to pick fruits; however, once pears start producing they will continue for decades.

- **Botanical name:** Pyrus
- **Family name:** Rosaceae
- **Growth characteristics:** Trees do best in a sunny location that is sheltered from the wind. They prefer a deep, loamy soil that will keep its moisture in the summer.
- **Hardiness:** Zone six through nine; or if a very sheltered spot pears could grow in zones four or five; trees can be damaged if temperatures get below 20°F or minus 29°C.
- **Pollination:** Blossoms usually start in late March or early April (in colder climates may not start until May) and they need to be pollinated to produce fruit. Two trees planted closely together—no more than 20 feet apart and both blooming at the same time—are needed so they can pollinate each other.
- **Water and fertilizer:** Water regularly; fertilize about two months before buds begin to swell.
- **Pruning:** Prune similar to an apple tree, just less severely to avoid forcing the development of soft new fruit growth that is susceptible to fire blight. Pear trees also produce fruiting spurs more easily, and these need to be thinned out in midsummer.

- **Care:** Some natural fruit drop is normal; however, poor soil and dry conditions can make the whole crop fail.
- **Harvest:** August to October. Harvest when fruits start to change color and pull easily away from the tree when gently lifted. If fruits remain on the tree too long they will rot at the core or become dry, mealy, and flavorless. Once fruit is picked, store in a cool room to ripen.
- **Grown in containers:** Dwarf varieties are available.

FACT

Small citrus trees are evergreen and thus require a similar temperature all year round. They are among the easiest fruit trees for indoors. They will tolerate room temperatures and fairly low humidity.

Plum, Damson, and Apricot

These are known as stone fruits. Plums are nearly as popular as apples, grow on smallish or midsized trees, and are attractive in a home garden. The apricot fruit is known as a drupe and is often allied to the almond. Fruits may only come once every six years or so in cooler climates; however, the trees are very ornamental and the harvest is worth the wait.

ESSENTIAL

"Apricot is a plum without downy covering as is the nectarine is a peach with the covering off."—Eugene Davenport in *Domesticated Animals and Plants* (1910).

- **Botanical name:** Prunus
- **Family name:** Rosaceae
- **Growth characteristics:** It is important to remove fruits so they do not touch each other to prevent any disease from forming; the touching fruits often will fall on their own. They like a sunny location that is protected from the wind, like a rich soil, and can handle

a heavier-type soil than other trees so long as it is well drained. They will bear fruit three to five years after planting.

- **Hardiness:** Zone six or higher; fruit buds can be injured at temperatures below 15°F or minus 23°C.
- **Pollination:** They need cross-pollination and are dependent on insects, especially bees; however, there are some self-pollinating varieties that will work well for a small garden. Even if trees are pollinated, a late frost can kill the flowers or tiny fruits.
- **Water and fertilizer:** Water is essential. If no rain falls, make sure the trees are watered once a week from full bloom to harvest. Fertilize in late winter or early spring, sprinkling the fertilizer around the tree to cover an area a little larger than the spread to the tree's branches. Do not fork the fertilizer in as this can damage roots; let the fertilizer work its way in naturally.
- **Pruning:** Once your tree is established and has reached its mature height, keep it at that height by cutting back the central leader to a strong lateral in the summer. You may need to do this every second or third year.
- **Care:** Tree branches are often brittle and may snap off if the fruit is too heavy. Start thinning heavy crops in late spring. Curl a finger around the stalk and snap off the fruit with your thumbnail, leaving the stalk attached to the tree. Complete thinning later, once the natural drop of fruit occurs. Leave one plum to each cluster.
- **Harvest:** Fruits ripen from midsummer to fall. For apricots, harvest when fully ripe and green has disappeared from the fruit. Fruit is prone to bruising so handle with care when picking.
- **Grown in containers:** Small varieties do well in pots; however, need to be wintered indoors. Apricots can be trained as espalier against a south-facing wall.

Tending Potted Fruits

Growing fruits in a container can make more demands on the gardener than growing them in the ground. With a container, the gardener has to make sure the tree is getting all the right requirements: warmth, water, nutrients, and pollination. A fruit tree in a container will often suffer more from over- or under-watering or extreme temperatures than a tree or bush in the ground.

The first thing is to make sure the container is large enough to accommodate the root size of the mature tree or shrub. Most dwarf trees need pots at least 18 inches across and deep (holding about five gallons of soil) to do well. Wooden containers have better insulation than pots made of plastic, ceramic, or cement. When choosing a container consider how you will move it around your patio or balcony. Plastic is the lightest in weight, however, not the sturdiest. Whatever kind you choose, make sure the pot has drainage holes and place gravel, plastic, or Styrofoam peanuts in the bottom of the pot to allow for better soil drainage.

ESSENTIAL

Providing a fig tree is kept warm, watered, and fertilized you will get a good crop. The type of fig grown in northern gardens requires no pollination. The small fruits remain dormant in the winter and will swell when the weather warms up.

Do not use only potting soil for your fruit trees and shrubs as there is not enough organic matter in it for the plant's needs. Compost is best, or mix the compost half and half with topsoil. For peaches, nectarines, apricots, and cherries, reduce the topsoil by one quarter and add in sand.

Once the tree is planted, mulch the top of the container with wood chips to help conserve moisture. Give potted fruit trees and shrubs a thorough watering whenever the top inch of soil feels dry. A little fertilizer, like an inch or so of compost or fish fertilizer, should be applied every spring when blossoms start to form. Most fruit trees or shrubs grown in containers will need to be brought indoors or at least protected from the colder winter weather.

CHAPTER 16

Bringing the Harvest to Your Table

Enjoying fresh tasty veggies from your own garden is the highlight to having a garden. Vegetables mature at different times; some are best picked early, some late, and still others need to be harvested regularly or the plant will stop producing. All this variation can make it difficult to know when start harvesting. In this chapter you will learn how to recognize when your plants are ready to be picked, which ones will keep producing for you, which storage methods will keep everything fresh, and which plants are best for freezing and canning for winter use.

Tips for an Easy Harvest

We are usually impatient to have our fruit, pods, and seeds ripe enough to eat. Eating fresh veggies is the reason for having a garden. The taste and crunchiness of freshly picked veggies is a real treat that you are not aware of until you actually do it.

Observation is the best way to learn when to harvest your veggies. If you are really organized, you can make a note on the calendar based on the maturity date of the variety you planted. For most gardeners this is too much work, so "pick and taste" is probably the best test to see if your veggies are ready to be eaten. If you harvest too early they may lack sweetness, size, and flavor. If you wait too long, many vegetables lose their flavor, become starchy tasting, and are tough. For instance, peas and corn become starchy tasting when older. Beans can become stringy and zucchini seems to become monster size overnight if not picked regularly.

Along with zucchini squash, other plants such as peas and beans need to be harvested regularly so the plant will keep producing more. If the pods or fruit are not harvested in a timely way, the vegetables plants will take that as a signal to stop producing and will start producing flowers and seeds rather than new fruits or pods.

FACT

Thinning plants provides more room to grow. When direct seeding it is difficult to know how many seedlings will germinate; however, it is important to pull out some of the seedlings to give the rest a better chance to grow. Check the seed packet for suggested spacing of plants.

Use sharp tools to harvest your veggies. Some fruit can be easily pulled or broken off which can damage the plants and they will not produce anything more for you.

It is generally a good idea to harvest early in the morning when there is still dew on the plants, especially leafy vegetables like lettuce or other greens. That way they stay fresher and keep longer. For root crops, it is great to have a bucket of water handy to quickly wash off the dirt. Otherwise you are tracking it inside the house. Use the muddy water to water your containers or other plants.

Harvesting can be fun and a great way to get your family together. Tasting as you pick is totally okay! Make it an event. If you have lots of veggies, get your neighbors involved and share the pickings or make a meal together with some of the harvested veggies. Canning is another great way to get a group of friends together to have fun now and enjoy later.

Knowing When to Pick Your Veggies

Different vegetables are harvested at different times and in many different ways. Certain vegetables need to be harvested on a regular basis to keep the plant producing more. Some you harvest at the peak of ripeness and the plant only produces one item; others will keep producing a crop over several weeks, and still others will produce a second crop but in smaller sizes.

Salad Veggies

Salad vegetables such as lettuce, spinach, Swiss chard, oriental greens, and salad greens can be harvested by cutting individual baby leaves or cutting the mature plants. For baby greens to be used in salads, cut when the leaves are 2 to 3 inches high. Do not disturb the roots. That way another set of greens will grow. You can usually get two cuttings before the plant will stop producing or start tasting bitter. For a mature plant, check the seed packet to see how long the variety is supposed to take to mature; if left too long, lettuce can have a bitter taste. A mature plant can be cut off at the base of the plant or individual leaves can be cut as well (most common in Swiss chard). Cut the outer leaves, leaving the center to produce more leaves; if the roots are not disturbed, the plant will grow again. A sign that the plant is finished producing is when the center stalk starts to grow taller and the flowers start to form. You can pinch off the flower and the leaves can still be eaten; however, they can start to become bitter once the flower starts growing.

FACT

To keep lettuce longer, moisten a clean kitchen towel and wrap it around the lettuce. Place this into a plastic bag and put it in the refrigerator. Do not seal the bag as it will keep better with air circulation. The lettuce will keep for up to two weeks stored this way.

Cabbage Family

Brassicas, sometimes also known as the cabbage family, include your cabbages, broccoli, and cauliflower. This family of vegetable plants usually produces one good-sized head. Some will keep producing smaller heads once the main one has been harvested. These vegetables can be harvested once the head reaches approximately 4 to 8 inches in diameter with the variety, your soil fertility, and garden conditions often determining the size of the head.

For cabbages you want a nice firm head. The heads can be harvested on the small size or left longer in the garden until they get larger. If the head begins to split you know it is getting old. After the main cabbage is cut from the plant, smaller heads will form if the plant is left in the ground. The newer growth will usually not get that firm, but the smaller heads are still tasty.

For broccoli you want to harvest the head when it is a bright green color and still firm. Once it starts to open, it is beginning to flower and will be less flavorful. Once you cut the center head, broccoli will produce side shoots off the main stem, and if cut regularly, can produce more shoots for several weeks. These will be considerably smaller in size and will go to flower quickly if not cut. Cauliflower will produce only one head. Make sure the head is filled out and firm before harvesting it. It is getting old when the florets start to open. The opening means the plant is starting to flower.

Peas and Beans

Peas and beans are two of the crops that are best picked on the early side as they are usually sweeter and tender when small. Common pea varieties grown are shelling peas (for the seed inside the pod), flat snow peas used fresh or for cooking, and the snap variety, which is grown for the crunchy pod. You want the pea pods to be full and for the pod to be easily opened if it is a shelling pea or sweet and crunchy if it is an edible pod variety. Once they get older the pods becomes wrinkly and the pea seeds begin to taste bitter and starchy. Once your peas are ready for harvesting, pick them every few days or the plant will stop producing more. Leave some pods on the plant to fill out completely; then shell the peas, dry, and save them for planting next season.

There are several different varieties of beans. Bush (green or wax), runner or broad beans, and varieties for drying, such as black beans, are some to the most common types grown. A fresh, bush green bean is best picked when it is slender and about 3 to 4 inches long. Runner beans usually grow much longer and larger in size than the bush varieties, and once you can start to see the bean forming in the pod, they are ready to be picked. If you are growing beans for the seeds, you want the pod to fill out as much as possible and dry on the vine. As beans get older they become stringy and less sweet, so it is best to pick them on the younger side.

Squash

Zucchini summer squash needs to be harvested regularly starting when the squash is 4 to 8 inches long. Tiny zucchini are a delicacy for many chefs as they are tender and taste best when small. They can grow several inches overnight, so check on them every few days. If you happen to miss one, and it is a foot long or more when you find it, still harvest it so the plant will produce more. The larger zucchini can be used for a stuffed zucchini recipe or used in baking.

Fresh cucumbers taste so much better than ones bought in the store and they are easy to grow. They can be trellised, which are great when growing in small spaces. There are slicing varieties, which are harvested when they are 6 to 12 inches long; check the packet for the size at maturity. Depending on the variety, some cucumbers are eaten with the skin on like the English cucumber, whereas others are peeled and the inner white flesh is sliced. You want to pick cucumbers regularly so that the plant keeps producing more.

For winter squash it is best to leave the fruit on the vine as long as you can; often a frost will make the squash even sweeter tasting. A quick test to see if they are ready to be harvested is pricking the skin with your fingernail. If it leaves an indentation, it is not ready; if there is no mark on the skin, the fruit can be harvested.

Root Vegetables

Root veggies are the plants that can be left in the ground such as potatoes, carrots, and beets. The advantage to growing root crops is that you can harvest as you need them rather than having to eat them up as soon as they mature. Carrots, beets, rutabaga, and potatoes can be harvested as small as you want them to be. Pulling baby carrots or beets helps to make room in the row for the rest of the plants to grow larger. Baby veggies are often sweeter tasting; however, the flavor of root crops usually does not change that much as they mature.

ESSENTIAL

For root crops a good garden fork is invaluable. Gently loosen the soil around the area where the plant is growing and then use your hands to pull up the tubers or the root. Be careful not to pierce you potatoes or break the carrots when digging them.

Once the potato plants starts to flower you can dig with your hands around the base of the plant, pulling out small potatoes, often known as nugget potatoes. This way the plant is left to produce more potatoes. Once the green top of the plant starts to brown and die back, you can pull the whole plant and dig up the rest of your potatoes. Potatoes can take up a fair amount of space; however, for one seed potato you can get at least ten more from the plant. Most root crops can be left in the ground over winter so long as the soil does not get too wet and the plants are well mulched so they do not freeze.

Heat-Loving Vegetables

Heat-loving veggies such as tomatoes, peppers, eggplants, cucumbers (in squash section as well), and corn all have specific indicators that tell if the vegetable is ready for picking or not. The tomato is easy. It starts out a green color, and then as it ripens on the vine, it will turn red, orange, yellow, or black depending on the variety. If left on the vine too long, the tomato will become soft, mushy, and fall to the ground. Peppers can be harvested at pretty much any size, usually when they are 3 inches or so in diameter. They also start out as green and are very often harvested at this stage; however, if they are left on the plant, they will turn red, orange, or yellow depending on the variety. For them to change color, you have to be patient. It can take several weeks once the green pepper is at its full size before it will have fully changed color.

FACT

The secret to a healthy pepper with good color and flavor is adequate water and fertilizer! The pepper plant does not need a lot of nitrogen—this will promote leaf growth but not fruits. Keep the plants mulched with grass clipping to keep the soil moist and weed-free.

You want your eggplant to be firm and have a shiny skin before harvesting. If the color becomes dull, the fruit is getting old. For cucumbers you can harvest pretty much at any size depending on the varieties you have planted. For the English variety, pick once they are about a foot long and at approximately 2 inches in diameter. The peeling varieties are best harvested at about 8 inches before they become too big. If a cucumber gets too large, it will become seedy and bitter tasting.

All these heat-loving vegetables like tomatoes, peppers, eggplant, and cucumbers will keep producing over several weeks if you continue to harvest the fruit. The exception to this is corn. Each stalk will produce one or two cobs and that is all. Before you harvest corn you want the cob to be filled out and firm to the touch. Gently pull away some of the husk and see if the kernels are a bright yellow (some varieties are white or a mix of yellow and white). If they look fully formed and are a good color gently prick the kernels with your fingernail. If a milky liquid shoots out they are ready to be harvested.

Storage Tips

You cannot buy vegetables with the kind of flavor and nutrition that you get from growing and harvesting your own. Since most people garden only seasonally, it is really great to be able to have some of our vegetables in the off-season. If you want to feed your family with your fresh veggies all year long, it is important to start at the planning stage. Make sure you estimate how much you will eat fresh and how much you would like to store, freeze, or can, and then plant accordingly. The natural course is for the vegetables eventually to rot, so it is important to store them properly to slow down the aging process. The next step is learning how and where to store and how to preserve these veggies.

ESSENTIAL

To make limp celery crispy again, cut off the end of the stalk and stand it upright in a jar or vase of cold water. Place it into your refrigerator and leave it in the water until it becomes crispy again. Then store it in a sealed plastic bag or airtight container in the refrigerator.

Some vegetables like salad greens have a very short life and need to be refrigerated. They will last for only a week at the most, whereas other vegetables like winter squash, potatoes, and onions, if cured properly, will store for several months.

The following are vegetables to store in the refrigerator unwashed and to use as soon as possible:

- Artichokes
- Asparagus
- Broccoli
- Greens—collards, spinach, salad greens, lettuce, kale, Swiss chard
- Eggplant
- Okra

- Peas
- Radishes
- Tomatoes

Here are vegetables to store in a cool and damp area:

- Beets
- Brussels sprouts
- Cabbage
- Carrots
- Cauliflower
- Celery
- Leeks
- Parsnips
- Peppers
- Potatoes
- Rutabagas/Turnips
- Squash, summer

Store these vegetables in a cool and dry area:

- Garlic
- Onions

These vegetables need to be stored in a warm and dry area:

- Pumpkins
- Squash, winter

You will need to have a proper storage space for the types of vegetables you want to store. If you are storing for resale, proper coolers that regulate temperature and humidity will be needed. However, for the home gardener this equipment is very costly and not necessary. If you are lucky enough to have an existing root cellar, it is a great place to store produce as it is usually cool, dry, and dark. A cool, dry area in your basement or a pantry will work just as well.

Which Veggies Can I Freeze?

Freezing your vegetables to use during the winter months is a great way to eat healthy all year long and to save money. It there is a certain veggie you love, plan in advance to make sure you plant a sufficient amount so you can freeze some to enjoy later. You may get a bumper crop of a certain vegetable, and freezing or canning is a great way to use the produce so it does not go to waste. Freezing will preserve the nutrients and flavor of the vegetables.

When you are planning to freeze your produce, pick it and freeze it the same day. That way you will be getting the full nutrients when you eat the food later. It is best to pick the veggies early morning when the temperature is lower. Choose the freshest and most tender veggies, and then keep them cool until they can be put into the freezer. If left at room temperature for more than two hours, the vegetables start to lose their nutrients so you want to work fast to preserve them.

▼ **TABLE 16-1**

Vegetables That Freeze Well	Amount of Time for Blanching
Asparagus	2 minutes
Beans (string)	2 minutes
Beet, collard, spinach, Swiss chard greens	2 minutes
Broccoli	3 minutes
Brussels sprouts	3 minutes
Carrots	5 minutes for whole; 3 minutes for sliced or diced
Cauliflower	3 minutes
Corn	4 minutes for whole cob; 1 minute for kernels
Peas	1 minute
Zucchini	1 minute
Tomatoes	1 minute

Blanching, also known as scalding, is done to destroy enzymes in your vegetables. Enzymes will affect the color and flavor of your vegetables if they are kept frozen for any length of time. If you are planning to eat your frozen veggies such as string beans, peas, or small carrots within a month, you do not necessarily have to blanch these items. However, if you will be eating them over winter, take the time to scald your vegetables as they will look and taste better when you get around to eating them.

To blanch your harvested vegetables, fill a pot with water and bring it to a fast boil. You can add a few teaspoons of lemon juice or salt to your boiling water to help with discoloration. Use a wire rack to hold the vegetables and lower them into the boiling water. Start timing immediately and closely watch the time, as just one minute over will give you mushy vegetables. Most vegetables will take one to four minutes (check the previous list for timing). You then need to plunge the vegetables into ice-cold water for the same amount of time as you blanched them to stop the cooking process. Continue the above process with each batch of vegetables, making sure the water is at a fast boil and adding more ice to the water for cooling. Drain the vegetables and then place them on a tray or cookie sheet and put them in the freezer for an hour or so. After that time you can portion them into bags or containers and return them to the freezer. This method prevents any water crystals from forming in your bags or containers.

Labeling is an essential part of freezing your vegetables. You can use whatever labeling system works for you. Label the top of the container if you have a chest freezer and the front if you have an upright freezer.

Canning for Later

Canned food is so readily available in the grocery stores that we have gotten out of the habit of preserving our own veggies. As we become more concerned about how our food is grown, where it is coming from, and what is in it, there has been a resurgence toward preserving some of our own food again. It is a great feeling to open a jar of pickles from your pantry in the dead of winter knowing you grew those cucumbers!

When canning vegetables make sure you choose the best quality of vegetables you have, especially if it will be stored over several months. You want to harvest and can the veggies, within a few hours if at all possible, so the vegetables retain their freshness and nutrition. You will need to wash the vegetables thoroughly as even a little dirt can contain bacteria. Wash small amounts at a time under running water or change sitting water several times to make sure the produce is clean. After washing, let the vegetables drain well; leaving them to soak in water will cause them to lose flavor. Try not to bruise the vegetables as this can cause them to rot or go moldy. Handle them gently.

ALERT

Some vegetables can be stored for several months if certain criteria are met. The ideal storage room is dark, dry, and cool (between 40° to 50°F or 7° and 10°C). Basements, cupboards, and garages can be used for storing your excess harvest.

Most vegetables can be canned either raw (cold pack) or precooked (hot pack). For cold packing you fill your jars with the vegetables and pour boiling water over them. In hot packing, your precook the vegetables and then pack the vegetables into your jars. Then you pour the cooking liquid or boiling water over them. With either method, the jars filled with the veggies will need to be processed in a pressure cooker.

These are great vegetables for canning:

- Artichokes
- Beans
- Beets
- Cabbage (sauerkraut)
- Carrots
- Cauliflower
- Corn
- Cucumbers (pickles)
- Onions
- Peas
- Peppers
- Squash
- Tomatoes (sauces, whole, ketchup)

When storing your canned goods, you will want to put them in a cool, dry, dark place. Dampness will erode the lids and cause leaking. Warmth can affect the quality of the vegetable, and freezing can break the jars. A basement room or pantry is a great place to store your canned vegetables.

CHAPTER 17

Watering and Fertilizing

Along with soil and sunshine, the correct amount of water and organic fertilizer are the next two important elements in producing great vegetables. The amount needed by your plants will depend on your climate, your soil, and the type of vegetable you are growing. Read on for suggestions on how best to water and fertilize your small-space garden. You will also find tips on how to tell what your plants may need more of in order to produce an abundant and healthy harvest.

Water: How Much Is Enough?

The plants' stems absorb water that brings along with it nutrients found in the soil. That is why water is so important for plants to grow. Every garden site has different needs and every gardener may have a slightly different outlook on watering. Some like to do it; others find it a chore. Most gardeners utilize a few different watering techniques like hand watering or a sprinkler or drip (seeping or soaker) system. The most important part of watering is to make sure your veggie plants are not getting too much or too little water. So what is just right, you ask?

Plants need approximately 1 inch of water a week to grow well. A once-a-week, deep watering of your vegetable garden is much better for the plants and more effective than frequent light watering. When plant roots seek out water and moisture found in the earth, they are encouraged to grow deeper roots, which give the plant access to even more nutrients.

FACT

When choosing to purchase new watering products, choose one brand and stick with it. That way you will know that all the parts will fit together. Metal or plastic ends and accessories are okay; just stick to the one brand.

Most gardeners get out and spray their garden every day or so, and that can work for some gardens. But often you are just giving water to the top inch or so of soil and never even reaching the plant roots. Most plant roots are at least 3 inches into the ground, so you want the water to reach at least that far down. Before and after watering, stick your finger into the ground up to your knuckle: if the soil is wet to that depth, your plants have enough water. If the soil is dry, give them some more. If you are growing your veggies in a container, a quick way to check is to lift the container up: if it feels light, it needs some water; if it is still quite heavy, it does not. If the pot is too heavy to lift, dig down a few inches to see if soil is still damp (the top inch or so will dry out first). If it is still damp, the plant still has enough water.

Watering Methods

There are several different ways you can water your veggies, each having their advantages and disadvantages when working in a small-space garden. There are three main methods: hand watering, overhead watering, and drip irrigation. You can decide which one is the best option for your vegetable garden.

Hand Watering

For a small-space garden hand watering may be the easiest option. Hand watering is done by using a container of some kind, or a hose connected to a water source, to water individual vegetable plants. The main benefits of hand watering are you can direct where the flow of water goes and you have control over when and how much water you give the plants. While doing it you also have time to observe your plants. Another plus? The equipment needed is inexpensive to purchase.

Any kind of container that will hold water can be used to water your plants, but a watering can made either of plastic or metal is the most common and it will be fairly inexpensive to purchase. When choosing a watering can, the nozzle may be the most important component to check. Each nozzle has as different number and size of holes that affects how much and how quickly the water comes out. If you are watering tiny seedlings you want a nozzle that will give a light spray of water. A Haws watering can is great as it naturally gives a very gentle spray of water. If you are watering larger plants, the holes in the watering can can be bigger as the larger plants can handle a heavier spray.

The size of the watering can or container is another consideration. A large can holds a large amount of water so fewer trips are needed to your water source; however, the container can be extremely heavy and difficult to lift and carry when full. Consider your strength, how much you will be watering, and the distance you have to pack the container.

If you choose to water with a hose, the nozzle is an important component to consider. Choosing one that has a variety of spray options is best; that way you can give a light or heavier spray depending on what kind of plant you are watering. Make sure your hose easily reaches to all areas of your garden site, which makes it easier to water the garden.

There are some plants that do better if they are hand watered. For example, containers are best hand watered since there is less waste than when using a sprinkler. Larger mature plants such as broccoli, cabbages, and cauliflower do better with hand watering (or drip), as the leaves can impede water from reaching the roots if using an overhead sprinkler. Plants like tomatoes, squash, and carrots attract pests and disease more readily if their leaves get wet, so hand-watering is beneficial in growing these as well.

ESSENTIAL

When seeding your garden it is important to keep your seedbed moist until the seeds have germinated. When setting out your transplants makes sure the seedlings are moist when planted and water again after planting. Young seedlings have very shallow roots so you do not want the soil to dry out.

Hand watering your vegetable garden can take up a lot of time even in a small space, and that is one definite disadvantage. But some gardeners find hand watering relaxing and enjoy this aspect of growing vegetables. Others do not have the patience.

Overhead Watering

Using an overhead sprinkler is easy and probably the most common way most gardeners water their vegetables gardens. All you have to do is set up your sprinkler, turn it on, and everything gets watered all at once, especially in a small-space garden. It takes approximately one hour of sprinkling (depending on water pressure) for the water to soak into the soil several inches.

FACT

When purchasing a hose, stick to a 50- or 100-foot length. Anything longer than that is very heavy and cumbersome to move around. If you get shorter lengths, make sure they are all the same brand and size of hose so they can be easily connected together if needed.

There are many benefits to using an overhead sprinkler:

- It is simple to set up and use.
- Equipment is fairly inexpensive to purchase; all you need is a water tap, hose, and sprinkler.
- A sprinkler saves time as you can do other gardening chores while the sprinkler waters your garden.
- Timers and automatic equipment are available to make it even easier.
- Sprinklers can be easily moved around your garden.
- Overhead watering is used to keep plants cool in warm weather.

Some vegetables that benefit from overhead watering are lettuce, spinach, salad greens, and Swiss chard. As it evaporates, the water on the leaves keeps them cool, lowering the temperature of the plant and preventing the plants from wilting or being scorched in hot temperatures.

Some disadvantages to using an overhead sprinkler:

- Too much water can be wasted through evaporation or the watering of areas that do not need water, such as your garden pathways.
- With some vegetable plants moisture on the leaves can cause diseases such as mildew and blight.
- In larger vegetable plants, such as those in the cabbage family, the moisture can be impeded from reaching the plant roots by the leaves. This stresses the plant, which in turn can draw pests and cause diseases.

ALERT

The best time to water your vegetables is in the morning. This gives the plants' leaves time to dry off and remain cool once the sun hits them. Plants do not like to be cold, especially young seedlings, so it is best to water when the temperature is increasing during the day rather than when it is decreasing at night.

Choosing to use or not to use an overhead sprinkler is a personal choice. If time is a factor in your life, then overhead watering may be the simplest solution. It is also important to look at what vegetables you will be growing and what adverse effects overhead watering may have on those plants. You will have to find out which method will work best in your situation. Another option is that if you have a larger garden, you can choose to water certain areas with a sprinkler and others by hand.

Drip Irrigation

Drip irrigation is a term used when a hose that has many little holes in it, or a flat, plastic tubing that has slits on one side, allows the water to seep slowly out into the soil. It is also known as a trickle or weeping system. Either hose or tubing is laid on the ground along the base of your plants and allows water to reach the roots where it is best utilized. The flat plastic tubing needs more setup and is commonly used in larger, commercial vegetable gardens. You will need irrigation connectors, attachments, and a water pipe in order to attach the tubing to your water source, which is most likely too much work in a small-space garden. A soaker hose, however, can be easily attached to a water tap as it has the same attachments as a regular hose. In a small-space garden a soaker hose can be a good option. You can purchase one—they come in varying lengths—from a gardening or hardware store. It is an investment that will save you time and will last for many years. With good water pressure, both the soaker hose or plastic tubing can give your garden soil up to an inch of water in approximately fifteen minutes, making drip irrigation a very efficient way to water your vegetable garden.

FACT

If you have an old hose lying around, it can be easily recycled into a soaker hose. Use a nail or another sharp object to punch holes every few inches along one side of the hose. Make sure the end is closed off; then lay it out into the garden bed, turn on your tap, and you now have a soaker hose working for you.

Advantages to using a drip system:

- You use less water because very little is lost to evaporation.
- The moisture reaches the roots where it is most needed.

- Soaking adds moisture to the soil slowly, allowing the water to soak in over time, which allows the roots to utilize it better.
- The soil is watered evenly and thoroughly.
- Hoses or equipment can be fairly easily moved around to where they are best utilized.

It is best to have enough soaker hose or plastic tube length to cover your garden area; that way you can place the hose out when you plant an area and pull it up after harvesting. For easier setup, place the hose along your beds as you plant your seeds or set out your transplants. The plantings will not be disturbed later. The hose and plastic tubing can either be mulched or just left on top of the ground. However, both can deteriorate over time if left exposed to the sun, so mulching is probably the better option.

Disadvantages to drip irrigation:

- It takes time and some effort to set up and to take down the equipment and hoses.
- The tubing can be easily punctured by a rake or hoe.
- It can become very costly if you have a large garden area; however, the equipment will last for a long time if handled properly.

Signs of Too Much or Too Little

The plant roots must continually grow for the plant to stay healthy and produce its fruit, seeds, or buds. The roots draw the nutrients from the soil up into the plant to make it grow. Water allows the nutrients in the soil to be absorbed into the plant, so if there is too little water the roots cannot draw in the nutrients. That means the plant will not grow and mature as it should. You can be watering the surface or even the top several inches of your soil, but the plant roots have already absorbed the nutrients in the surface soil and need to go deeper to get more. This is why it is essential for you to provide regular, deep watering when growing vegetables.

Signs of Under Watering

One easy-to-spot sign that your plants may not be getting enough water is wilt. If the plant can draw enough water to replace the amount that evaporated from its leaves, it will remain upright and strong. If the plant is not getting the water it needs, the lack will cause severe stress and the plant will quickly collapse and often die. If a plant gets wilted, it is important to water it as soon as possible.

ALERT

If you have to ration water because of drought conditions, it is important to know which plants have the deepest roots, making them more tolerant to drought conditions. Beets, asparagus, tomatoes, and Brassicas can do with a bit less water. Never stop watering celery, lettuce, cucumber, squash, and peppers as they are very sensitive to drought conditions.

It is important to take the time every day to observe your plants. That way you can quickly fix what could be wrong. If you have young transplants, they will need a drink of water every day if there is no rain, as their roots are very shallow and the top few inches of your soil can dry out very quickly. Once your vegetable plants have begun to mature, watering them once a week is usually sufficient. For some plants, such as onions and potatoes, it is best to stop watering them altogether once they are nearly mature.

Here are some signs that your plants need more water:

- The plants appear small and very slow growing.
- The vegetable plants are not producing very many fruits, seeds, or buds, and the ones being produced are often misshapen.
- Your plants are diseased.
- The plants are yellowish or pale in color rather than having a bright green color.
- Your plants are wilting. Some natural wilting may occur in the heat of the day; however, if plants do not perk up by late afternoon, you have a problem.

Too little water can lead to poor root development, which will make for an unhealthy plant. Take the time to walk through your veggie garden at different times of the day to make sure your plants appear strong, have a bright color, and look healthy.

Signs of Over Watering

There are some clear signs that your plants are not getting enough water. But over watering your vegetable garden can also be a concern. Most gardeners go to great lengths to make sure there are enough nutrients added to their garden beds in the form of amendments and fertilizers. When the soil is moist the water helps to hold the nutrients to rock particles in the soil so the plant roots can absorb them. If there is too much water in the soil it drains lower into the soil taking a lot of the nutrients with it. This is called leaching.

ESSENTIAL

One way to conserve water is to install a rain barrel to capture water from your eaves troughs; another is to recycle water from dehumidifiers, air conditioners, and household grey water to use to water your vegetable garden and containers.

Along with moisture in the soil, plants need good air circulation for the plant to have access to oxygen and to release carbon dioxide. If the soil is saturated, the water is filling up all the space in the soil, leaving no room for air circulation. If the air supply is cut off for any length of time the plant roots will rot, killing the plant. The bottom line is gardeners need to know their own soil conditions. When it comes to moisture, it is good to keep a record of rainfall and regularly check the moisture in your soil with either a moisture meter (small tool that can be purchased at your local garden center) or by digging into the soil with your hands or a small shovel to see how far down the moisture is. Then water when needed. If you are a beginner gardener it can take time to get to know your soil and climate. Especially at first, it is important to observe and jot down some notes so you can refer back to them the following season.

Is Fertilizing Necessary?

Soil fertility is always changing; nutrients are used up by growing vegetables, the soil structure is disturbed by tilling, nutrients are leached out by the rain, and top soil is stripped from the beds by the wind. To grow great vegetables, it is important to fertilize so the plants have access to all the nutrients they need to grow well. The three main elements needed for good plant growth are nitrogen, phosphorus, and potassium. These are needed for leaf, stem, and root growth as well as for forming the buds, flowers, and ultimately, the vegetables you will be eating.

There are two ways to fertilize—you can choose to feed the plant or feed the soil. To feed the plant you use chemical fertilizers, which will make your plant grow, but do not benefit the soil in anyway. Feeding the soil involves using organic fertilizers as well as amending the soil by adding different organic materials to it. The organic fertilizer adds nutrients while the organic matter decomposes over time adding to the soil fertility.

Choosing how to fertilizer is a personal choice; however, if you are planning to have a long-term healthy garden it is best to use organic methods. Soil is a living thing. Keeping it healthy is important to getting great tasting, chemical-free vegetables. Using organic growing methods are better for your health, the health of your family, and the health of the environment.

ESSENTIAL

There are eight common trace elements that are needed for good vegetable plant growth. They are calcium, sulfur, iron, boron, copper, manganese, molybdenum, and magnesium. There are usually sufficient amounts of these elements in garden soils so you do not need to add them in.

Some examples of organic soluble fertilizers (meaning they dissolve in water) are liquid kelp, or liquid fish emulsion, which you mix with water and put into the soil when watering your garden. Some common nonsoluble organic fertilizers are cottonseed meal, blood meal, bone meal, green sand, and rock phosphate. These are best added to your garden bed directly in the spring and tilled under. Nonorganic fertilizers, also known as chemical fertilizers or pesticides, are man-made from petroleum products and should be avoided if possible, as the chemicals will be ingested when you eat the vegetables.

How Much Is Needed?

Amending your soil on a regular basis with organic materials and organic fertilizer is important in any garden. As often discussed, plants need nutrients to grow and often will use up everything they can reach in one season. So it is important to keep adding in more nutrition each year. Plants require three main elements to grow: nitrogen, phosphorus, and potassium. All these elements are found naturally in the earth but not always in the quantity needed for growing vegetables in your back yard soil, and especially not if you are growing veggies in containers.

Nitrogen (N) is needed for leaf and stem growth, and it gives the plant the green color. Some organic sources of nitrogen are blood meal, fishmeal, alfalfa meal or pellets, and cocoa shells. Some animal manure such as chicken manure has a high nitrogen concentration. Some signs your soil may be deficient in nitrogen are the leaves of the plant are turning yellow, the leaves are falling off, or the plant is looking stunted and not growing well. On the other end of the scale, too much nitrogen in the soil may lead to leggy, spindly plants or plants that have lots of green leaves but are not producing any fruits or pods.

FACT

The code for nitrogen is an N, for phosphorus it is a P, and for potassium it is a K. This is a universal code displayed on bags of fertilizer and can be used as a quick reference when purchasing specific types of fertilizer.

Spreading the fertilizer gently around the base of the plant and watering it in can help a troubled plant fairly quickly. If you are going to be planting a new crop, rake or till the fertilizer into the first 6 inches of the garden bed. If your soil is very low in nitrogen, add five pounds per 100 square feet of vegetable garden. If it is just a bit low, add in two-and-a-half-pounds per 100 square feet. To maintain a consistent amount, add one pound per 100 square feet every year. If you find your soil has an excess of nitrogen, try planting vegetables that need a lot of nitrogen, such as leafy greens, and make a note to do a soil test before adding any in the bed the following year.

Phosphorus (P) is needed for healthy plant roots as well as for the flowering and fruit growth of your vegetables. Some easy to access sources of phosphorus are bone meal, fish emulsion, rock phosphate, and some animal manures such as horse manure. Plants that are stunted, very slow growing, or have dull-looking leaves with a purplish tint to them are all signs of a phosphorus deficiency in your soil. Few gardens have an excess of this element in the soil; fortunately, too much phosphorus will usually not have any adverse effect on your vegetable plants.

If your garden is low in phosphorus, add in six pounds per 100 square feet. If your plants are producing well, all you have to do is maintain a good amount of phosphorus in the soil by adding in one pound per 100 square feet each year.

FACT

There are many multipurpose organic fertilizers on the market if you do not want to add in several different types of fertilizer each year. Every garden is different, so make sure you take the time to observe your plants for signs of any deficiencies and add whatever may be needed.

Potassium (K) is needed for plants to produce leaves, buds, healthy roots, and flavorful fruits. Some common sources are potash rock, wood ash, and greensand. If your soil is deficient, your plants will be short and stocky and have a loss of color in the veins and brown spots on the underside of the leaves. Like phosphorus there is not often an excess of this element in the soil, and if there were, it would not have an adverse effect on your plants.

If your soil is low in potassium, add ten pounds per 100 square feet of some of the organic sources. If you just want to maintain the amount you have in your soil, add two-and-a-half-pounds per 100 square feet each year.

Water and Fertilizer Chart

▼ **TABLE 17-1: COMMON VEGETABLE WATERING AND FERTILIZING CHART**

Vegetable	When to Water	When to Fertilize
Beans	Regularly once pods begin to form	After heavy bloom and once pods set
Beets	Only during dry conditions	At time of planting
Broccoli	Only during dry conditions	Three weeks after transplanting
Brussels sprouts	At transplanting and during dry spells	Three weeks after transplanting
Cabbage	Only during dry conditions	Three weeks after transplanting
Carrots	Only during dry conditions	Preferably in the fall for the following spring
Cauliflower	Only during dry conditions	Three weeks after transplanting
Celery	Once a week	At time of planting
Corn	When tassels appear and cobs start to swell	When 8 to 10 inches tall and again when silk first appears
Cucumbers	Frequently, especially when fruits are forming	One week after bloom and again three weeks later
Lettuce	Once a week	Two or three weeks after transplanting
Melons	Once a week	One week after bloom and again three weeks later
Onions	Only during drought conditions	When bulbs begin to swell and again when plants are 1 foot tall
Parsnips	Only during dry conditions	Preferably in the fall for the following spring
Peas	Regularly once the pods begin to form	After heavy bloom and set of pods
Peppers	Once a week	At first bloom and after first fruit set
Potatoes	Regularly	At bloom time or time of second hilling
Pumpkins	Only during dry conditions	Just before vines start to grow usually when plant is about 1 foot tall
Radishes	Once a week	Preferably in the fall for the following spring
Spinach	Once a week	When plants are one-third grown
Squash, summer	Only during dry conditions	Just before vines start to grow usually when plant is about 1 foot tall
Squash, winter	Only during dry conditions	Just before vines start to grow usually when plant is about 1 foot tall
Tomatoes	Deep watering once a week	Two weeks before and after first picking

CHAPTER 18

Choosing the Right Tools

Planting and tending your vegetable garden is easy and fun if you are working with the right tools for each job. If you are a beginner gardener, you will need some basic tools to get started. These are usually easy to find and fairly inexpensive. This chapter explains how to choose the top ten vegetable-gardening tools for your small-space garden, how to stay on budget when purchasing them, and how to keep everything in good working order.

What Tools Do I Need?

Vegetable gardening is definitely "hands-on," so knowing which basic tools you need can make it easier and more fun than if you try to work with the wrong equipment. The basic tasks start in the spring with digging the garden beds, getting them ready for planting, moving amendments and debris to and from the garden site, and then planting the seeds and transplants, watering, harvesting, making compost, and of course, keeping track of everything you are doing. If all you have is a few containers on a balcony you will need to do most of these tasks, just a bit differently and on a smaller scale.

TEN BASIC TOOLS NEEDED FOR VEGETABLE GARDENING

- ❑ Shovel
- ❑ Garden fork
- ❑ Rake
- ❑ Hoe
- ❑ Hand trowel
- ❑ Wheelbarrow or bucket
- ❑ Garden hose or watering can
- ❑ Sharp knife
- ❑ Garden gloves
- ❑ Garden journal

Some of the above tools will be used more often than others and there are smaller versions of each tool available for your small-scale garden.

Shovel

You need a shovel for digging, tilling, and amending your garden beds. There are two basic types, a round-edged one and flat-edged one. Each has different functions and both may not be needed depending on what kind of garden site you have. A round-edged shovel is used for scooping and lifting soil. This type of shovel is great for turning your garden beds and adding in organic amendments such as compost or aged animal manure. A shovel with a flat, rectangular blade is used most when prepping a new garden bed.

This type of shovel works well for cutting edges, removing or turning sod, digging holes, and for prying up rocks.

You want to choose a shovel with a smooth, rounded shoulder at the top of the blade to protect your feet when pressing down on the shovel. When moving material from one area to another, turn your whole body, not just your hips. Stand up straight while digging, and bend your knees when lifting. This will help prevent any back strains or injuries.

Garden Fork

There are two different garden forks that can come in handy; one is used for digging and the other for turning your compost. The digging fork (sometimes called a spading fork) is used for turning over soil, mixing in soil amendments, lifting and breaking up clumps of soil, and for harvesting root crops. The compost fork (or sometimes called a pitchfork) is ideal for turning and moving compost, mulches, straw, green manures, and other organic material used in or around your garden beds. If you are planning to make a layered garden the compost fork will probably come in very handy.

QUESTION

What tools do I need to make compost?
Firstly, you need a bin of some sort. You will need a good quality garden fork to turn your pile, a thermometer to tell if the compost is heating up, and a tarp or plastic to keep your pile covered unless you are using a commercial bin that already has a cover.

Your digging fork should have four broad, flat metal tines with V-shaped ends. You want a solid fork with a bit of weight to it so that you can easily turn soil or lift out rocks without the tines bending. The compost fork has four curved tines that are fine so that they easily penetrate and hold on to the organic matter. You want this fork to be lighter as you will be doing more lifting and throwing of materials with it.

When choosing a fork you want to make sure the size and weight are a good fit for you. Always choose the best quality tool you can afford.

Rake

The rake is used for preparing and cleaning your garden bed, for planting, and for collecting organic matter like garden debris and leaves that are found around your yard. You want to use a garden rake which has small tines attached to a bar that is attached to the handle. This type of rake is used for leveling and cleaning any larger pebbles and debris from your planting bed. A finely raked, clean bed is necessary when planting seeds like carrots, radishes, turnips, rutabagas, and salad greens.

The garden rake can be used for gathering up leaves, grass clippings, and other garden debris; however, a leaf rake is much easier to work with for these jobs. The leaf rake or landscape rake has longer teeth and they are arranged in a fan style. The tines or teeth are usually made of steel, plastic, or bamboo. This allows you to rake up a larger amount of debris.

ALERT

You have seen it happen in slapstick comedy. Someone steps on a rake and it swings upward, hitting the person in the face. This can look funny in a movie, but it can cause serious injury to a person if it happens in your garden. Be aware of where you leave your rake and never leave it with the tines facing upward!

When choosing a rake, make sure it fits your body. You want to be able to stand upright while raking so as not to injure or strain your back. If the rake handle is too long or too short it is difficult to work with. Purchase one that will fit your body and the needs of your garden.

Hoe

The most common use for a hoe is keeping your garden free of weeds. It can also be used to mark rows when planting seeds or transplants. The basic hoe is a goosenecked hoe which has a flat edge used for digging and chopping weeds. The stirrup hoe is easier to use when weeding large garden beds as it slices the top inch or so of the soil, cutting the weeds off just below the soil surface. This motion is easier on your back and shoulders than the digging motion used with the goosenecked hoe.

In a small-space garden all you may need is a handheld hoe for digging deep, stubborn weeds. Hand weed the rest. If you choose to purchase a regular hoe make sure the length of the handle is long enough so you can work standing upright. Keep the blade sharp to make it easier to work with. Hoe in the evening just before the sun goes down to discourage the weeds from germinating. It is easier to hoe when the soil is moist; however, if it has been dry and there is a rainfall predicted, hoeing hard soil will help it to absorb the moisture better.

Hand Trowel

The hand trowel is a handy little tool for digging a hole when setting out your transplants or when planting bulbs like garlic or your seed potatoes. A hoe will do a similar job, but a hand trowel might be much easier to work with in a small-scale garden as you are usually closer to the ground. Having a tool with a long handle can make the job more difficult. Another good use for the hand trowel is as a measuring stick since having a measurement marker makes it easier to get the correct depth when planting your seeds, bulbs, or seed potatoes. When purchasing, look for a trowel that has depth measurements written on the blade, or if you cannot find one with the markings, take time to make your own using a permanent marker.

FACT

Reuse items around your home such as aprons with large pockets, wicker or plastic baskets, a backpack, or a child's wagon as a tool holder. Having all your tools in one place makes it easier to grab everything you need quickly.

Using the trowel and hoe together is a great way to make a straight garden row for placing your seeds. Use the handle of your hoe as a marker for the row and then use the trowel to make a trench along one side of the handle to the depth you need.

Wheelbarrow or Bucket

Something easy to move and big enough to carry items around your garden is essential. A wheelbarrow can come in very handy even in a small space. If you are only growing in a few containers, a sturdy bucket may be all you need. Either one is used for hauling items like compost, amendments and manure to and from your garden site so they can be added to your garden beds. The wheelbarrow can be used for transporting vegetables you have harvested, hanging your garlic or onions over the sides of the wheelbarrow so you can easily move them in and out of the sun, and for carrying plant material you have collected to your compost area.

There are many different types of wheelbarrows and they come in varying price ranges. They can be made of plastic or cloth and be lightweight, or of heavy-duty metal or aluminum. Two-wheeled ones make hauling heavy loads easy. The most common is the single-wheeled type with two handles for pushing. Before choosing a wheelbarrow make sure you know what you will be using it for and the amount you will be hauling in it. Are you going to be carrying heavy loads? Choosing a sturdy metal one is probably best. Do you have a small garden and are only going to be using it for lighter loads? Then a lightweight plastic or cloth type may work better for you. A wheelbarrow that can be easily stored might be another consideration for a small-space garden. When purchasing a wheelbarrow, take the time to push it around in the store. If it feels heavy for you when it is empty, go for a model that is more lightweight as it will only get heavier when full!

Garden Hose or Watering Can

No matter how small your garden is, if you have to pack water, you will be less likely to water your plants adequately. This is where the garden hose or a proper-sized watering can comes in. When planning your garden make sure you have a water source nearby and that the hose reaches to all corners of your garden. Hoses come in different lengths and can be easily connected together to make the length that works best for your garden site.

Hoses come in a variety of styles and are usually of ½ inch to 1 inch in diameter. The bigger the hose diameter, the faster the water will come through, although the rate may vary depending on what kind of water pressure you have. Larger diameter hoses are usually heavier to move around. Try to choose a "no kink" hose for ease of moving around as it can become frustrating when your hose kinks at one end of the garden and shuts off the water while you are at the other end! You can spend a lot of money on hose carriers and systems to roll them up; some are better than others and what you choose will depend on your garden site and the amount you wish to spend. Purchase the best quality hose you can afford and take care of it by remembering to take it inside during the colder months so that it does not crack.

ESSENTIAL

When moving a hose around your garden it can become frustrating if it knocks over plants or pulls mulch around your garden. One solution is to place a curved drainpipe (with the curve downward) securely into the ground, allowing the hose to be easily guided through it.

Attaching a water wand or nozzle to the end of your hose can make gardening easier as it allows you to reach the base of the plant more easily without straining or having to bend. There are a variety of water wands available. The best option is to purchase one that has several spray functions and gives you different ways of watering your veggies.

Sharp Knife

You can find all kinds of gardening items in your local gardening store or in seed catalogues. All of these gadgets have their place in the garden if you can afford them; however, they are usually not necessary in most gardens. For the home gardener a good sharp knife is one of the most flexible tools you can use. A simple knife is great for opening bags of fertilizer, cutting string, cutting your vegetables when they are ready to be harvested, cutting off stems of plants for composting, cutting off diseased or pest-infected plants (just make sure you disinfect the knife afterward), and for slicing into a tomato or cucumber to eat it! A good quality knife is one of the handiest tools to carry with you when in your garden.

Garden Gloves

A good pair (or a few pairs) of garden gloves is needed to help keep your hands soft and prevent blisters on your hands when doing heavy work. Working in soil or with other organic materials can give your hands a beating, and digging or shoveling for any length of time is a sure way to give yourself a blister if you are doing it with bare hands. Weeding can be hard on the fingernails and fingertips as well. A good pair of gloves will help to protect your hands from all these hazards.

When choosing a pair of gloves make sure they fit snuggly but are not too tight. If they are too large, every time you put down your tool they will have a tendency to fall off. It is harder to grip anything if a glove is too big! A well-fitting pair of gloves made with a breathable material that is easy to wash is the one you want to choose. An inexpensive option, especially if working in wet soil, is a pair of kitchen rubber gloves. They will protect your hands and keep them dry as well.

Garden Journal

Number ten on the list of the Ten Basic Gardening Tools is a garden journal. The importance of jotting down where you planted certain things, how they grew, and what worked or did not work is invaluable for planning and troubleshooting next season. The journal can be as fancy or as simple as you want it to be. Choosing some kind of bound book or folder is better than using scraps of paper as a book or a folder is easier to carry with you and can be put away once the growing season is finished.

Here are some important items for your journal:

- A drawing of your garden site
- A section for each type of vegetable (or family of vegetables) listing the variety you planted and where, the maturity date, how well it grew, how successful the harvest was, and would you grow this variety again
- A place to note when you fertilized each vegetable, how much was given, and whether it seemed to make a difference.
- A note about any pest or disease problem, actions taken, and whether it made a difference

Writing in a garden journal is one the best habits a vegetable gardener can have. It is important to jot down your thoughts about what worked or did not work in your garden to make it easier to plan for next season. You may think you will remember certain details from one season to the next. But often you might not even recall where certain vegetables were planted so you can do a proper crop rotation. Just little notes about the weather or whether you saw butterflies or ladybugs in your garden are interesting to write about. Often the little things are the most valuable when looking back at how our garden grew in past seasons.

New Gadgets

There are always new gardening gadgets being advertised. Some ads claim to promote healthier, more productive plants while saving you time and energy. Some claims are valid, whereas others are not, and a huge amount of money can be spent on gardening tools and supplies that are never used and definitely not needed. If you are just starting out as a new gardener or on a budget, stick to the basic items you know you will need. Once you are more familiar with your garden site and your gardening habits, you can do some research on other tools and gadgets.

How to Stay on Budget

Basic gardening tools can be purchased at garden centers, hardware stores, and garage sales or flea markets. When purchasing secondhand make sure the tool is in good shape. Examine the handles for cracks, make sure any joints are solid, and check that the tines or blades are straight. Used tools can easily be cleaned and sharpened, but they can also be expensive to fix; unless, of course, you are handy with that type of thing.

When you go looking for your vegetable gardening tools you want to make sure you purchase the right tool for your size and needs. You want to be able to dig, hoe, or rake without straining your back or arms. A 5-foot woman will need a different size tool than a 6-foot man in order to use it properly and with ease. Choose a handle that works for your height and make sure the circumference of the handle fits comfortably in your hand.

When starting out as a new gardener, buying tools and equipment can be daunting and expensive. Setting a budget is important when purchasing tools as they can vary in price and you will be less likely to overspend on gadgets that look great but are really not needed. Deciding what you need right now and making a list before you go to the gardening store are both helpful habits when trying to stick to a budget. Spend some time at the garden center or hardware store trying out the different tools and checking the size, fit, and weight. Imagine how the tool will feel when working with it for a few hours. Is it comfortable?

ALERT

Proper footwear is important in the garden, especially if you will be doing any digging. A heavy-soled boot will make it easier to press down on a spade or shovel when digging or moving any amendments or compost. If your garden is uneven, proper footwear can prevent tripping or falling.

Always choose the best quality you can afford! Blades should be forged from a single piece of metal and should have a solid-socket construction where the blade meets the handle. Studies have shown that a D-shaped handled tool is easier to use as the handle is easier to grip. For the most longevity, choose a tool with a handle made of strong wood, metal, or good quality plastic. By purchasing good quality tools you are making an investment that will pay for itself over many years.

Maintaining Your Investment

A good-quality tool can be expensive to purchase. If it is properly used and cared for, it will last you several decades. Every gardener should get into the habit of cleaning off any dirt and wiping the tool after every use. Do a thorough cleaning of all your tools at the end of the season before you put them away into storage. To do this, rub off any debris with a cloth or burlap sack. If the dirt is dried on, use a wire brush or steel wool to scrape it all off. Wipe all metal parts lightly with oil (car oil works well), and then wipe wooden handles with linseed oil. Store tools in a dry, clean garage or storage shed. Hanging them on a wall is one way of using your space more productively.

During the growing season, if you knowingly have used your tools in an area where you were working with diseased plants, it is extremely important to clean your tools, pots, and work surfaces immediately after finishing the task. If you do not take the time to clean, the disease can easily and quickly spread throughout your whole garden. Soil clings to shovels and trowels and can carry organisms. So scrape off all the soil away from the garden beds. Then wipe the tool clean. Brush or sweep all benches or surfaces that could have been affected as well. Clean pots or pails in which you carried the diseased material in with a one part bleach to nine parts water solution. The last thing you want to do is work hard at containing a pest or disease and then forget to clean your tools.

ALERT

Having a large well-organized garden shed is a luxury most gardeners do not have. However, it is important to organize your tools and equipment in the storage space you do have. Keep frequently used items easily accessible. If you have an organized space you will be less likely to purchase duplicate tools. Organization will save you money!

Tools such as a hoe or shovel should be regularly sharpened as having a sharp tool will make gardening tasks easier. Tools should be sharpened before you start to work, and when hoeing or digging a large area, sharpened again during the time you are working. Once you work with a sharp tool, you will never go back!

To sharpen your tools, use a flat file and draw it smoothly down the blade from top to bottom. Do not go back and forth; just move the file in one direction. File the blade until all the nicks are smoothed out. When the blade is sharp to the touch, move the file over the back edge of the tool to remove any build up on that edge.

CHAPTER 19

Simple Solutions to Small-Space Problems

It can be disheartening to put so much effort into planting a garden or container just to have all your hard work destroyed by some unforeseen problem. There are ways to help ensure more success with growing veggies in your garden and you'll find them in this chapter. You'll learn how to choose healthy plants to get you started, how to keep them growing and happy with tips on weeding and deterring animals, and how to identify and manage pests and diseases.

Smart Plant Choices for a Healthy Garden

In a small-space garden you can grow a variety of plants: however, you may have more success by choosing dwarf varieties, plants that grow upright to maximize your space, or specific types that will grow best in containers. Seed catalogs will indicate some of the benefits of each variety. Some have shorter or longer maturity dates. Some grow smaller than other plants; others do better in different temperatures. There can be various reasons for choosing a certain variety. Take the time to read and choose the plants that will work best for your situation.

Before purchasing your seeds or plants make sure you have planned your garden layout. You will save time and money by purchasing only the items you need. Buy from a reputable seed company or nursery. If there are any companies that do growing trials in your area, check them out first. You will know that those varieties will have been grown in a climate similar to yours and will have a greater chance of success in your garden.

Make sure you purchase your seedlings (also known as transplants) from a reputable business as well and choose the healthiest seedlings it sells. Insects and disease can be easily brought into your garden with unhealthy transplants. Look closely at transplants. Check for any insects in the soil or on the undersides of the leaves, holes in the leaves, and evidence that insects have chewed the leaves. These are all signs that your transplant may be damaged and infected.

ALERT

A hybrid variety is made when seeds from two parent plants are crossed for the purpose of improving the plant's productivity. Often vegetable plants are hybridized in order to create disease-resistant varieties and to increase vegetable size, color, and shape. The problem with hybrid plants is that the seeds cannot be saved for future use.

A healthy transplant is bushy and compact, not spindly or leggy; the stems are a healthy color and strong, and the plant is not root bound. If the plant roots are showing through the drain holes, it is a sign the plant may be root-bound. Gently pop the plant out of its container and look at the roots. If they are tightly wound around the soil, do not look healthy, or are discolored at all, choose another plant. A plant that is root-bound or unhealthy looking will potentially take longer to get established and is less likely to grow well. When bringing your transplants home make sure you are ready to plant them into the garden as soon as possible to ensure greater success.

What to Do with the Weeds

There are three types of weeds—annuals, biennials, and perennials. Annual weeds live for only one season and produce thousands of seeds; that way their survival is assured. They germinate in the spring, produce seeds in the summer, and die in the fall. The best way to control annual weeds is to pull them out or cut them off with a hoe before they go to seed. Annual weeds grow quickly and they need to be removed regularly so they do not go to seed and spread. Some examples of common annual weeds are knotweed, pigweed, purslane, lamb's-quarter, and chickweed.

A biennial weed grows in the first year; however, it does not produce a flower or seeds until the second year of growth. The best way to control these weeds is to remove them from your garden in the first year of their growth so they have no chance of spreading their seeds. Common biennial weeds are burdock, mullein, and Queen Anne's lace.

ESSENTIAL

Because they offer water for drinking and bathing, birdbaths and ponds are magnets for birds. The water bath should be no more than 2 inches (6 cm) deep and needs to be kept clean. Scrub the bath regularly with a stiff brush.

Most weeds like similar growing conditions as vegetables so a lot of weeds can indicate that your garden soil is healthy. You can look at it as a blessing or a curse. Weed seeds are exposed by digging or tilling the soil. They are brought into the garden by birds, wind, and the bottom of your shoes. Once the seeds have found a nice place to germinate, they will grow. Weeds have a tendency to grow quickly stealing the light, nutrients, and space from your vegetable plants.

Some common perennial weeds are dandelion, thistle, bindweed, chicory, plantain, wild sorrel, and dock. Perennial weeds will continue to grow for many years. Some produce seeds to propagate whereas others spread by their root system or with bulbs. Perennial weeds usually die back once they have gone to seed; however, they will continue to grow year after year with great vigor if the root system is not completely removed.

Weeds such as poison ivy, kudzu, morning glory, and Japanese honeysuckle have deep roots that creep underground. Some of these plants can multiply quickly and can be very difficult to eradicate. All they need is a piece of stem to touch the soil and they start growing. To control these you will regularly need to dig and remove as much of the root system as you can. Another invasive perennial weed is grass. Various grasses can make some of the worst weeds because they produce a lot of seeds and the plants are difficult to uproot. Some common grasses that are considered weeds, especially in the vegetable garden, are quack grass and some varieties of bamboo. These plants are difficult to remove because they have underground roots and stems that produce new plants several yards away from the parent plant.

Weeding Your Garden

Do not avoid weeding! Putting off weeding is often a new gardener's downfall because weeds can grow rapidly, and before you know it, they are taking over. The situation can become overwhelming and you may not be sure where to start. Weeding can be time-consuming; however, setting a bit of time aside each week can make it easy to stay on top of things. Spring is the best time to put some focused energy in to weeding your garden. Weeds often grow faster than vegetable plants at this time of year, stealing light and nutrients that your veggie plants need to grow. It is easier to kill weeds when they are small and the soil is moist rather than later in the season when the soil can become hard and dry. Always remove weeds before they go to seed so they do not have a chance to spread!

Getting on your hands and knees and pulling out the root of the plant is probably the best way to get rid of it. As a new gardener it can be confusing to decide what is a vegetable plant and what is a weed. Some veggie plants look similar to weeds, especially when they are small. For example lamb's-quarter looks like a radish when young and wild sorrel looks like spinach when it first starts to grow. If you are not sure if a plant it a weed or a veggie, delay the weeding until you see your row or the pattern of your vegetables (another important reason to take the time to mark where you are planting your seeds).

ALERT

If you have missed a few weeks of weeding and some of the weeds have gone to seed, carefully pull out the plant and immediately put it into a plastic garbage bag. This will help prevent the seeds from spreading.

Hoeing is another way to keep weeds in check by scraping the hoe over the top inch of the soil. It is easier to hoe when the soil is moist so do your hoeing after watering your garden or after a rainfall. By scraping the top of the soil you will be slicing off the top of the weeds preventing the weed from going to seed. However, you may not be killing the roots system so the plant may grow again. If you keep hoeing, though, sooner or later the root will die as it needs the green part of the plant to keep growing. Keeping your hoe blade sharp will make this job easier to accomplish.

Deterring Animals

Larger pests and animals can cause a lot of damage to a vegetable garden. Deer, elk, bears, raccoons, squirrels, opossums, skunks, gophers, rabbits, rats, and mice love vegetables and garden debris. Even in urban gardens some of these animals can be a problem. If you see signs of your plants being eaten or damaged, take the time to observe what kind of animal is entering the area. Often they come in at dusk or dawn. Watch more closely at these times of day. If it is not a wild animal, perhaps it is your neighbor's cat or dog sneaking in and digging up your garden.

Building a fence around your garden plot is probably the best way to keep out dogs, cats, raccoons, and other larger animals. If mice or rats are a huge problem in your area, traps are often the only effective way of controlling them.

Aquatic animals such as toads, box turtles, and frogs love to eat insects, so encouraging their presence in your garden can be beneficial. Make a pond or fill a shallow container with water to give them a source of water. For a shelter, place a clay flowerpot upside down in your garden and chip the side to make a little space for them to enter.

Birds are often a mixed blessing in a fruit or veggie garden. They feed on damaging insects; thus, it is great to put up birdhouses and water gardens to attract them. On the other hand, some birds will eat tiny seedlings or fruits such as tomatoes or cherries, and therefore are unwelcome. It is difficult to decide what to do. Again take the time to watch and observe what birds are coming in and what they are doing. One defense in keeping away unwanted birds is to hang metal foil strips on stakes extended 2 or 3 feet above your garden bed. A more extreme and costly measure would be to enclose your garden completely (sides and top) with netting or chicken wire held up with posts. Fruit trees may need to be totally covered with netting to keep the birds from eating all your fruits. Cherries are often the most desired fruit for birds.

Common Pest Problems

When you first begin to garden there is a lot to learn about which bugs are good for your garden and which are potentially harmful. It takes time to get to know what is living in or entering your garden and each year you may have to play detective for a new problem. Learn to identify and problem solve by talking with fellow gardeners, reading books, searching the Internet, or asking questions at your local nursery or garden center. If you have a certain problem in your garden, do not be afraid to experiment with different methods to control the problem and keep trying new varieties to see if they can make a difference.

No garden is pest-free—nor do you necessarily want it to be. There are beneficial and sometimes-harmful insects and organisms living in soil and both are needed to create a healthy garden. It is important to take the time to document your pest problems and what you did to control them. Every season may be different with new pests, but if you have documented what happened in previous years, your records can help you know what to do this time around. Your records can save you time on having to experiment. It is best to stay away from chemicals or pesticides when it comes to your vegetable garden. They will not make your soil healthier nor will they help attract more beneficial insects to your garden site.

Tilling your garden beds is one way to make it harder for pests to survive by exposing insects and larvae to the elements and their natural predators. Planting a cover crop or using mulch will keep your soil healthy, which also helps to fight off damaging pests. Keeping your garden clean is another way of keeping unwanted pests out by not providing them any safe place to hide.

Birds, bats, toads, and snakes are all animals you want in your garden. They will keep the slugs, snails, and many insects under control.

There are as many beneficial insects as there are harmful ones. It just takes time to learn which are which. Each garden site has a variety of different insects and soil animals.

COMMON BENEFICIAL GARDEN CREATURES

- Earthworms
- Ground beetles
- Honeybees
- Lacewings
- Ladybugs (sometimes known as ladybird beetles)
- Praying mantis
- Spiders
- Syrphid flies
- Tachinid flies
- Braconid wasps
- Yellow jackets (also known as hornets)

Planting flowers among your vegetables or letting some of your vegetable plants flower rather than pulling out the plant is another way to attract beneficial insects to your garden. The flowers are colorful, some are edible, and they can make your garden more attractive overall.

POPULAR FLOWERS THAT ATTRACT OR REPEL INSECTS

- Broccoli flowers
- Calendula
- California poppy
- Celery flowers
- Dill flowers
- Lemon balm
- Marigolds
- Nasturtiums
- Parsley flowers
- Sunflower

By having a healthy ecosystem in your vegetable garden, nature will be able to take care of things for you. Start with healthy soil, plant healthy seeds and plants, and create an environment that will keep everything and everyone in your garden in balance.

Plant Diseases

You can physically see a pest or insect. It is more difficult to diagnosis a plant disease because the symptoms can be similar to those caused by other factors like excessive heat or cold, nutrient deficiencies in the soil, or poor drainage. If you have healthy soil, give your plants proper water and fertilizer, and maintain good garden practices, you will not have many diseases show up on your plants. If you do have a recurring problem year after year, it is important to learn what it is and try to correct the cause.

There are four main types of disease-causing organisms (also called pathogens) in vegetable plants—bacteria, fungi, nematodes, and viruses. These all attack plants in different ways with some common symptoms like wilting, yellowing, and stunted growth. The pathogens can be spread in various ways. They can be blown around by the wind or carried in water. Animals, humans, garden tools, and other equipment can also transfer these organisms from plant to plant. An insect can carry a pathogen in its saliva and transfer it from plant to plant. When you are trying to diagnosis a disease it is important to learn what the life cycle of the pathogen is so you can avoid spreading it.

ALERT

Aphids are the worst offenders when it comes to insects spreading many viral and bacterial diseases. Often by controlling the aphids you will stop the spread of the disease. Control aphids by attracting braconid wasps, hoverflies, lacewings, and ladybugs to your garden. An alternative is knocking the aphids off the plant with a strong stream of water. Repeat this several times.

Before any disease can occur there have to be three elements present—a susceptible plant, a pathogen, and favorable conditions for the pathogen to survive. To control or manage plant diseases you need to remove one or more of these elements. Planting disease-resistant varieties can remove a susceptible plant from this equation. Pulling out and destroying the infected vegetable plant removes the pathogen. We cannot control the weather; however, we can make it difficult for pathogens to survive by creating an environment that is not compatible for them. For example, avoiding overhead watering or taking time to trellis a plant so it has better air circulation will help to make the conditions less favorable for the pathogen to survive.

The best way to keep your vegetable garden free of pests and disease is to have healthy soil, give your plants the proper amount of water, use crop rotation, and keep your garden and tools clean. No vegetable garden will be totally free of all pests or disease (and some insects are actually beneficial). Just remember, a healthy plant will be able to fight off anything that comes its way!

Answers to Your Problems

There are many different things that could potentially go wrong when gardening. The weather, pests, diseases, and animals all can affect how the plants grow. Most problems usually affect only one or two plants or a family of plants. So plant a variety of different veggies and you will pretty much guarantee that you will be able to harvest some vegetables. Gardens are living things, so a little damage or a few pests are normal. Just welcome them and learn from any mishaps.

ESSENTIAL

Here are five steps to controlling pest and disease in your garden: identify the problem, check the level of injury to the plant, determine the most sustainable and organic treatment needed, evaluate how effective the treatment was, and then make notes for future reference.

The most common problems in a veggie garden are often caused by over watering, under watering, poor soil fertility, poor drainage, and poor air circulation. These factors can all be managed with a little extra knowledge and attention from the gardener. If your soil it healthy, then your plants will be healthy and be able to fight off any pest or disease that may try to attack them.

Here are some signs that your soil may not have the nutrients your plants need to grow strong and healthy.

▼ **TABLE 19-1: NUTRIENT DEFICIENCY GUIDE**

Nutrient	Symptom	Causes	Solutions
Nitrogen	Plant leaves are light green or yellowish in color	Easily leaches from the soil	Mulch or plant a cover crop
Phosphorus	Plants are stunted and have a purplish color	Wet, cold soil; low pH (acidic soil)	Plan to lime next spring
Potassium	Leaves are brown and curling	Excessive leaching	Mulch or plant a green manure
Calcium	Stunted plants, stubby roots, and blossom-end rot on tomatoes	Very acidic soil, excessively dry or wet soil, too high levels of potassium	Add lime, check for drainage problems, fertilize carefully
Magnesium	Yellowish color on older leaves	Very acidic soil, too high potassium levels	Add lime and fertilize carefully
Sulfur	Yellowish color in young leaves and stunted growth	Low organic matter often found in sandy soil	Add in compost and aged manures fall and spring

Nutrient	Symptom	Causes	Solutions
Boron	Leaves distorted, growing point of the plant dies	Soil pH above 6.8 or below 5.5, low organic matter usually in sandy soil	Soil pH test to see if lime or sulfur needed
Copper	Yellowish leaves that become thin and elongated	High pH (too alkaline)	Add sulfur to the soil in the spring to lower the pH
Iron	Youngest leaves are light green or yellow colored	High pH (too alkaline), low organic matter, and excessive phosphorus in the soil	Add sulfur, compost, and aged manures in the spring and fall
Zinc	Yellow beet leaves, rust spots on beans	High pH (too alkaline), cool wet soil in the spring, and excessive phosphorus in the soil	Add sulfur and fertilize carefully
Manganese	Mottled yellowish areas on younger leaves	High pH (too alkaline)	Add sulfur in the spring
Molybdenum	Distorted leaves, curling at leaf edges, yellowish outer leaves	Low pH (acidic soil)	Add lime in the spring

What's Wrong with My Plants?

The following table will help you identify what could be causing problems with your vegetable plants and some suggestions of what you can do about them.

▼ TABLE 19-2: PLANT PROBLEM GUIDE

Symptoms	Possible causes	Possible cures
Stunted plants yellowish or pale colored	Low fertility, low pH, poor drainage, insects	Soil test for fertility recommendations, add lime, add in organic matter
Stunted plants, purplish colored.	Low temperature, lack of phosphorus	Plant at the recommended temperature, add phosphorus to the soil
Holes in leaves	Insects	Identify the insect by looking on the leaves to see if there are any insects on them. Remove leaves if severely damaged.

▼ **TABLE 19-2: PLANT PROBLEM GUIDE** (continued)

Symptoms	Possible causes	Possible cures
Wilting plants	Dry soil, excess water, and disease	Irrigate if dry, drain if too wet, plant resistant varieties
Weak spindly plants	Too much shade, too much water, too much nitrogen in the soil, planting is too thick	Place in a sunnier location, avoid excess fertilization, thin plants to proper spacing
Fruit not forming	High temperature, low temperature, too much nitrogen, insects	Plant at the recommended times, avoid over fertilization, identify insects and find the appropriate control
Abnormal leaves	Virus disease	Remove infected leaves
Spots, molds on stems and leaves	Disease	Identify and use appropriate controls

Your vegetable plants are a wealth of information when it comes to problems in the garden. They will wilt if they get too much heat or not enough water. They will turn yellow if they are not getting the nutrients they need. And they may even die if they are not taken care of properly. Every garden is different so take the time to get to know your soil, climate, and plants.

CHAPTER 20

Gardening on a Budget

We all want stay on budget, find the best deals, and still get what we want and need. Growing some of your own food is a great way to save money on your grocery bill. Gardeners can spend a small fortune if they are not aware of what is needed and how to find the best deals. So how can you get the best bang for your buck when starting a garden? Read on to learn ways to save money when planning and growing your garden. You will also find tips and specific growing plans to get you started.

Vegetable-Gardening Budgeting Tips

Finding ways to cut costs is important for most people in our tight economic times. When on a limited or tight budget, growing some of your own food will definitely save on your grocery bill. No matter if we are new gardeners or experienced ones, most of us are concerned about how much money we are spending when purchasing items for the garden. Statistics show shoppers spend millions of dollars every year on plants and materials for their gardens.

You just have to walk into a garden center or hardware store to know there is an overwhelming number of gardening tools and materials and a staggering selection of plants. There seems to be a tool for everything. Do you need them all? What materials are best purchased? Are there ways to recycle or reuse other things? How do you choose the best items to get the best bang for your buck in your small-space garden? Which plants are best to buy as transplants and which are better to start from a packet of seeds? These are all valid questions, especially for someone who is on a tight budget. So how can you save a few dollars and still have a healthy abundant food-producing garden?

Plan Before You Shop

Taking the time to so some research and making a plan of your space and what you want to grow will go a long way toward saving you money.

What size of a garden do you have? Before you purchase anything measure the area you want to grow in and do a rough sketch on a piece of paper. Even if all you will be growing will be contained in a few pots, it is important to know the size of the area in which the pots will be placed.

ALERT

If you are a new gardener or have kids, choose quick-growing plants such as lettuce, spinach, mustard greens, cress, oriental greens, radishes, green onions, and scallions to see the results more quickly.

Where are you growing your garden? Growing veggies in the ground in your back or front yard, growing in raised beds, or in containers on a balcony or patio will make a difference in what you will need. Knowing how you will be watering and maintaining your garden will help when choosing the equipment needed.

What are the growing conditions of your space? The amount of sunlight or rainfall your area gets will determine what plants will grow best for you.

What it is you want to grow? Grow what you want to eat. If you and your family will not eat something, even if it will grow well in your area, it will be a waste of your money. Once you have your list of plants you will also be able to determine whether or not you need to support or stake them. If you do, will you need to purchase materials for this project or do you have something you currently own that can be used?

How many plants or seeds will you need? The size of your garden and what you want to grow will determine the number of plants you will need. Buying seeds and transplants can get expensive, and knowing what you need will save you from bringing home more plants than you need or have space for.

FACT

Choosing plants that will produce an abundance of veggies for the amount of space they take such as beans, Brussels sprouts, cucumbers, Jerusalem artichokes, peas, radish, salad greens, spinach, tomato, and zucchini will make your small-space garden even more productive.

Are you growing your garden in containers? If so, how many containers will you need? Do you have some old containers in the garage or under the back steps you can clean up and use or will you need to purchase new ones? Containers can be very expensive and heavy to move around once filled, so planning ahead it important. Choosing to use recycled or creative items rather than traditional containers can save you a small fortune.

Trade or Save Seeds

A packet of seeds seems to be getting more expensive to buy every year. Finding alternatives to having to purchase seeds every year will save you some cash. Saving your own seeds is probably the most economical way to go but this is not always easy if you are growing in a small-spaced garden or in containers. To save seeds, you need to plan in advance and mark the best plant; don't harvest it until it has produced seeds that you can use the next season.

Another option is to trade seeds. Chat with other gardeners in your area who may be willing to give or trade seeds; start up a seed-trading club, or check out Seedy Saturday, which is a day event every spring in many Canadian towns and cities.

▼ **TABLE 20-1: VEGETABLES BEST TRANSPLANTED OR DIRECT SEEDED**

Vegetable best transplanted	Vegetable best direct seeded
Beet	Bean
Broccoli	Carrot
Brussels sprouts	Corn
Cabbage	Cucumber
Cauliflower	Muskmelon
Celery	Pea
Chard	Turnip
Eggplant	Watermelon
Lettuce	
Onion	
Pepper	
Tomato	

Purchase Healthy Transplants

If you are growing lots of veggies, the cheapest and ultimately the best way to get transplants is to grow your own. However, this option is not usually available or the necessarily the best option for a small-space garden if you need only a few of each vegetable. Always purchase plants from a reputable nursery or garden center. If you purchase healthy transplants you will not bring disease or insects into your garden space.

A healthy transplant is bushy and compact, not spindly or leggy. The stems should be strong, hold the plant upright, and have a healthy color. Avoid plants that are root-bound as they are older and may not grow as well.

If the roots are coming out of the bottom of the pot they may be root-bound; you can gently knock the plant out to its container to check. If they are tightly holding the soil together or are discolored at all, do not bring them home.

When you go to purchase your transplants, make sure your garden area is ready to be planted as it is best to get them into the ground or containers as soon as possible. Make sure the pots are well watered before transplanting and then give the plant another watering once it has been placed in the soil. Water helps the plant's root system get established.

ALERT

For early tomatoes, purchase plants with flowers. The flowers may fall off when the plant is transplanted but more will form. These plants may not yield well after the early crop. Young flowerless plants will fruit later but bear more.

If you are adding perennial herbs or flowers to your garden for companion planting, check with your neighbors or friends to see if they have some cuttings from plants that need to be divided. Offer to help dig them up in exchange for taking a piece. If you cannot afford to purchase a larger plant but want the instant impact, try buying two smaller ones. Plant two lilies, lavenders, or roses together and double the impact. Over time, the plants will merge and you will not realize it is two plants.

Recycle and Reuse Items

If a gardener starts purchasing every little thing needed, it can cost a small fortune. Tools, hoses, sprayer, watering cans, mulching materials, baskets, harvesting tools, and other odds and ends can quickly add up and break the budget. Before going out to purchase the latest gadget, take a look around the house or garage to see what you already have or what could be used instead of spending money on something new.

Some basic tools are needed and you want good quality and proper fitting tools, so purchasing some of these might be the best option in the long run. Make a list of necessities and then check out flea markets or garage sales. It is easy to clean up or sharpen gardening tools, but make sure they are in good working order.

A pail or plastic milk jug makes a cheap watering can. A clam shell that fits into the palm of your hand makes a great digging tool, an old apple corer will dig up tough weeds, a shoehorn will make planting holes, an old spoon will make small holes for smaller transplants, and an old fork can be used for cultivating a small area. There are many uses for other common items. Have fun being creative rather than buying the latest gadget.

Collect leaves and grass clippings from neighbors for mulch and to add to your compost bin. Just make sure the items are not sprayed with pesticides if you want to grow organically. You can use almost anything that will hold soil as a container, just make sure there is some way for the soil to drain.

Make Compost

Healthy soil produces healthy plants that give you more veggies to harvest. Compost is an inexpensive way to keep your garden and container soil healthy. Compost is made out of your kitchen and garden waste so it is costing you nothing to make, perhaps even saving money on your garbage bill. You can purchase a compost bin (they are pretty reasonable) or you can easily make your own out of a garbage can or some recycled wood. Compost can even be made in a pile in your back yard if you are not concerned about how it looks while it is being made.

FACT

According to some estimates, in countries such as the United States and the United Kingdom, food scrap represents around 19 percent of the waste dumped in landfills. The scrap ends up rotting and producing methane, a greenhouse gas. The social, economic, and environmental impact of food wastage is enormous (*www.epa.gov*).

Compost can be used as a mulch to keep the weeds down. It is a great soil amendment, adding organic matter to your existing soil, and is a soil fertilizer since all the decomposed food and garden waste will add nutrients to your garden beds and containers. Veggies, herbs and fruits love compost so save money by making it rather than purchasing expense mulches, amendments, and fertilizers.

Rent Large Equipment

Large garden equipment and tools such as rototillers, shredders, weed-eaters, and cultivators can save time and energy in tilling or maintaining even a small-space garden. They are, however, very expensive to purchase and renting them is a less expensive option. Check with local equipment-rental companies as most will carry these items. If you are not able or do not want to use larger machinery, hiring someone can be an economical way of turning your garden each spring.

If you grow in a community or collective garden, sharing the cost of purchasing larger equipment and even general gardening tools like shovels, hoses, and wheelbarrows can be a worthwhile option, especially if the garden area is large. You can then even make money by renting the larger equipment to other gardeners or groups in your city. Purchase the best quality tools and equipment you can afford and make sure it is used and maintained properly. Your investment will pay for itself in a few years and you will use the equipment for decades.

Getting the Most Out of a $25 Garden

So all you have to spend is $25. What kind garden can you have? If you can be creative, even with this little amount you can enjoy some of your own lettuce, tomatoes, and herbs. Here is what you need for a container garden on your balcony, patio, or front porch—just make sure the area gets lots of sun. Note prices may vary a little depending on where you live and the time of year.

List of items needed:

- ❑ One 18-liter bag of organic potting soil ($6.00)
- ❑ One 16-inch container ($8.00)
- ❑ One tomato plant (in a 6 inch pot) ($3.50)
- ❑ Four lettuce plants ($3.00)
- ❑ Two basil plants ($1.50)
- ❑ Two parsley plants ($1.50)
- ❑ Four pansies ($1.50)

❑ Four 4- to 6-foot lengths of wood stakes or a wire tomato cage (you can often find these for free; tree branches or bamboo will work)
❑ Masking or packing tape

Place the stakes to the inside edge of the pot and secure them to the pot with tape. Plant the tomato in the center of the pot, filling up the pot with the soil and making sure the stakes are secure. If you are using a wire tomato cage, you can place it around the tomato plant after is has been planted into the soil. Plant the lettuce, parsley, and basil around the tomato plant. Wash out the pot that the tomato plant came in and then plant the pansies into it. You now have a minigarden that you can put on your balcony or patio. Cut the outer leaves of the lettuce and parsley, nip the top of the basil every few days, and you will be enjoying food from your minigarden for several months.

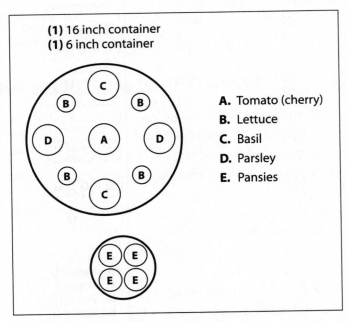

▲ $25 container garden design

If you wanted you could exchange the lettuce for spinach or other greens, use any annual herb you liked rather than the basil or parsley, and switch out the pansy for another annual flower. Enjoy.

Getting the Most Out of a $50 Garden

In this garden plan we are assuming you have an area of soil that is ready to be planted. If you do not, you can make a raised bed out of wood, cement blocks, or rocks, or bring in soil and plant in containers. Both approaches will add to the cost unless you can be creative with finding inexpensive materials. Any extra seeds can be kept in a cool, dry place and used the following year. Note prices may vary a little depending on where you live and the time of year.

List of items needed:

❑ Three tomato plants ($10.50)
❑ Six basil plants ($3.00)
❑ Four pepper plants ($3.00)
❑ Four cabbage plants ($3.00)
❑ Four broccoli plants ($3.00)
❑ Four marigold plants ($2.00)
❑ Three cucumber plants or one packet seeds ($4.50)
❑ Six lettuce plants ($3.00)
❑ One packet peas seeds ($3.00)
❑ One packet bean seeds ($3.00)
❑ One packet radish seeds ($3.00)
❑ One packet beet seeds ($3.00)
❑ One packet carrot seeds ($3.00)
❑ One packet spinach seeds ($3.00)

(2) 8 feet by 4 feet areas

A. Tomato (3)
B. Basil (6)
C. Peppers (4)
D. Peas (16)
E. Beans (16)
F. Cabbage (4)
G. Broccoli (4)
H. Marigolds (4)
I. Radish (32)
J. Beets (16)
K. Carrots (32)
L. Cucumber (3)
M. Lettuce (6)
N. Spinach (4)

▲ $50 garden design

If you wanted, you could exchange some or all of the cabbage or broccoli with cauliflower, Brussels sprouts, or kale plants.

Getting the Most Out of a $100 Garden

This plan is for three containers and one hanging basket to place on your balcony or patio. The plan calls for plastic or resin containers; if you prefer ceramic, clay, or wire they will cost more than what is stated here. The first year you will be investing in the containers, so your costs will be less in the following years unless you want to expand your garden with more containers. Any extra seeds can be kept in a cool, dry place and used the following year. Note prices may vary a little depending on where you live and the time of year.

List of items needed:

- ❏ Four 18-liter bags organic potting soil ($24.00)
- ❏ Three 16-inch round plastic pots ($24.00)
- ❏ One 16-inch plastic hanging basket ($8.00)
- ❏ Four 6-foot length stakes, made into a teepee ($3.00)
- ❏ One rosemary plant ($4.00)
- ❏ One thyme plant ($4.00)
- ❏ One oregano plant ($4.00)
- ❏ One kale plant ($3.00)
- ❏ Two lettuce plants ($3.00)
- ❏ Two Swiss chard plants ($3.00)
- ❏ Two bok choy plants ($3.00)
- ❏ One packet of pole bean seeds, twelve seeds altogether, three at the base of each stake ($3.00)
- ❏ Six colorful annuals of your choice ($3.00)
- ❏ One tomato plant ("Tumbler" variety) ($5.00)
- ❏ Four basil plants ($3.00)
- ❏ One packet of nasturtiums, 12 seeds needed ($3.00)

If you want you could exchange the herbs for other perennial ones, the pole beans for peas, and the kale for a cauliflower, Brussels sprouts, or broccoli plant.

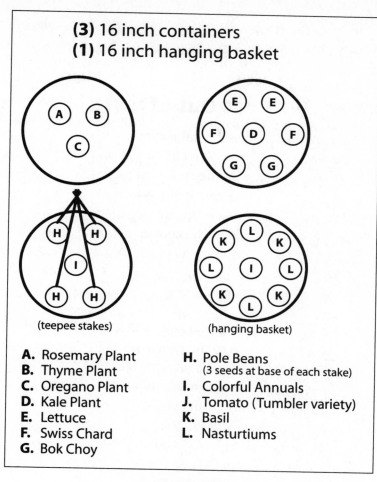

(3) 16 inch containers
(1) 16 inch hanging basket

(teepee stakes)

(hanging basket)

A. Rosemary Plant
B. Thyme Plant
C. Oregano Plant
D. Kale Plant
E. Lettuce
F. Swiss Chard
G. Bok Choy

H. Pole Beans
(3 seeds at base of each stake)
I. Colorful Annuals
J. Tomato (Tumbler variety)
K. Basil
L. Nasturtiums

▲ $100 garden design

Getting the Most Out of a $250 Garden

This plan is for two 8-foot by 4-foot raised beds for your front or backyard, plus one plastic container, and one plastic hanging basket to be placed in the garden area or on your balcony or patio. The raised beds can be built out of wood (6–8-feet by 12-inches deep by 2 inches wide) or cement blocks (32 blocks). The plan calls for plastic or resin containers; if you prefer ceramic, clay, or wire, they will cost more than what is stated here. The first year you will be investing in the raised beds, soil, and containers, so your costs will be less in the following years. Any extra seeds can be kept in a cool, dry place and used the following year or exchanged with friends. Note prices may vary a little depending on where you live and the time of year.

List of items needed:

- ❑ Material for two 8-foot by 4-foot raised beds, wood or cement block ($61.00)
- ❑ Three yards of soil/compost mix ($90.00) (Three yards = 2300 liters)
- ❑ Two 4.75-gallon (18-liter) bags organic potting soil ($12.00)
- ❑ One 16-inch plastic pot ($8.00)
- ❑ One 16-inch plastic hanging basket ($10.00)
- ❑ One box seed potatoes, 12 seed potatoes ($5.00)
- ❑ One packet corn seeds, 16 seeds ($3.00)
- ❑ One squash plant, zucchini ($3.00)
- ❑ One packet pea seeds, 32 seeds ($3.00)
- ❑ One packet bean seeds, 32 seeds ($3.00)
- ❑ Six lettuce plants ($3.00)
- ❑ Six spinach plants ($3.00)
- ❑ Eight onion plants ($3.00)
- ❑ Eight leek plants ($3.00)
- ❑ One tomato plant, "Tumbler" ($8.00)
- ❑ Two basil plants ($2.00)
- ❑ Two parsley plants ($2.00)
- ❑ Four viola plants ($2.00)
- ❑ One dwarf cherry tree, "Stella" ($26.00)

If you wanted to exchange for different vegetables you can use the plantings in the $50 garden design in place of one of the boxes in this design. The cherry tree can be exchanged for a pear tree "Conference" or an apple tree "Greensleeves." All three trees are dwarf varieties that will grow and produce fruit on their own.

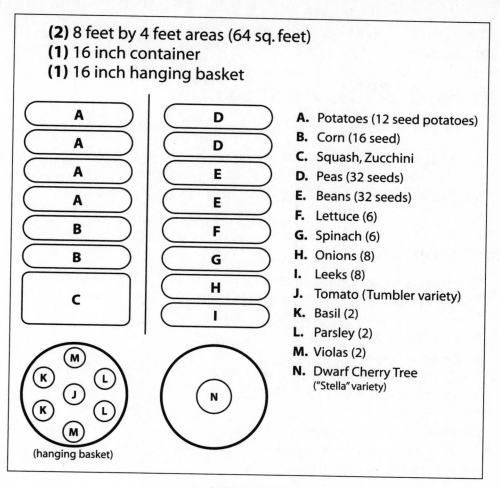

(2) 8 feet by 4 feet areas (64 sq. feet)
(1) 16 inch container
(1) 16 inch hanging basket

(hanging basket)

A. Potatoes (12 seed potatoes)
B. Corn (16 seed)
C. Squash, Zucchini
D. Peas (32 seeds)
E. Beans (32 seeds)
F. Lettuce (6)
G. Spinach (6)
H. Onions (8)
I. Leeks (8)
J. Tomato (Tumbler variety)
K. Basil (2)
L. Parsley (2)
M. Violas (2)
N. Dwarf Cherry Tree ("Stella" variety)

▲ $250 garden design

Web and Book Resources

The author acknowledges the following websites and books for the inspiration they gave during the research and writing of this book. If you want more information, check out these resources on small-space gardening.

Web Resources

Your Vegetable Gardening Helper
This site has some great "how-to" steps and some garden design books to help you to have a fabulous vegetable garden.
www.your-vegetable-gardening-helper.com

Kitchen Gardeners
A site teaching the importance of growing your own food in order to live a healthier lifestyle, and have a healthier community and planet.
www.kitchengardeners.org

Backyard Food Production
This site promotes and gives instructions on growing food in your backyard.
www.backyardfoodproduction.com

Straw Bale Gardening
A site introducing straw-bale gardening.
www.strawbalegardens.com

The Rooftop Garden Project
Learn about rooftop gardening.
www.rooftopgardens.ca

Fine Gardening
An online magazine with a variety of gardening topics.
www.finegardening.com

Mother Earth News
Online magazine with articles promoting self-sustainability, organic gardening, and living off the land.
www.motherearthnews.com

Urban Garden Casual

This site promotes and gives information on setting up urban gardens.
www.urbangardencasual.com

About.com

A site with a variety of topics promoting organic gardening.
www.organicgardening.about.com

No-Dig Vegetable Garden

This site promotes and teaches the no dig gardening method.
www.no-dig-vegetablegarden.com

Food 4 Wealth

Videos giving tips and instructions on how cost garden tips for growing organic vegetables.
www.HomeOrganicGarden.net

Book Resources

Catherine Abbott. *The Everything® Grow Your Own Vegetables Book.* (Massachusetts: F+W Media, Inc., 2010).

Catherine Abbott. *The Everything® Root Cellaring Book.* (Massachusetts: F+W Media, Inc., 2011).

Catherine Abbott. *Vegetable Garden Plans for Row Gardening.* (Canada: Self-published, 2008).

Catherine Abbott. *Vegetable Garden Plans for Square Foot Gardens.* (Canada: Self-published, 2008).

Catherine Abbott. *Vegetable Garden Plans for Your Raised Beds.* (Canada: Self-published, 2008).

Mel Bartholomew. *Square Foot Gardening.* (New York: St. Martin's Press, 1981).

Graham Bell. *The Permaculture Garden.* (Hampshire, UK: Permanent Publications, 2004).

Jennifer Bennett. *The Harrowsmith Book of Fruit Trees.* (Canada: Camden House Publishing, 1991).

Sally Jean Cunningham. *Great Garden Companions.* (Emmaus, PA: Rodale Press Inc., 1998).

Eugene Davenport. *Domesticated Animals and Plants.* (Boston and New York: Gin and Company, 1910).

Nigel Dunnett and Noel Kingsbury. *Planting Green Roofs and Living Walls*. (Portland: Timber Press Inc., 2008).

Bob Flowerdew. *The No-Work Garden*. (Canada: Whitecap Books, 2002).

Marjorie Harris. *Pocket Gardening: A Guide to Gardening in Impossible Places*. (Canada: Harper Collins Publishers Ltd., 1998).

D. G. Hessayon. *The Container Expert*. (London: Transworld Publishers Ltd., 1995).

Erin Hynes. *Rodale's Weekend Gardener*. (Emmaus, PA: Rodale Press Inc., 1998).

Patricia Lanza. *Lasagna Gardening with Herbs*. (Emmaus, PA: Rodale Press, Inc., 2004).

Patricia Lanza. *Lasagna Gardening for Small-Spaces*. (Emmaus, PA: Rodale Press, Inc., 2002).

Clare Matthews. *Great Gardens for Kids*. (London: Octopus Publishing Group Ltd., 2002).

Duane Newcomb and Karen Newcomb. *The Postage Stamp Garden*. (Massachusetts: Adams Media Corporation, 1999).

Sue Phillips and Neil Sutherland. *A Creative Step-by-Step Guide to Patio Gardening*. (Canada: Whitecap Books, 1994).

Sue Phillips. *A Creative Step-by-Step Guide to Urban Gardens*. (Canada: Whitecap Books, 1995).

Ruth Stout. *Gardening Without Work*. (New York: The Devin-Adair Company, 1963).

Ruth Stout. *How to Have a Green Thumb Without an Aching Back: A New Method of Mulch Gardening*. (New York: Exposition Press, 1955).

Sunset Book. *Plant Containers You Can Make*. (Menlo Park: Lane Publishing Co, 1976).

APPENDIX B

Glossary

Annual: A plant that completes its growing cycle in one season. It grows and does not come back the following season.

Arbor: A small-scale garden shelter usually made of wood or lattice with plants climbing all over it.

Biennial: A plant that requires two growing seasons to complete its life cycle. Leaves and stems grow the first season with the flowers and seeds forming the second year.

Companion planting: Plants that have an influence on each other, either beneficial or harmful.

Compost heap: A compost heap is made up of vegetable scraps and plant discards. When you pile all of this together it will begin to rot over time, making a great fertilizer to put back into your garden.

Cool crops: Vegetables that grow and produce better in cooler weather, such as peas, lettuce, spinach, and cabbage.

Crop rotation: Growing annual vegetable plants in a different location in the garden each year. This helps to control insects, improves soil fertility, and helps to prevent soil erosion.

Cultivate: To prepare soil for planting by plowing, digging, and fertilizing or it can mean you cultivate the earth by digging around the root of a plant.

Drainage: The running off of water gradually from the earth where your plants are growing. Good drainage ensures your plants get the moisture they need but the moisture does not collect, leaving the roots waterlogged.

Dwarf rootstock: A rootstock of diminished vigor, which produces a smaller mature plant or tree.

Espalier: A lattice made of wood or wire on which to train fruit trees by selecting lateral branches to grow horizontally on each side of a main stem.

Fertilizer: Extra nourishment for your plants. Air, water, and nutrients are essential for plant growth. Sometimes the soil does not have enough nutrients so additional nourishment needs to be added, usually in the form or organic matter or man-made fertilizer.

Fertilizer tea: A mix of organic materials intended to bolster the health of growing vegetable plants.

Gazebo: A garden pavilion, usually designed to offer a view, shelter, or a place to sit.

Germinate: To begin to grow or sprout a plant from a seed.

Green manure: Crops such as legumes or grasses grown in the fall to be dug under in the spring. Used to increase the organic matter in garden soil, which will improve the soil structure.

Humus: Partially or totally decayed vegetable matter, which is food for plants and helps soil retain moisture.

Interplanting: Planting to get maximum production from your garden or container. This is done by planting vegetables that mature early in the season alongside plants that mature later in the season.

Leggy: Weak-stemmed and spindly vegetable seedlings. This is usually caused by too much heat, too much shade, crowding, or over fertilization.

Lime: A compound containing calcium and magnesium. It is applied to garden soil to reduce acidity.

Loam: Soil that consists of a mixture of sand, silt, and clay. It is an ideal garden soil for growing vegetable plants.

Manure: Animal waste used as a soil amendment and fertilizer. You want to use aged manures in order not to harm the plants.

Microclimate: A climate particular to a specific situation, which differs from the overall climate of an area, against a wall or hedge as an example.

Microorganism: A microscopic animal or plant that may cause disease or may have a beneficial effect when a plant is decomposing.

Mulch: A protective covering of rotted organic matter such as straw, leaves, peat moss, wood chips, and grass clippings used to keep the weeds from growing as well as protecting plant roots.

Nematodes: A variety of parasitic worms that live in the soil.

Organic matter: A portion of the soil that is a result of decomposition of plant and animal residue. It helps maintain good soil structure and promotes microorganisms in the soil.

Peat Moss: A kind of moss that grows in very wet places. It is gathered, processed, and then sold to be used in mulching, as plant food, or mixed into soil.

Perennial: A plant that lives for more than two years.

pH: A chemical symbol used to identify the level of acidity and alkalinity in soil. The scale ranges from 0 to 14, with 7.0 being neutral. Readings of less than 7.0 indicate acidic soil and readings of above 7.0 indicate alkaline soil.

Pergola: A walk of pillars and cross members with plants trained to grow up over it.

Plant residue: Plant parts such as leaves, stem, and roots that remain after a vegetable has been harvested. These parts can be used to make compost.

Potager: A French term for a small vegetable garden.

Propagate: To cause plants to increase, spread, and multiply. Bees, insects, and the wind carry pollen from flower to flower to fertilize plants.

Prune: To cut off branches or leaves to make room for healthy new growth on trees and plants.

Ripe: The stage of maturity at which the fruit or vegetable is ready to be harvested and eaten.

Rootstock: Root or plant on which can be grafted certain species that are difficult to propagate from their own roots.

Seedling: A very young vegetable plant.

Self-fertile: Describes a plant whose ovule is fertilized by its own pollen and grows into viable seed.

Self-seeding: Describes a plant, usually an annual, that will regenerate from year to year by dispersing its seeds around an area.

Self-sterile: Describes a plant whose ovules require pollen from another plant (the pollinator) in order to grow viable seed.

Short-season vegetable: These are vegetables that are ready for harvesting one or two months following planting.

Silt: Soil particles that are between the size of sand and clay.

Slow-release fertilizer: A substance that releases the essential nutrients for the growth of a plant over a long period of time.

Soil: This is the upper layer of the earth's surface. It is composed of organic matter, minerals, and microorganisms, all making it capable of supporting plant life.

Sow: To scatter seed over the ground you have prepared for planting.

Stake: To tie plants to a sturdy stick for support to grow upright.

Tender: Describes plants likely to be damaged by low temperatures.

Thin out: As plants grow you must take some of them out of the ground to leave room for others to have enough space to grow bigger.

Transplant: To move young plants from one place to another. You take a plant from a pot and put it into the ground.

Tying in: The action of securing climbers to a support, a wall, trellis, or a stake.

Variety: Closely related vegetable plants forming a subdivision of a species that have similar characteristics.

APPENDIX C

Garden Vegetable Recipes

Cheddar-Parmesan Potatoes

This is a tasty and easy dish for your fresh potatoes. This dish can be made in advance and frozen.

INGREDIENTS | SERVES 6–8

¼ cup butter
½ cup all-purpose flour
2 cups milk
½ teaspoon salt
1 cup shredded Cheddar cheese
½ cup grated Parmesan cheese
5 cups cooked, peeled potatoes (about 5 medium)
¼ cup bread crumbs

1. In saucepan melt butter and stir in flour until smooth. Gradually add milk; cook and stir over medium heat until mixture thickens. Remove from heat.

2. Preheat oven to at 350°F. Add salt, Cheddar, and Parmesan cheeses. Stir until cheese is melted.

3. Add potatoes, stirring gently to mix.

4. Place in a 2-quart baking dish. Sprinkle with bread crumbs and bake uncovered for 30 minutes until browned.

Crustless Spinach Quiche

This is a great recipe to hide the healthy spinach that some may not like.

INGREDIENTS | SERVES 6

1 large onion, chopped
1 tablespoon oil
1 bunch fresh spinach or 10 ounces frozen
5 eggs
12 ounces Muenster cheese, shredded
¼ teaspoon salt
1 dash black pepper

1. Preheat oven to 350°F.

2. Sauté onion in oil in large skillet until tender. Add spinach and cook until excess moisture evaporates; cool.

3. Combine eggs, cheese, salt, and pepper; stir into spinach mixture. Pour into greased 9" pie plate.

4. Bake 30 minutes, until set.

Fabulous Bagel Spread

Serve this wonderfully cool and refreshing spread for a brunch with family or friends.

INGREDIENTS	SERVES 6–8, ABOUT ⅓ CUP SPREAD

3 green onions
½ small cucumber, seeded and cut into chucks (about ½ cup)
1 (8-ounce) package cream cheese, softened
1 teaspoon Worcestershire sauce
⅛ teaspoon salt

1. Trim away roots from base of green onions. Place in a food processor or blender.

2. Add the cucumber to the food processor or blender; cover and process until coarsely chopped.

3. Add cream cheese, Worcestershire sauce, and salt. Cover and process until almost smooth. Transfer to a bowl. Cover and refrigerate at least 6 hours or overnight.

4. Spread on toasted bagels.

Fried Eggplant

This tasty recipe is easy to make and a great way to introduce eggplant to your family.

INGREDIENTS	SERVES 4

1 egg, slightly beaten
1 cup milk or soymilk
3 tablespoons olive oil
1 cup chickpea flour
½ teaspoon salt
1 medium eggplant, sliced into ½" pieces
Parmesan cheese, to taste

1. In small bowl combine the egg, milk, and 1 tablespoon olive oil.

2. To make the batter, mix the flour and salt together and slowly add it to the egg mixture. Mix until smooth.

3. Heat the rest of the oil in a large skillet. Dip the slices of eggplant into the batter and fry in the heated oil for 2–5 minutes.

4. Drain on a paper towel. Serve with Parmesan cheese.

Garlic French Dressing

Why spend money on salad dressings when it is easy, cheap, and much healthier to make your own?

INGREDIENTS | SERVES 4

1 cup oil
⅓ cup ketchup
¼ cup apple cider vinegar
1–2 cloves garlic, crushed
1 tablespoon honey or other liquid sweetener
1 teaspoon sea salt
1 teaspoon paprika
Several dashes cayenne pepper

1. Blend or beat together all ingredients.

2. Chill and serve. Keeps seven or more days in the refrigerator.

Garlicky Snow Peas Sauté

You'll love this tasty recipe—it works as a great side dish for any meat or chicken dinner.

INGREDIENTS | SERVES 4

2 tablespoons olive oil
2 cloves garlic (up to 3), finely chopped
4 scallions, chopped
1 large sweet pepper (red, yellow, or green), diced or chopped
1 pound fresh snow peas, trimmed
½ cup jicama or water chestnuts; cubed
2 teaspoons soy sauce

1. In a wok or deep skillet, heat oil.

2. Add garlic, scallions, and sweet pepper and sauté until softened and fragrant, about 1 minute.

3. Add snow peas and jicama; sauté until cooked but still very tender-crisp, 2–3 minutes.

4. Add soy sauce and toss together. Taste for seasoning, adding more soy sauce if desired.

Green Beans with Stir-Fried Onions

Make this easy dish to add a bit of variety to your next dinner party.

INGREDIENTS | SERVES 4

2 medium onions, sliced
3 tablespoons butter
½ cup chicken broth
1 tablespoon sugar
1 tablespoon red wine vinegar
1 pound of green beans

1. In a heavy skillet cook the onions in 2 tablespoons of butter until well browned.

2. Add in the chicken broth, sugar, and red wine vinegar; whisk until sugar dissolves and mixture comes to boil.

3. Cook the green beans in large pot of boiling water until crisp-tender, about 5 minutes. Drain well.

4. Return beans to same pot. Add remaining butter and toss to coat.

5. To serve, pour the onion mixture over the beans.

Jumping Vegetable Juice

This is a healthy beverage that can be canned and enjoyed just like you would with commercial vegetable drinks. It can also be frozen.

INGREDIENTS | MAKES 6 QUARTS

15 pounds fresh, ripe tomatoes, chopped
1 small yellow, orange, or red pepper, chopped
1 small green pepper, chopped
1 cup diced celery
2 diced carrots
2 bay leaves
2 teaspoons dried basil
1 tablespoon salt
1 tablespoon freshly grated horseradish root
½ teaspoon pepper
1 teaspoon sugar
2 teaspoons Worcestershire sauce

1. Place all ingredients in a nonreactive pot; simmer 45 minutes. Stir periodically.

2. Place entire blend through a sieve or juicer to remove any fibers, skins, and seeds. Repeat to get a fine consistency.

3. Return to pan; boil. Pour liquid into hot quart jars, leaving ½" headspace.

4. Process in hot water canner 30 minutes. Let cool, then test lids.

Kale and Potato Soup

Kale is one of the most nutritious vegetables you can eat.
This is a great way to introduce kale to your family.

INGREDIENTS | SERVES 4–6

1 onion, chopped
1 tablespoon extra-virgin olive oil
2 cups chopped white potato, with skin
2 cups water or vegetable stock
3 cups kale, stems removed and chopped
¼ cup chopped fresh parsley
2 tablespoons tamari soy sauce
1 teaspoon salt
¼ teaspoon cayenne pepper

1. Sauté the onion in the oil until slightly browned.

2. Rinse the potato thoroughly to remove the excess starch.

3. Add the water or stock, potatoes, and kale to the pot.

4. Simmer everything together on low heat until the potatoes are soft.

5. Add the parsley, soy sauce, salt, and cayenne and cook for 5 minutes longer.

Raw Vegetable Relish

This relish is wonderful with meat, chicken, pork, vegetarian dishes, or in place of tomato sauce on pizza.

INGREDIENTS | MAKES 4 QUARTS

12 onions
1 large cabbage
8 carrots
4 green peppers
4 red peppers
1 tablespoon salt
1½ pints white vinegar
6 cups white sugar
2 teaspoons celery seed
2 teaspoons mustard seed

1. Grind the first 5 ingredients together in a food processor or blender. Mix in salt.

2. Let mixture stand for 2 hours, then squeeze out juice.

3. Add in last 4 ingredients and mix thoroughly. Pour into jars and seal. Let it stand for 2 weeks before using.

No-Fat Carrot Muffins

Yes, you are eating veggies in these tasty, low fat, and healthy muffins. Enjoy!

INGREDIENTS | **MAKES 6 LARGE MUFFINS**

1 cup plain yogurt, low fat
1 egg
½ cup water
1 cup carrots, grated
2 cups flour (rice flour can also be used)
1½ teaspoons baking soda
1 teaspoon cinnamon
1 teaspoon allspice
1 teaspoon nutmeg
½ cup shredded coconut, optional

1. Preheat oven to 350°F. Grease a large muffin tin.

2. In a medium-size bowl mix yogurt, egg, water, and carrots.

3. Mix the flour, baking soda, cinnamon, allspice, nutmeg, and coconut together in another bowl.

4. Slowly add the dry ingredients into the wet ingredients and mix thoroughly. Pour batter into the muffin tin, about ⅔ full.

5. Bake for 30 minutes or until knife inserted comes out clean.

Parsley-Buttered Corn

The creamed butter can be made ahead of time and will keep in the refrigerator or freezer.

INGREDIENTS | **SERVES 6**

¼ cup salted butter
½ teaspoon lemon juice
2 tablespoons organic fresh parsley, finely chopped
6 fresh ears organic corn

1. Beat the butter until soft.

2. Add the lemon juice slowly to the butter and mix. Then add the parsley and mix thoroughly.

3. Chill the butter mixture until it is a good consistency for spreading, or make into shapes.

4. Cook ears of corn in boiling water for 6–8 minutes. Cool for 5 minutes before serving. Use the creamed butter to spread over the fresh ears of corn.

Rosemary-Roasted Beets

Foil-roasted beets are juicy with locked-in herb and garlic flavor.

INGREDIENTS | SERVES 6

6 beets (1½ pounds)
4 cloves garlic, minced
3 tablespoons chopped fresh rosemary
2 tablespoons olive oil
½ teaspoon salt
½ teaspoon pepper
1 tablespoon minced fresh parsley or rosemary

1. Preheat oven to 400°F.

2. Cut beet tops to leave 1" attached, leave tails. Place beets on 16" square piece of foil. Sprinkle with garlic, rosemary, 1 tablespoon oil, salt, and pepper. Fold to form a packet.

3. Place on a rimmed baking dish and roast at until fork-tender, about 1 hour.

4. Wearing rubber gloves, peel and trim beets; cut into ¼"-thick slices.

5. Arrange on a warmed platter; drizzle with remaining oil and sprinkle with fresh parsley or more rosemary. Serve warm.

Sesame-Steamed Broccoli

This dish is great served over rice for a lovely lunch or used as side dish for any meat or vegetarian dinner.

INGREDIENTS | SERVES 2

2 cups broccoli
1 teaspoon oil
1 tablespoon sesame seeds
1 tablespoon soy sauce
1 tablespoon lemon juice
1 tablespoon maple syrup

1. Steam the broccoli until just tender; set aside.

2. Heat oil in a saucepan, then add sesame seeds. Cook until nicely browned, about 3–5 minutes.

3. Add soy sauce, lemon juice, and maple syrup; stir.

4. Add in the steamed broccoli and toss until well coated.

Speedy Tomato-Basil Soup

This quick soup needs minimal preparation—it's an easy lunch or a starter for dinner.

INGREDIENTS | SERVES 2

1 onion, finely diced

2 tablespoons extra-virgin olive oil

1 cup dried red lentils

4 cups vegetable stock (freezing left over water from your steamed veggies makes a great stock)

4–6 fresh tomatoes, diced, or 1 (28-ounce) can diced tomatoes

Sea salt and freshly ground pepper, to taste

2 tablespoons dried or fresh basil, finely chopped

1. In a soup pot, sauté the onion in olive oil over medium-high heat.

2. Add the dried lentils and stock. Cover, bring to boil, then reduce heat to medium-low and simmer for 20 minutes.

3. Stir in tomatoes, salt, pepper, and basil; serve hot.

Zucchini Pancakes

This is a great way to use up those zucchini that were missed and grew into giants overnight.

INGREDIENTS | MAKES 10 PANCAKES

2 cups zucchini, grated

½ cup grated Parmesan cheese

1 teaspoon grated onion, or 1 chopped green onion

3 eggs

3 tablespoons flour

2 tablespoon yogurt or buttermilk

Seasoning salt, to taste

1. Blend all ingredients together.

2. Drop by spoonfuls onto an oiled skillet. Spread into circles, and turn once. Cook each side until browned, 4–5 minutes.

3. Serve at once or keep in oven until all are ready.

Swiss Chard Frittata in a Pita

A quick and easy alternative for dinner. Your kids will not even know they are eating healthy greens!

INGREDIENTS | **SERVES 2**

4 eggs

1 tablespoon water

1 teaspoon olive oil

¼ cup chopped onions

½ teaspoon minced garlic

2 cups packed, chopped Swiss chard

2 tablespoons chopped fresh basil or parsley

¼ cup grated Parmesan cheese

2 small (6") pita breads

1. In a small bowl, whisk together eggs and water. Set aside.

2. In an 8" nonstick skillet, heat oil over medium-high heat.

3. Add in onions and garlic; cook for 1–2 minutes.

4. Stir in chard and basil (it will cook down; if necessary add it in two batches); cook for 3–4 minutes or until chard is wilted. Remove from pan; set aside.

5. Wipe skillet and place over medium heat.

6. Add half the chard mixture and half the egg mixture. Cook for 3–5 minutes or until browned on the bottom with some of the top still not set; sprinkle with half of the cheese.

7. Flip frittata over; cook for 1–2 minutes or until browned and completely set. Remove from pan and cut in half.

8. Repeat procedure with remaining ingredients to make second frittata.

9. Cut warmed pitas in half; place frittata halves inside the pita bread.

Index